WHATEVER HAPPENED TO THE BRITISH MOTORCYCLE INDUSTRY

Bert Hopwood

ISBN 0 85429 459 7

© H. Hopwood

First published March 1981, reprinted May 1984 and March 1986.

A FOULIS Motorcycling book

Printed in England by the publishers
Haynes Publishing Group
Sparkford, Yeovil, Somerset BA22 7JJ, England

Distributed in North America by
Haynes Publications Inc
861 Lawrence Drive, Newbury Park, California 91320. USA

Editor: **Jeff Clew**
Cover design: **Phill Jennings**
Layout design: **Lynne J. Blackburn   Sandra M. Whitaker**

Contents

Dedication

During the Summer months of this year, I had paused to look around a village in Hampshire and was puzzled by a crowd of forty or so people who were gathered together in animated discussion.

I found, at the centre, simply six motorcycles which were resting on their stands while their owners were elsewhere refreshing themselves. There were three Triumph machines, two BSAs and one Norton. Six British motorcycles, all of them at least ten years old, had generated a sizeable crowd and, as I mingled, I was quite astounded that these people, of a diversity of ages, were so drawn together.

The older men were reminiscing and swapping experiences and outlining some of the technical details, while the teenagers, and one or two a little younger, were bent in what seemed to be a microscopic survey of all six engines.

I must confess that I had not realized that many of our younger teenagers were little more than toddlers at the time the fragments of the British motorcycle industry were being shaken out and probably some of them have never seen a group of six British bikes

My mind was to wander back through a maze of uneasy and troubled years to a period, little more than a generation ago, when the factories of our industry were humming with life, busy supplying world demand. Since then world demand for motor cycles has increased enormously, and we need no reminder that the British motorcycle industry had disappeared.

The specialists who were employed in the industry, who spent much of their working life skillfully coping with the wandering policies of the Board rooms, particularly in the last two decades, are now mostly scattered in fields afresh. Many of them will, I am sure, often pause and savour the nostalgia of happy and distant memories and it is to these people this book is dedicated.

Acknowledgements

The author is deeply indebted to the following people, without whose help this book would have been far less complete.

Jeff Clew, the enterprising Editorial Director of our publishers, whose fund of knowledge of motorcycle matters is vintage and whose help and friendly advice has been generously given.

Bob Currie, Midland Editor of *Motor Cycle Weekly,* whose journalism thrills me today as it always did. His generous help is reflected in many parts of this book.

Mrs. Dalton, probably more commonly known as Brenda Price who, as Charles Parker's second in command, did so much to preserve the lovely simplicity of the financial system through the glorious years at Meriden.

Ivor Davies, former Publicity Manager with the Triumph Engineering Co., whose work so reflected his knowledge and all round involvement in the industry.

Doug Hele, a close friend and worthy adviser, who did so much to improve the Norton, BSA and Triumph image.

Mrs. Alan Jones who, as Miss Gwen Arey, is best remembered as the dynamic private secretary of Jimmy Leek, the great BSA man who knew what business was all about. From her closeness to 'the Chief' Gwen, more than most, is able to appreciate "what happened".

Mrs. Loach or the young Gladys Pickering, former telephone operator with Components Limited, a Company which later was to resolve itself into Ariel Motors (JS) Limited.

Arthur Lupton, who spent a lifetime as a prominent figure in the design and technical department of BSA. His encyclopaedic knowledge of the products and personalities of Small Heath is much sought after and his advice has been generous and helpful.

7

Acknowledgements

John Nelson, ex-Service Manager of the Triumph works, who helped generate the remarkable liaison factor which Meriden enjoyed.

Mrs. Round, whose late husband, Frank, was the proud owner of both the first and the last of the Ariel square four motorcycles to flow from the production line.

Stan Truslove, mechanical engineer and diplomat extraordinary without whom the Triumph Engineering Co., and the author in particular, may have had a much rougher ride.

Henry Vale, ex-Competition Manager of the Triumph Engineering Co. and best known for his work in the progress to success of the off-road Cubs and the brilliant flying twins.

Charles Waller, ex-Service Manager of Ariel Motors and now in peaceful retirement deep in Somerset, whose advice on very early Ariel matters has been most helpful.

Jack Wickes, without whose particular brand of philosophy, Meriden may have been much less bearable. Designer, Project Engineer and Stylist, whose exceptional skills in the latter sphere characterise every Triumph machine.

And, not least, the publishers of *Motor Cycle Weekly* for their premission to use photographs from *The Motor Cycle* and *Motor Cycling*.

Chapter One

A small enterprise from a sound foundation

THROUGH the 1920s, the grand and massive showrooms of Birmingham's motorcycle dealers interested me greatly and there is no doubt that this early window gazing served as my introduction to the world of motorcycles. They kindled an interest which later was to attract me to an industry which never, at any time, lost the power of fascination which drew me in those early days.

I remember, best of all, Frank Hallams in Bristol Street, who I think sported the rather flowery title of Motor Cycle Emporium, a description to which the Hallam establishment did ample justice. They certainly knew, inside out, the craft of displaymanship. Frank Hallam was an ex-competition rider who had graduated to the role of dealer and he must have had the franchise of almost every make of British motorcycle which was significant, for there were over 100 firms in the manufacturing business at that time. These showrooms were vast and magnificent, with a roomy forecourt which enabled one to examine every make of machine through huge plate glass windows, while under cover.

The motor car showrooms did not attract me. After all, motor body shapes seemed to be very much alike and I felt that their engines all seemed to be very similar water-cooled chunks of metal so that it was of little consequence that they were out of sight. Not so the engines of the gleaming two-wheelers, with every detail there to see. No draping of sheet metal over these beautifully finned air-cooled masterpieces. Each nut and bolt was polished to perfection, some having elegant dome shapes, and even each wheel spoke and nipple was a shining piece of engineering.

I was twelve years old in 1920 and I remember making these pilgrimages to the Hallam windows very frequently, with my nose pressed hard on the glass. The exclusive Velocette, the big BSAs with the proud piled arms badge, the rather severe and simple looking Ariels of that time, the splendid engineering of the AJS in smooth black and gold, the P & M Panthers with the unique frames and, of course, my favourites, the famous Nortons, purposeful in their livery of silver and black.

It was very comfortable viewing in Bristol Street, often with the rain bucketing down, and I learned, from a distance, about oil pumps, which lubricated the engine if the driver did not forget to operate the plunger every so often. I remember the hand gear changes with their elegant control mechanisms and I was much puzzled by the Velocette throttle control which looked tatty but which I was to learn later was a push-pull piano wire device. Though not so neat as the more conventional cable type, it probably worked a good deal better.

Above all else it was the engines, those handsome finned monsters, that were critically compared and I know that those which sported 'fat' exhaust pipes in flashing serpentine curves, came off best. All this, I am afraid, was far from being an enlightened excursion into design engineering, but at least it was a start.

My family was poor and it was essential that I should start earning as soon as possible. At 14 years of age I commenced my working life in a malleable iron foundry doing, what seemed to me, all the most filthy jobs. But it seemed that I learned something in the process for much later in life my rather sparse, though practical, foundry experience was to be of great benefit.

For the next few years I drifted through a variety of works jobs, none of which had any future. Oddly enough, throughout this rather soul-destroying period I had the good sense to lay the foundation of a sound technical training by attending evening classes at Birmingham Technical College.

I could not afford ambitions, otherwise apprenticeship with an engineering company might have become a reality, but it is a source of wonder to me that I pressed on regardless with my technical education in the whole of my spare time right through to my acceptance, many years later, as a member of my professional institution. I am grateful to the genie whose influence it must have been, for steering me through this side of my training. Sometimes in those very early days it did seem to appear somewhat futile.

However, I was fortunate enough to win a college memorial prize for design engineering and somehow news of this reached the chief designer of Ariel Works who gave me a job, at 18 years of age, as a junior draughtsman.

The great man who became my boss was none other than Val Page, who had recently left J.A. Prestwich Ltd. to join Ariel Motors in the top design job. This was the start of a long association with this brilliant engineer, first as office boy and much later as a colleague.

Ariel Motors was, in those days, part of a huge manufacturing group which traded under the rather insignificant company name of Components Ltd. It was a misleading title for a mammouth business engaged in the manufacture of Ariel and

Fleet bicycles, Ariel motorcycles, Ariel cars, Fleet three-wheeler commercial

Val Page – Chief Designer at Ariel Works during the late 1920s.

A group of Fleet 3 wheeler commercial machines standing outside the directors entrance to Components Ltd in 1930. The price tag for this 10 cwt vehicle was £87.5 and the running cost was claimed to be one penny per mile.

vehicles, cycle wheel rims under the name Endless Rims, forgings and solid drawn tubes under the name of Midland Tube & Forging Co., and malleable iron castings under the trade name of Oak Foundry Ltd.

The commercial three-wheeler vehicle, not to be confused with the glorious flop of 1970, was a well engineered and sturdy vehicle with two front wheels and a 10 cwt. capacity. During its day it was a success and would probably be so even today.

The Ariel car was first the Ariel 9, with a two cylinder Harper-Bean engine, but this model was not too reliable and was quickly replaced by the Ariel 10, which had a four cylinder Swift engine. Its general lines were rather spartan.

Rumour had it that the great new designer, Mr. Page, was working on wonderful new motorcycles with saddle tanks and here was I at 18 years of age feeling like a million dollars in what I felt was a terribly important job. Although in those non-pampered days it was customary for the most insignificant members of the staff to make and serve the tea and run a few errands, I was happy and having very good training by absorbing all the knowledge and expertise which was mine for the asking.

My technical training was, of course, all arranged at another place and in my own time. It was all so enjoyable that I become puzzled by many of today's so-called problems in relation to job training and preparing young people to face the future. It seemed simple enough to me at the time, for we were training while actually performing the job in a junior role and there is no doubt that the expertise and knowledge was transmitted by natural absorbtion, a very simple process. Unfortunately it was a form of training which most of today's non-practising career training experts would tear to pieces.

Ariels were then marketing a comprehensive range of motorcycles, the smallest of which was a 250 cc machine powered by an ohv Blackburne engine, but the economic climate of the late 1920s was heading towards the depression in the early 1930s, which was to thin out many of the 100 or so British manufacturers of motorcycles. Already rapidly dwindling, they were sharing a fluctuating market.

Reliability trials, hill climbs and time trials were growing in popularity and such giants as Harry Perrey, Jeff Butcher, Allan Rollason and several others were reminding the buying public of the extreme reliability of Ariel machines by their successes in the competition field.

At a later stage came Graham Goodman, the sidecar wizard, Hartley the tuner who coaxed so much horse power from the side valve Ariels that they went like the wind, and Ben Bickell whose later exploits at Brooklands, on the Red Hunter models, secured for Ariel many first places and speed records that established their reputation in the world of pure speed.

Publicity stunts were common and Harry Perrey climbed Snowdon on his Ariel. Similarly mounted, he rode across the English Channel with floats attached and a crude means of propulsion. Harry had a keen sense of humour and I well remember his rather dramatised step by step account of his achievements. I recall that Harry seemed to feel that all designers 'played around and wasted far too much metal'. One of his favourite examples when he was making this point was the street gas lamp post of those days, which he claimed weighed 10 cwt and which held up an incandescent gas mantle which weighed only a fraction of an ounce. An obvious case of over indulgence, he felt. How could designers be so stupid and wasteful?

Val Page was not altogether convinced but Harry made his point and indeed was such a character and was so persistent that many weight saving experiments were made and incorporated into the production specifications.

At that time, Charles Sangster was Chairman of Components Ltd. and his son, Jack, was brought into the business as general manager of the motorcycle and car operating unit. The younger Sangster had good engineering and management training and was bright and shrewd, so it was not very long before he made his presence felt.

I shall never forget first meeting him at the time when the Ariel 9 car was prone to break rear axles so regularly that no one with any sense would think of driving more than two blocks without having one or two spares aboard. Jack, of course, was determined to end this nonsense forthwith and instructed the car designer, a man named Tippen who was a brilliant mathematician, to re-stress the axle and come up with a trouble-free answer in terms of a modified shaft diameter.

Although I was very much a junior, I was present when Jack Sangster and Tippen met to discuss the several pages of high mathematics leading eventually to a new shaft diameter, guaranteed not to break and stressed to the nearest three places of decimals. Jack was simply in no mood to go through all this stuff and cut Tippen short by asking for the new shaft size, which was something like 1.154 in. Quick as a flash Sangster said 'Right, make it $1\frac{1}{4}$ in'. The whole discussion, if it could be called that, was over in seconds and I was surprised that this designer of high calibre should meekly accept this snap upgrading which must have been grossly wasteful of metal and unnecessarily expensive.

This little episode would often flash through my mind in the later years during similar discussions with Jack, when I occupied the engineering 'hot seat'. I am sure that it served as a practical lesson for it was never any good beating about the bush when dealing with this needle-sharp man who, like the businessman that he was, never had time, on such occasions, for anything but conclusive and convincing comment. No one knows, to this day, whether Jack Sangster's rule of thumb philosophy was the medicine which we needed, but I can say that the breakage problem was firmly put to bed.

In those distant days, being elevated to the drawing board meant an end to odd jobs such as making tea and running errands. A junior was normally seconded to a senior draughtsman, from whom he received instruction. I have always felt that, in learning, it is best to model oneself as closely as possible on an expert one respects

13

The 497 cc Ariel sloper of 1934. An exceptionally quiet machine which proved costly to manufacture.

The first new Ariel designed by Val Page was a 497 cc ohv model introduced in 1926.

and admires. Near perfect teamwork will follow and the flow of expertise will be very rapid.

I have deliberately followed this principle twice in my life for I made sure that I graduated to the drawing board under the tuition of the best engineering draughtsman I have ever known. At a later stage in my career I employed a similar approach with Edward Turner, whom I admired mostly for his down to earth business common-sense and for his ingenuity.

As a practising junior draughtsman I felt that now, at last, I was on active service in the design field, although in reality this was far from being the case. Nonetheless, I remember my first solo job was that of having to re-design the valve springs for the 500 cc ohv Ariel, the current components having been condemned for persistent breakage. I was pleased and eager to exploit the science which the Technical College had drummed into me and although these first calculations were not too academic, I felt like a million dollars.

The incident of the Ariel motor car axle shaft calculations and their ignominious despatch to the waste-paper basket was always in my mind, but tutor and pupil had the situation quickly under control. The redesign was successful and the breakage problem solved with very little time lag.

A new sales team, headed by Vic Mole, soon arrived at Ariel Motors and Vic came up with the bright idea of featuring, in his advertising propaganda, the twenty horse-power which was then being developed by the 500 cc ohv engines. The new cradle-type frame was linked with a snappy and very rewarding publicity splash in a sales drive, which offered the motorcycling public 'Twenty horses in a cradle' for the modest cost of the machine. Although this may sound a little weak when compared with the punch of some of today's advertising, the horse idea caught on with the public and for a time, the Company had full order books.

The Ariel Red Hunter of the mid-1930s.

Chapter One

The Ariel Colt, a very light 250 cc machine, and the baby of Vic Mole's stable, was launched on a successful production run and the famous Red Hunter variants were on the way, with two models in 350 cc and 500 cc ohv form.

A young man named Edward Turner had joined the Company as a forward design engineer, and a senior draughtsman and myself were seconded to him, forming a team of three to cope with forward design work. We were not exactly overstaffed but, nonetheless, there was a prodigious outflow of new products over a very short period of time and the Ariel range was re-vitalised. The Red Hunters had started to out-perform our competitors' products, Ben Bickell had become the 'King of Brooklands' riding Ariels exclusively and many successes were being achieved in trials and similar events with the great Len Heath in the saddle. The Ariel 'slopers' in two and four valve form, had been introduced and the Square Four model was rapidly taking shape in the experimental shop. The Ariel Square Four engine was, of course, Edward Turner's special 'baby' and it is this particular design which undoubtedly stamped his name indelibly on the minds of the motorcycling public.

I met Mr. Turner for the first time a few days after he joined the company; he as the boss and I as his junior assistant. At that time his draughtsmanship was very weak but nonetheless he knew what he wanted. I, still a raw junior with everything to learn, had to resort to real diplomacy in resolving our first basic engineering drawings.

Fundamentally, any fool can draw, but the thought and expertise behind the shapes, and the amount of clarity of information transmitted in the process, is really all that matters and it is small wonder that a man of Turner's calibre was master in no time at all. Soon, we were away to a new era of product design, which was to further the Ariel name throughout the motorcycle world.

Charles Sangster, the Company Chairman, had taken a great liking to Turner and it was not very long before this new young engineer, with his undoubted abilities of persuasion, had taken the Board with him on his new type of engine. With four cylinders in coupled pairs it was later to blossom as the famous Square Four.

It seems that Turner was given very scanty terms of reference and no commercial guidelines whatsoever. My feelings were that if this had originated from a board composed mainly of financiers with an ex-racing cyclist and a gentleman farmer thrown in, they would have been hopelessly short sighted. As a result, Turner seemed to have a free hand, with no restrictions, so that he started with a clean sheet of paper and designed a completely new motorcycle.

His brilliance as an inventive designer was never better and this classic new design had an engine of 500 cc capacity with the cylinders arranged in a square four formation, a gearbox built in-unit and wet sump lubrication. The chassis and wheels were brilliant in conception and the whole machine weighed no more than motorcycles of half the engine capacity which were then being made. This design, which the public never saw, was undoubtedly much more outstanding and

The 500 cc ohv Ariel 4 valve 'Sloper' of 1931. This machine was manufactured by the Ariel subsidiary of the Components Ltd complex prior to its bankruptcy in 1932. The rider is the late George Wheeler who was then part of the Sales staff.

commercially worthwhile than the type which later was to go into production.

By now I was working very closely with Mr. Turner and we were both certain that this original machine would have been a world-beater, had it been allowed to go into production, permitting the company to reap a rich harvest. Small wonder that the testers, who were engaged in proving the two prototypes, raved about this new machine, which was so easy to handle and so exciting to ride with its revolutionary power to weight ratio and its zestful zooming exhaust note. We were, of course, plagued with the typical coupling gear knock which characterised its later production relatives but it was not nearly so pronounced and we had outlined a development programme which, we felt, would ease the problem considerably.

On tick-over the machine had what I would describe as a 'sewing machine' noise, a ticking rather than a rattle characteristic, which was not unpleasant to the ear and indeed infinitely more acceptable than the noises emanating from normal motor-cycles of the day, with the exception, perhaps, of the Scott. Very little trouble was experienced during the test period and in fact it would be true to say that most of our problems were caused by crashes due to the exuberance of one tester. Of rather portly proportions, Turner had nicknamed him 'his ball of leather' simply because he seemed to spend so much of his time separated from the motorcycle and rolling at high speed along the hard road.

Reprinted from MOTOR CYCLE *September 18th, 1930.*

"Ixion" tries a Mystery Four

With a 1931 Multi=
cylinder Machine on
the Road.

No Vibration: Super
Silence: 5 m.p.h. "On Top":
Amazing Acceleration.

FOR about a week I have been riding an experimental four-cylinder. It is a machine which is definitely intended to form the basis of a commercial model for next year. It is designed and produced in one of our foremost British factories.

The best-laid schemes of mice and men gang aft agley; and even now I dare not definitely promise readers that they will see it at Olympia. But only one event can stop its figuring on a Show dais—namely, the receipt of such innumerable orders for the firm's conventional machines that no plant would be available for making fours; and in the present state of trade no factory is likely to book record orders this November. So I would gladly take on a substantial bet that this machine will be at Olympia; that it will be the chief sensation of the Show; that it will sell in great numbers; and that it will prove a great success on the road during 1931.

I hate to be tantalising, but my lips are largely sealed by solemn promises to the designer, and if mysterious sentences annoy readers they will, at any rate, breed thrilling anticipations of Olympia, or of any earlier "release" which the factory may permit. So here goes for a veiled description of the machine.

Orthodox Appearance.

I have been riding it over crowded roads and among keen motor cyclists for a week past; yet hardly a soul has spotted anything unusual about the bus. There is nothing of the dachshund about it—it is not eight feet long, or anything of that sort; its wheelbase, on the contrary, is approximately 53in., which would be quite a normal dimension for a single-cylinder. It does not look in the least like a four to a casual observer; and when I am sitting on it in road garb there is much excuse to be made for a pump attendant who mistakes it for something entirely different.

Being a hand-made experimental model, no weight-saving has been attempted, and it scales 376 lb. with tanks full. That figure would be slightly on the heavy side for a hot-stuff 500 c.c. single, but when the production machine appears it will weigh rather less; and, anyhow, this figure is not out of the way for a full-sized touring bus.

There is no vibration. I contrived to balance a tumbler of water on it with the engine ticking over and the gear in neutral, and a brimming tumbler did not spill, though there was a faint ripple on the surface of the water. If a hand is placed on the tank, frame or head lamp, with the engine running, it is barely possible to detect by the feel whether the engine is running or not. In other words, it has the smoothest motor cycle engine I have ever encountered.

Phenomenal Silence.

The silence is phenomenal. It is only possible to create any exhaust uproar by racing the engine on one of the lower gears; and thus raced the engine emits a smooth, subdued roar, entirely devoid of the staccato racket usually associated with motor cycle power units; it is a roar reminiscent of a Baby Austin. In normal, sensible use the engine would, of course, never be accelerated hard enough on first or second gear to emit any roar at all, as the gear would be changed up before the noise became insistent or aggressive; and such engines, handled with even moderate consideration, would eliminate *all* public prejudice against motor cycle exhausts.

The power unit is extremely flexible. It will fire evenly and pull smoothly down to about 5 m.p.h. on top gear, on which I rode it up a kerb, through a gate, and round a sharp corner into my garage. In heavy traffic it is almost too silent, as pedestrians are often unaware of its approach, and additional hooter-blowing is needed

One of the leading technical journalists of the day enthuses about the Ariel Square Four experimental model which did not reach the production stage.

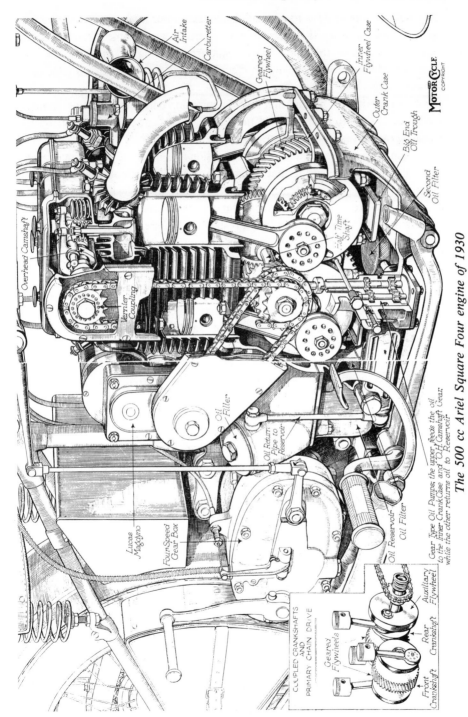

The 500 cc Ariel Square Four engine of 1930

Chapter One

Eventually it was decided to produce the Square Four in a very much modified form and so watered down that as a money spinner it was doomed from the start. How could a board of this kind know right from wrong in the complex and specialized world of motorcycles and how could they venture an opinion relative to the forward prospects of such a project?

In all fairness, it must be said that severe depression had overtaken the economy but one might reason that this should have been the incentive to press on with a world beater, rather than an also-ran.

The engine was re-designed as a 600 cc version and much of the old magic was sacrificed on the way in ensuring that our out-of-date machine tools could cope. We were instructed to make use of the largest frame and wheels which were then in production and the result was a 'camel' of huge proportions with a shocking power to weight ratio and no performance. As a result, the Square Four dribbled through years of minute production figures; certainly an unusual motorcycle for the sparse following which it attracted. I shall never understand why this machine was allowed to survive for so long and clutter the real production lines.

By 1934 the Triumph Company of Coventry had created a sensation by announcing the introduction of a new motorcycle which had a parallel twin engine unit of 650 cc capacity. This was the work of Val Page, who had departed from Ariels and was now Triumph's chief designer. The technical journals made a big splash featuring the new Triumph which appeared to be workmanlike and was certainly a handsome machine. Edward Turner threw a tantrum because he felt that he had been robbed. While Page was still with us we had modified a Square Four engine by discarding two pistons and had developed a parallel twin in this way. It took some little time for my boss to recover from what seemed to me a matter of small consequence. Later on, Turner was to 'inherit' the Page machine when he joined Triumph and he went on to redesign it and create the Speed Twin.

In 1932 Components Ltd. went broke and this created a gap in the Ariel saga, fortunately to be of short duration. Each separate manufacturing unit was sold off, with the bicycle rights and goodwill going to a large competitor in the same business. The Endless Rim Co. was taken over by Dunlop. The Midland Tube Co. became part of the Tube Investment empire and the Midland Forging Co. was sold to a former general manager of the now bankrupt group, named Morgan, to become a new company under the name George Morgan Ltd.

Jack Sangster, as a member of the board, must have seen the danger signs and he had already secured for himself premises which were, hitherto, used mainly for wheel rim manufacture. He then very quickly negotiated with the official receiver and secured the manufacturing rights of the motorcycle activity to set up his own private company, which he named Ariel Motors (J.S.) Ltd.

Most of the essential machinery and tools were bought by him at give-away prices; items like lathes were being auctioned at a few pounds and one might say that the severe economic depression enabled Sangster to organise a smooth, worry-free transition which, by and large, involved moving equipment a mere 500 yards or so. He was able to pick and choose his personnel, for we were all on the dole, and he set up a very nice compact manufacturing unit with an absolute minimum of non-producers.

The cream of the motorcycle personnel from Sangster's recently deposed kingdom were thankful to be re-employed and on the move once more and it is no small wonder that the new Ariel Motors (J.S.) Ltd. got off to a flying start in its first

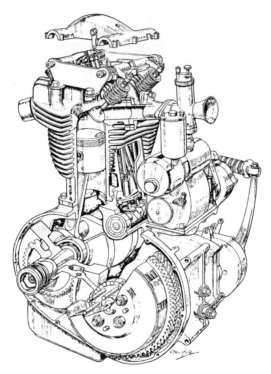

The 650 cc vertical twin engine designed by Val Page for the Triumph Co. in 1933. An exceptionally advanced design for the period.

venture. In no time, it seemed to me, machines were operating and motorcycles were rolling off the production line with absolutely minimum overhead expenses and very low production prices.

Edward Turner was in charge of design work with myself, the chief draughtsman, and two supporting drawing office personnel. There was soon evidence that the new company was very much a going concern with a limited range of Red Hunter single cylinder machines and eventually a dribble of Square Fours. In spite of the difficult economic climate our limited output was much in demand.

21

The engine assembly shop at Ariel Works after the 1932 collapse. This picture gives some indication of the close packed activity of the new organisation.

The early 1930s were difficult years for most businesses for there was massive unemployment and many concerns had gone to the wall. The new Ariel company was fortunate in its new-found sparseness and efficiency, with its limited range of products, its floor space geared tightly to production figures with not a foot to spare, and most of all the skimpy group of hand-picked employees, each eager to make a going concern from the rubble of the crash.

During those hard years this small unit was able, better than most, to withstand the economic pressures of the day. Although many suppliers had lost considerable sums of money with the crash of the old Company, they nonetheless carried on supplying us with parts and materials and indeed helped Sangster to get off the ground by extending generous credit. These people deserve the highest praise and I would like to think that Sangster felt the same, particularly in his later years of extreme prosperity, for without their generous help at a time when they themselves were struggling to survive, he would not have had the easy ride that it turned out to be.

Edward Turner was beginning to feel frustrated and unsettled by the limited nature of the new operation and he felt that there was no likelihood of outlet for his inventive talents for many years, if ever. We were working on many projects and he fitted up a drawing office at his home. To supplement the working day we both would work well into the night on a variety of projects, ranging from simple engines suitable for motorcycles or cars to diesel engines with some resemblance of modular concept. I remember that we completed the design of a four cylinder light aircraft engine which, we felt, was badly needed at that time.

His brain was very active and it was obvious that a man of his ability could not be constrained in his present capacity by such a small and insignificant manufacturing unit. Matters were made worse by the vexing time he was having in trying to cope with the Works Manager, with whom he seemed to be constantly at loggerheads. Some indication of the spartan nature of our operation is that the Works Manager was also the company Buyer, a stupid arrangement which created problems that needed exceptional diplomacy to resolve.

I found myself involuntarily acting as a kind of buffer between my boss Turner and the other man, and these were the two most important executives which the company boasted. My sympathies, not unnaturally, were with my boss and I had a busy, but not too difficult time, sorting out and getting things back on the rails, often after a fight.

It is strange that both men seemed to regard me as some sort of referee and this helped somewhat, although I now find it difficult to believe what went on. A serious problem was that although each separate item in the specification of the products we made was controlled by full instructions as to the correct material requirement, the Buyer would often be tempted, by lower prices, to reduce the quality. This did not seem to bother our Buyer cum Works Manager, who was not an engineer, yet the bogus material which found its way into the Ariel machines of that day caused many headaches.

It took me a long time to sort this one out but we got to grips with it finally and dramatically when Edward Turner was personally demonstrating a new motorcycle to a group of rather important people; the frame broke and my boss hit the deck rather sharply. It had been made from inferior welded tubing instead of the specified solid drawn material which, in those early days before extensive development gave us the present quality, and was an unforgiveable lapse on behalf of the Buyer.

Late in 1935 Jack Sangster made a bid, which was accepted, for the motorcycle manufacturing and trading unit of the Triumph Company of Coventry. Triumph, whose main interest was motor cars, were anxious to dispose of the two-wheeler subsidiary and Sangster was able to take over this section of the Coventry plant intact and in-situ at, what Turner described to me later, as a 'give away price'. All this necessitated was the appointment of top management and continuing to manufacture the same range of Triumph motorcycles in exactly the same production shops in Coventry. Edward Turner was appointed General Manager of this new venture and Sangster, very cleverly, killed two birds with one stone by satisfying, to some extent, Turner's ambitious manoeuvring. At the same time, he separated the warring elements at Selly Oak.

I was not keen to stay on with Ariel Motors for I felt the absence of real forward policy would now become more acute. I had been offered a job in the aircraft industry but Turner invited me to join him as his design assistant and although **23**

The 600 cc. Ariel Square Four with an engine of 56 x 61 mm bore and stroke. This is the 1932 model and features an instrument panel sunk into the petrol tank which was something of a novelty at the time. The rider is the late George Wheeler.

Sangster would not, at first, hear of it, he finally agreed and I moved to Triumph early in 1936.

Jack Sangster

Chapter Two

A second famous brand name is absorbed

BY NOW Turner and I were dovetailing, to some extent, in a partnership which was paying off in speedy execution of new designs which his very impatient nature demanded. I certainly knew his strengths and weaknesses and I am sure that he was aware of mine, although his nature was such that he was ever shy to acknowledge muscle of any sort in his assistants.

He was, quite definitely, the most egotistical man that I have ever met and when I first joined him at Triumph, I was foolish enough to refer, in an unguarded moment, to his Works Manager. He got really mad with me and pointed out, in no uncertain manner, that he was the Works Manager, the Sales Manager, the General Manager and the Buyer! He retained this strange attitude to the end of his working career and it is a pity because he was fortunate enough, at the height of his career, to be supported by a management team which must be classed as one of the finest ever to be assembled in the motorcycle industry.

At a later stage, Turner negotiated an agreement which enabled him to be absent in the USA for six months each year, an arrangement which was illogical and unnecessary. Nonetheless the Triumph company survived and prospered, notwithstanding these sunny excursions, which underlines the nature of this dedicated team of experts, some of whose capabilities extended far beyond the job titles under which they had been employed.

As an engineer, Edward Turner seemed to lack the technical knowledge which must be embraced if engineering design is to be anything but guesswork. Indeed, he dismissed as 'academics' most of the people whose job it was to make sure, by mathematics, that the company's products had reasonable factors of safety. However, he was an inventive genius and had a flair for pleasing shapes and an uncanny ability to 'smell out' what the buying public would readily accept. This, **25**

Part of the Triumph manufacturing unit at Dale Street, Coventry, just prior to the Sangster take-over in 1935.

The first Triumph motorcycle of 1902

together with a down to earth business sense, was the key to his very successful industrial career.

His original designs were, to me, dangerously lacking technically and always needed 'vetting'. Unless someone with a robot-like determination accepted this task soon enough, the results could be, and often were, catastrophic.

It was inevitable that he and I should all but come to blows on occasions, but by this time I had achieved technical levels of a reasonably high standard. In addition, I was becoming 'case-hardened' against emotional emergencies so that I was an expert in the mixing of the right dosage of mathematics. We generally managed, although not always, with good grace.

Through all this our business relationship, which was necessarily close, was at times so stormy and we were so extremely rude to each other that, on reflection, it seems very strange that the partnership was not terminated at a very early stage.

I shall never know whether he really appreciated what I was doing for he certainly gave me no such impression. But I remember feeling that mine was a unique experience for if I could master problems so fundamental with a character such as this, there was no need for concern about future mixes of design entrepreneurs.

The Triumph works was a rather larger version of the Ariel manufacturing unit and once again Mr. Sangster was able to pick and choose employees. Consequently

The famous Ricardo model Triumph. A four valve engine was standard equipment on this 1923 single cylinder model.

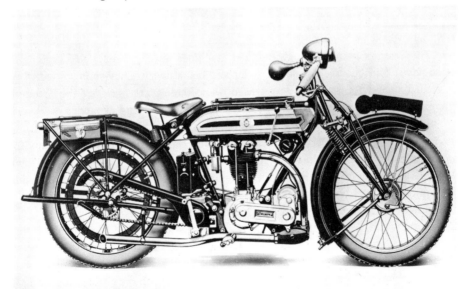

Another famous Triumph – the 1926 model P.

this unit was so sparse and efficient that the target production figure of 100 machines per week was achieved and exceeded very rapidly.

We were manufacturing a comprehensive range of single cylinder machines, all with ohv specification, from 250 cc to 550 cc and in addition we had 'inherited' the 650 cc parallel twin which Val Page had recently designed and had given Turner such high blood pressure back at Ariel Motors.

The Triumph range of single cylinder machines were injected with a little more horse-power and given a face lift of silver and black livery. They soon started to be in great demand for the economy was now becoming 'set fair' and the Triumph manufacturing unit, under Turner's leadership, blossomed and expanded.

Val Page's parallel twin was in small quantity production and quite contrary to the popular belief that Edward Turner pioneered this particular type of engine for motorcycles, it was, I think, the first motorcycle of this type to be mass-produced. Actually an engine of this sort was in being as early as 1913 and the accompanying illustration indicates clearly a very distinct parentage to the many varieties of parallel twin power units eventually to be produced.

Turner had set his mind on scrapping Page's twin cylinder machine and replacing it with one of his own design. It was a snap decision which struck me, at the time, as being near criminal, for this motorcycle was comparatively new in production and was far from being a failure. I felt that with the engineering strength we now had, this model would have responded very quickly to development and would have proven to be a very satisfactory product. However, no consideration was

Exhaust Ports

Inlet Ports

Exhaust Lifter

Magneto Drive

Details of a much earlier Triumph parallel twin engine. As early as 1913 the Triumph company had produced this interesting machine which had many novel features.

given to this possibility and it seemed to me that Turner had the obsession that this motorcycle, born of Val Page's brain, must be out of production forthwith. As a result, the model came to an undeserved end on the scrap heap.

There is probably no other industry which would have tolerated such obsessions and it seems to me that the motorcycle world has a history which is littered with examples of perfectly good products being cast aside purely because of whims and fancies of this sort, invariably when new management had been installed.

Edward Turner's new machine was to have a 500 cc engine, a parallel twin of course, and firstly an ohc version was designed. After several weeks, a clean snappy layout was produced which would be ordinary in terms of today's sophisticated standards, but was quite unusual for the year 1936. However, after much consideration and many interpretations on the drawing board when seeking alternative methods of camshaft devices, it was decided to abandon the ohc version and resort to the more conventional ohv operation. This was undoubtedly a wise decision for at that time, we knew very little about attenuated camshaft drives. I remember we felt that the overhead camshaft lubrication problems may have been difficult but, most of all, adequate drainage of excess oil from the valve spring chambers did not look at all easy to achieve. How right we were!

So the 500 cc Speed Twin was on the way and the design was utterly simple with a similar geometrical layout of valve gear to that used in the famous Riley car engine.

The Speed Twin engine had a rather small bore and consequently long stroke by today's standards, in order to achieve compactness in engine width and to allow enough space for a modicum of air to circulate between the cylinders, which were badly obscured by the push rod cover tubes.

Chapter Two

I remember that we were greatly concerned that a train of five gears were needed to drive the two camshafts and Magdyno but Turner's designs were always scrupulously compact (a chain drive may have been more quiet in operation but would have resulted in a more bulky package). Although the Speed Twin was fundamentally a rattler, the design proved to be so sound and reliable in most other respects that the characteristic ticking and clicking noises seemed to be accepted and forgiven by Triumph enthusiasts.

The new machine was launched in 1937 with an engine developing 27 bhp and was a complete success. It was smart and compact in appearance, it had a first class performance, was reasonably light in weight and sold at the modest price of £77.15s. The foundation had been laid for an era of prosperity and from that day the company was never, at any time, short of orders. Machines of this type were in such demand that Triumphs were able to operate year after year (in fact for the next 35 years) with steadily increasing output and with no record of short time working through lack of demand.

At about this time a young development engineer, Freddie Clarke, joined us for the express purpose of developing a sporting version of the Speed Twin. Freddie, who had established an enviable reputation at Brooklands developing and riding motorcycles very fast, was a down to earth character who did not suffer fools gladly. Although he was very small in stature, this was more than compensated for by an extremely peppery attitude. Freddie was brilliant and in fact one of the 'greats' in motorcycling. Had he not been killed in an accident, a few years later, he would, I am sure, have become a figurehead of the British motorcycle industry.

He soon got down to the job of upgrading the Speed Twin power unit, now in quantity production, and did his job too well, so it would seem, for Turner. When he pushed up the power by a massive 22% from 27 to 33 bhp, things began to break. My department became a graveyard of broken crankshafts and connecting rods and Edward Turner threw a fit. He seemed to think that someone had ulterior motives, but eventually, after lengthy persuasion, he became convinced that problems of this sort would not right themselves. Remedial action was taken and the Tiger 100 was on the way. Undoubtedly the Speed Twin would have continued quite satisfactorily without change, but if something happens that causes the maximum engine revolutions to be increased dramatically, it is not surprising that some re-design may become necessary.

However, although we invariably got things right in the end, much time was always wasted in procrastination of this nature and a prime example of this was the original Triumph spring wheel design. It seemed to me that the major part of design time was spent convincing Turner that springs made from the world's finest material would be overstressed by around 40% if they were to be squeezed into the space which was shown on his original sketch. He had a vexing habit of suggesting that most calculations were a waste of time and were a relic of schooldays, which should

The 1937 Speed Twin Triumph.

be forgotten and not mixed with the serious business of work. Frequently this led to turbulent scenes before work could be continued.

The 'Tiger 100' with its distinctive trim of silver sheen and styling that suggested rapidity of movement, proved to be a world beater, always in demand. It quickly established itself as the yardstick of performance, reliability and value for money, setting a standard which was was unequalled for a very long time.

Output was rising steadily, the Company was prospering and the management team was strengthened with the arrival of E.J. (Ted) Crabtree as Chief Buyer. We were also fortunate enough to have as Company Secretary C.W.F. Parker, a man who had a love for motorcycles and was a first class qualified accountant, who had somehow drifted from finance to motorcycle journalism and had joined us from Temple Press. Both of these men were giants in their field of operation, with motorcycles in their blood and seemingly limitless enthusiasm and energy. They formed strong links indeed in the team of professionals which was to steer the Company through a successful decade of achievement.

Turner was anxious to delete all the single-cylinder machines from the product range and to replace them with models having twin cylinder power units. In consequence, a 350 cc parallel twin motorcycle was designed and developed for production in the near future. The new power unit was not, however, nearly so satisfactory as its larger counterpart and was never destined to be such a success, **31** largely because of its weak and flabby performance figures upon which it was virtually impossible to improve. It was a 'lanky' engine with a small bore and a long stroke, and the push rods were over-long and whippy, causing excessive lost motion at the valve gear. The most important engine component, the crankshaft, was a somewhat pitiful design of three piece construction, unbelievably whippy mainly because of skimpiness in the clamping arrangement.

Small wonder that this machine, the 3T, never made the headlines, for it was quite impossible to coax a reasonable power figure from the engine in spite of all the wizardry that Freddie Clarke could muster. He finally gave up the struggle in despair.

By now Triumph were building up a very fine export market which grew steadily and a notable achievement was a breakthrough in the USA which, through the efforts of Johnson Motors of Pasadena, marked the beginning of a demand for substantial numbers of Triumph machines, particularly the Tiger 100 models.

Bill Johnson, the proprietor, was an ex-lawyer and a quite rich man who simply loved motorcycles. He built up a very fine business indeed with an exclusive Triumph franchise, developing a dealer organisation which was the envy of many. Its marketing performance was so effective that the Triumph production flow rate became an ever-rising figure and a happy workforce enjoyed complete freedom from any periods of short time working from the later 1930s until the debacle of the early 1970s. Bill Johnson and Edward Turner became firm friends and it is perhaps not surprising that Edward, who loved a change, was attracted to the exciting and sunny parts of the USA. He began to spend more time in the States and less time at his desk at Coventry.

Jack Sangster did not seem to mind in view of the arrangement referred to earlier, whereby Turner was free to spend 6 months of each year in the USA. I am not sure at what exact point of time this rather strange arrangement started to operate, but certainly by 1939 he was spending long periods away from Coventry.

During his periods 'in residence' so to speak, we began to notice that Turner's personality was beginning to deteriorate and as time went on, the situation got worse, for he seemed unable to concentrate or follow through a conversation. He developed an aggravating habit of giving sometimes strange instructions to all and sundry and bypassing the heads of departments who were, of course, unaware that members of their staff were thus advised. It became quite impossible to discuss a problem or to reason with the man and I was convinced that he was heading for a breakdown. As a last resort I tried to offer personal help as a friend. This sort of thing had done some good on a past occasion, but now it was doomed to failure for he was so rude and violent that it was very obvious that my type of psychology was not the medicine.

The clouds of war were gathering and the Government invited most motorcycle manufacturers to submit designs for a motorcycle to a specification suitable for war

The 1939 500 cc Triumph Tiger 100.

The Triumph assembly track at Dale Street, Coventry in 1939. Speed Twins are being assembled.

service. A machine of very low weight and high ground clearance was necessary, with a desirable power output of around 15 bhp. Reliability was, of course, a must and it was understood that substantial orders were waiting for the machine which was found to be most suitable.

Triumph responded to the challenge by re-vamping the 350 cc twin engine, for its flabby power curve matched the modest requirement. A tiny gearbox was grafted on and the lavish use of light alloy, wherever possible, helped to satisfy the weight problem. A very delicate little frame with wheels and brakes rather reminiscent of pedal cycle practice were designed and the combined result enabled us to produce a motorcycle of 350 cc capacity with a dry weight of 230 lbs.

Most motorcyclists of the day would have considered this a dream machine specification; a featherlight answer to a maiden's prayer. But no, it was the result of a sickness which had driven a capable designer to ignore practically every fundamental law of engineering. This machine, during its initial road test period, had more breakdowns of a really serious nature than could be coped with by the Experimental Department under the very able leadership of Freddie Clarke.

Our Managing Director refused to accept that the breakages and wear problems were even remotely connected with his design and steadfastly refused to agree to any corrective action by re-design. He seemed to think that Freddie and myself were in some sort of plot. After making frantic but vain efforts to deal with the situation, which was of course purely an engineering problem easily corrected by massive re-design, we resigned ourselves to a strange situation which could have been dealt with only by Jack Sangster.

At about this time, Sangster had acquired the design and goodwill of the New Imperial motor cycle company, which had gone out of business. Both he and Turner felt that a very simple, lightweight, single-cylinder motorcycle sold under the New Imperial trademark, but manufactured by Triumph, would broaden our market spread and strengthen our dealers considerably.

This was good thinking for, by now, the Triumph range of products were powered by multi-cylinder engines and the Company image was very strongly aligned to this rather more exclusive type of machine. So it seemed to be good business sense to market a cheap lightweight motorcycle under the New Imperial name. It was a foregone conclusion that the New Imperial designs would be scrapped out of hand, for Turner seemed to find it difficult to believe that any other designer had talent. His present mood certainly did nothing to enable us to be open minded in arriving at decisions.

When the New Imperial company ceased production, they had in their range a small machine of 147 cc capacity called the Unit Minor which was a handsome little motorcycle and reasonably trouble free, so the grapevine told us. After studying the design drawing I could see no fundamental problems which would prevent us from

producing this machine at Triumph, perhaps with slight alterations and a little re-

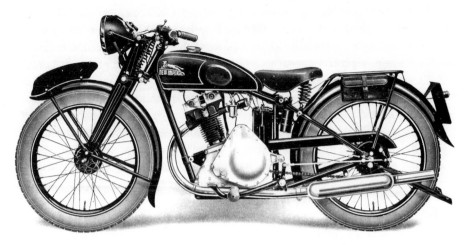

The 1936 New Imperial Unit Minor, then selling at £29/15/- complete.

styling here and there. This would have been a short cut to the production stage of a very desirable product aimed at a new and promising market sector, both at home and abroad, which would have produced results for us in the shortest possible space of time. The tooling layouts were complete and available and much of the heavy cost of production equipment had already been met.

Predictably, Sangster was persuaded to throw overboard the current New Imperial machine, which had been in production a comparatively short space of time. Instead, he had been prevailed upon to embark on a completely new design on which Turner himself became engaged and in about six months we had the first prototype undergoing road tests.

It is almost frightening and certainly depressing to compare this rate of progress with that of a similar operation today and one cannot help but wonder what has gone wrong. I am certain that the time factor would be trebled on present ratings and it is difficult for me to believe that so much work was done and so many new models were designed and made, even though some of these never reached the production stage. However, history confirms these facts for the Triumph Engineering Company did not start operating until 1936 and the Second World War commenced in 1939, cutting short the freedom of normal activity. I confess I found it difficult to realise that during three short years a manufacturing unit had been re-organised and launched to a very profitable beginning, an exciting new range of twin cylinder motorcycles were comfortably in mass production, and a further two new models had been designed and prototypes were undergoing road tests. A tremendous performance and a noteworthy comparison with our pitiful achievements several decades later, when resources had multiplied enormously and the industry had been invaded by swarms of experts in every business field.

Chapter Two

The Triumph-cum-New Imperial newcomer had a 200 cc ohv engine which was very simple. I remember that the valves were upright in the cylinder head and the power unit, which had a longish stroke, was somewhat tall, which tended to detract from the machine's general appearance because engine clearance problems necessitated the petrol tank to be positioned way out high. The cylinder was upright and it would have been a very simple matter to correct the appearance problem by sloping the engine forward a little. Indeed, I remember re-designing the machine in this simple manner and achieving more acceptable styling. But Mr. Turner had what can only be described as a 'bee in his bonnet' about motorcycles which had sloping engines and although I reminded him that his own Ariel 'sloper' of some ten years previously had an engine as its name implied, with a very exaggerated slope indeed, it did not make any difference. We persevered with the ugly duckling.

It so happens that it was of little importance for by then we were half way through 1939 with a state of war rapidly approaching and our activities on projected new products proved to be of only academic interest. Turner had been planning a simple machine with a good deal of structural enclosure, not like a scooter but a motorcycle which had more ample mudguards and panels, to give much more weather protection. It was intended to carry sufficient appeal to cater for, what he termed, a vast untapped potential market of riders who simply would not consider the normal motorcycles which were somewhat messy at times. Also the time had arrived, he felt, to dispense with spoked road wheels and to replace these with the disc type, reminiscent of those which are fitted to most metal wheelbarrows. Consequently, the enclosed machine exercise, for want of a better term, was coupled with the New Imperial project, and we were soon operating two types of experimental machines which looked vastly different, although each had similar engine and frame structures.

We were concerned with the problems of cross winds and the effect these would have on the stability of a machine which had a large proportion of enclosure, but in the main, we were unsure as to the effect of disc wheels on the handling ability of a single-track vehicle.

Freddie Clarke was a superb rider and he spent much time riding the enclosed version of the New Imperial in all weathers, making test after test with many modifications until he arrived at the stage where he was quite satisfied that the unusual wheels were not a hazard. He had gone through many changes to steering angle and wheel trail and several other variations, which had transformed the handling ability of the motorcycle to such a degree that he felt that the Speed Twin and Tiger 100 machines, now being produced in substantial quantities, would benefit from a similar development programme.

It will be known to most Triumph enthusiasts of that era that our machines were far from outstanding in handling characteristics and indeed I had witnessed Freddie developing a lock to lock steering wobble a few weeks previously, while riding a very fast Tiger 100 machine. This was an unforgettable experience, with the handlebars of the motorcycle out of control, making loud clanging noises as they went from left to right lock in rapid succession.

I am sure this experience spurred on a programme of improved stability for the Triumph range of products but Turner would have none of it. Although he must have been aware of this shortcoming in an otherwise very satisfactory product range, he would never admit that changes were necessary. The facts were that he was a fine rider himself and never got into trouble but Clarke also was a very fine rider, and in addition, was capable of riding much faster than the boss.

Freddie so transformed the Triumph test machines with modifications to steering angle, engine position and trail that every tester and many others were agreed that the changes were a must and should be put into production with all urgency. But this was not to be, for Turner went near berserk when this was suggested. He had never found anything wrong and he ruled a no-change policy. It was a strange situation for a company to be producing motorcycles which were a little dangerous under certain conditions, with our own testers admitting the fault and the riding public knowing and accepting the fault purely because of the satisfaction they had with the product as a whole. All this was jeopardised by the decision of a Managing Director who said no because he had never been flung off. I feel sure that because of the very severe safety regulations which had come into force by the late 1960s, every machine which had been exported to the USA would have been returned to the factory for modification, otherwise the Managing Director would have been found guilty of law infringement.

This incident convinced me that the designer should not be allowed to indulge in the riding or testing of products which are created by him until such time as they are satisfactorily in production, for he naturally regards the new project as his baby and this tends to blur the picture. The responsibility of proving prototypes through to the production stage is that of the Development Engineer and his staff of expert engineers and testers. Thankfully, this man is not normally also the designer.

Triumph were stuck with the weave and wobble characteristics and it was not until the early 1960s that another Development Engineer named Doug Hele came to similar conclusions and made the changes which transformed the handling characteristics of the whole range of products. It brought with it an enhanced reputation for Triumph, which was second to none.

The New Imperial prototype and the War Department machine had been designed at about the same time. Not surprisingly, the state of the art was not improving, and I am sorry to say that the design of the former was far from satisfactory either. The engine had a cylinder which was fabricated from a thick piece of tube, the inside diameter forming the bore and the cooling fins made from a series of pressings in sheet copper with alternate spacers which were then brazed together as a whole. I believe that Turner followed the same principle as that of the Franklin **37** car engine, an air-cooled power unit of American origin, but the Franklin unit was blower-cooled with close ducting, so that cooling air was forced, under pressure, between the fin spaces.

Not so with our unit, which relied on natural cooling and even at speed it was difficult to imagine air completely penetrating the depths of the incredibly fine spaces. It is not surprising that we never could prevent the piston from seizing on almost every test run.

The gearbox was so minute and over-stressed that problems arose every day and the gearchange mechanism was so skimped and clearances were so fine that, on occasions, two gears tended to be selected simultaneously. I remember that the clutch was actuated by a ball mechanism which Turner seemed to think had a rolling motion, but in fact the ball did not rotate when in operation and produced a skidding motion, causing the mechanism to destroy itself.

The frame was so whippy that sometimes a rider would feel momentarily lost when trying to make quick changes in direction and the brakes got so hot, probably because the disc wheels had some deterrent effect on cooling, but also because of their skimpy proportions. Braking effect would fade to nil and the machine became dangerous to ride.

In short, like the 350 cc War Department machine now labelled the 3TW, it was a flop and I consider that the intervention of war spared the motorcycling public the agony of coping with this horror. We were, of course, at war in September 1939, and Triumph ticked over for a month of two, but soon our manufacturing capacity was earmarked for the production of motorcycles for service use, although the Authorities had left it a little late as there did not seem to be any suitable machine for this purpose.

It is true that we and other manufacturers had been invited to submit a suitable machine, hence our effort with the 3TW, but plans were far from mature and indeed I believe that many of the makers who had been approached had barely commenced design work.

We were the exception for we had two prototypes of the 3TW machine, both of which had completed moderate road mileages.

Chapter Three

The ashes of World War 2 bring a transformation of facilities

THE MILITARY Authorities were now anxious to provide the British Army with suitable two-wheeled transport but it seems strange that crisis point had been reached before urgent thought was given to this matter.

A hasty decision was made to take a catalogue machine for immediate use, and press on as quickly as possible with the development of the 3TW. There were some doubts about the suitability of our production range of twins, mainly because of weight, and eventually it was agreed that we should resurrect the 350 cc single cylinder machine and switch the factory to the exclusive manufacture of this motorcycle.

At the same time, it was agreed to produce a pilot batch of 50 of our new 3TW motorcycles as quickly as possible, for user trials, in the hope that it would become the standard motorcycle for use by the armed forces. I must confess that I found this decision a strange one since Army riders had not had an opportunity to test the prototype in their own environment. However, the situation was desperate and Turner was a superb salesman. He had most certainly donned his 'rose tinted spectacles'.

So Triumph became a busy unit, mass producing the resurrected 350 cc single cylinder version of their discarded range and in addition, the 50 special 3TW machines were made and assembled. These were packed in their cases and were on the loading deck of our Despatch Department on the night of the big Coventry blitz. They were destroyed together with the factory and most of its contents. I still feel that, so far as the 50 specials were concerned, Hitler did our War Office a favour. I am sure, and so was Clarke, that these would have proved troublesome in all respects and most certainly were not suitable for the rigours of warfare usage.

Chapter Three

There was no question of making 50 replacement machines because the Triumph works had been completely destroyed overnight and all was gone. The factory was a write off and our immediate job was to get back to a situation, somehow or somewhere, which would enable us to produce once more the rather nondescript but thoroughly reliable 350 cc single cylinder motorcycle. Sangster and Turner had been considering having company records and drawings and designs copied and stored in a safe place but nothing had been done and we were left with a smouldering shell and no records.

It was essential that the technical staff were organised to bring some order back from the chaos and we rigged up temporary cover, much of it being of strong paper or cardboard. We also purchased new drawing boards and tools and tried to make a brave new start, but we were blasted again, night after night. After three or four such efforts, each time with new equipment, we gave up the struggle and moved house to a semi-derelict set of buildings alongside the canal at nearby Warwick. At last, there seemed to be reasonable prospects of a permanent roof over our heads.

There is no doubt that the hammerings we were being given by Hitler's air raids were uniting the British people and this had to be seen to be fully believed. Night after night our cities were heavily bombed and most of us were in the thick of it with little or no shelter, snatching what sleep we could. Although we were very weary indeed, we were determined to survive and we became more determined, after each battering

The Triumph 3TU prototype machine. A simplified offshoot of this design was to be marketed as a New Imperial. This particular machine was equipped with a simple form of 350 cc ohv parallel twin engine, but never reached the production stage.

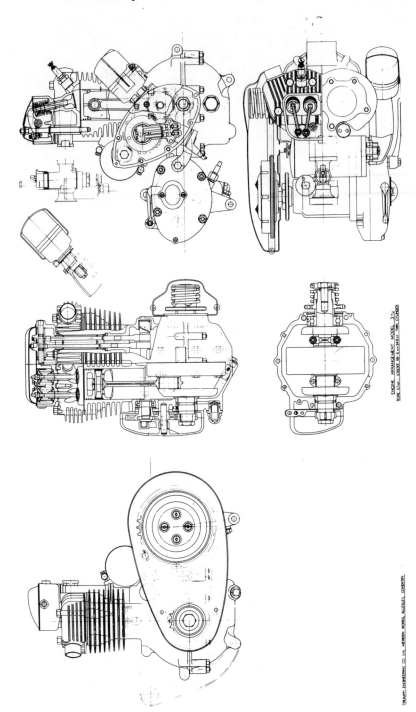

ENGINE ARRANGEMENT MODEL 3TU
BORE 55 mm. STROKE 68.6 m=349 cc TWIN CYLINDER

TRIUMPH ENGINEERING CO LTD, MERIDEN WORKS, ALLESLEY, COVENTRY.

The Triumph 3TU engine, a simple parallel twin 350 cc ohv unit. This failed to reach the production stage.

The Triumph 3TW, a 350 cc ohv twin designed for military purposes and weighing only 230 lbs dry. A pre-production batch of 50 of these machines were ready for delivery but were destroyed in the Triumph despatch dept during the night of the great Coventry blitz.

Part of the Triumph Coventry plant after the great blitz.

to set up shop again. And so it was that out of the rubble everyone, from the manager downwards, took off his coat and just got on with what was seen to be necessary, in a superb effort to get the wheels turning.

The least damaged machine tools were moved to Warwick and those which were out of action were repaired. I remember one huge twin spindle vertical boring machine, which was lying in two separate pieces, being disassembled by willing hands. The huge casing was welded together and in what seemed to be no time, the machine was in running order in its new home. This machine was to give excellent service for the next thirty years and the great rough line of welding which had re-united the monster was always there. It brought back vivid memories for me each time I walked through the machine shop in later years.

Things were moving very rapidly and at last the machine shop started to make parts. The commercial staff were housed in a derelict chapel next door, and slowly motorcycles began to trickle along the improvised assembly shop, producing a machine for which we had no drawing records. The drive, interrupted only by the blitz, had taken over and memories were doing the rest.

It was vital, of course that we should have drawing records, not only of the model we were making but, more important, of the Speed Twin and the Tiger 100 models which we hoped to re-introduce at the end of hostilities. The next twelve months or so proved to be the most unrewarding and miserable of my career. **43**

The Triumph organisation gave up the struggle in Coventry and moved to very spartan premises at 'The Cape' on the canal-side at nearby Warwick. It was nicknamed 'The Cape of Good Hope'; the 'tin' structure shown was the general office of the Triumph company. The testers are taking out two military machines of 350 cc single cylinder ohv type.

The design dept of Triumph in wartime 'Cape of Good Hope' days. The entire staff is shown with the author (in background), two designers, a clerk and a print boy.

The assembly track at the Warwick 'Cape of Good Hope' temporary premises in 1942.

Chapter Three

It is a most difficult operation to re-create, on paper, facsimiles of a range of products from drawings in suppliers hands, from the few records which were found at Turner's home (which were not up to date) and from memory. It was essential that every size and tolerance on the new records should be identical with the original, otherwise replacement parts would probably not be exactly suitable for machines which were already in use.

It may seem to be much ado about nothing as far as most readers are concerned for many can not possibly realize the difficulties, but the whole technical team were left with a sense of despair which was difficult to describe. After all this, all we had achieved was the re-drawing of records of machines which had been designed several years before!

To add to our problems the vermin, with with the old canal-side buildings were riddled, seemed to have formed a fifth column. The mice, in particular, relished the flavour of our nice new drawing paper and until we were able to install metal filing cabinets, which were extremely scarce, we seemed to be fighting another losing battle.

In 1942 Sangster and Turner had a quarrel, which resulted in the latter's resignation, and since trouble had been smouldering for some time, I was not very surprised. Indeed, it had seemed inevitable since Turner had become hostile to

The new Triumph factory built at Allesley, near Meriden, into which we moved in late 1942.

Engine assembly unit at Triumph, Meriden in 1943.

Sangster, whom he regarded as 'the faceless one who prospered greatly from my brilliance'. Turner became obsessed with this idea but, even if it were true, it seems to have been a minor hardship. There is no doubt that his financial reward, as an employee in the motorcycle industry, was one of the best on record, which seems to be a reasonable arrangement.

Long before this upset, the Directors had come to an arrangement with the Government to build a factory on a country site at Meriden. Work was already well under way and we moved into the new works in late 1942. It is quite amazing how quickly things were moving again in those troubled days.

The transition from slum to palace, so to speak, was a great boost to morale and it would have been a good time to have given some thought at least to the likely product line when peace came. However, it seemed that Sangster felt the post-war period could be satisfied with our pre-war products and no serious work of this nature was tackled.

Instead, time was frittered away designing and making prototypes based on a rather odd idea, emanating from Sangster. It took the form of a very light track laying vehicle which would be capable of propelling a man, in prone position, over rough terrain. Powered by a 50 cc two-stroke engine and having an armour-plated front end, the vehicle was 6 feet long by 2 feet wide and had a height of roughly 12   **47**

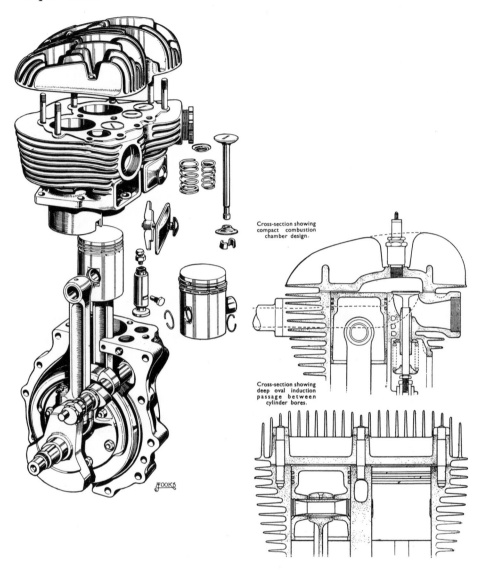

Cross-section showing compact combustion chamber design.

Cross-section showing deep oval induction passage between cylinder bores.

The Triumph 500 cc sv twin cylinder engine, designed by the author in 1943.

inches, weighing a little over 75 lbs. It was a proposed military vehicle for surprise attacks, capable of being carried by the operator to the attacking point and presenting to the enemy the minimum possible target. Because it operated on miniature tracks (like a tank) and was extremely light, it was considered likely to negotiate minefields with minimum problems. These were the parameters set for this machine, soon nicknamed 'the magic carpet', but although we had some fun and games with two prototypes on the field at the back of the works, the military authorities did not seem interested and the project was dropped.

We had a second journey into the realms of fantasy, which was such a time waster that I am disgusted to this day. Edward Turner had been engaged by BSA as Chief Designer and Sangster had heard, over the grapevine, that he was designing a 500 cc side-valve twin cylinder machine, presumably for Army use. It was understood that the new BSA motorcycle would be ready for assembly in about three months and I was instructed to design and make one prototype of a similar machine for Triumph, with the proviso that we demonstrate the new model at a press gathering which we should organise in two months time.

A tall order indeed but the punch line was that the machine would not go into

The Triumph 500 cc sv twin cylinder machine designed by the author in 1943. Although this motorcycle, designed and made in 7 weeks, was purely a publicity gimmick laid on by Mr. Sangster, it proved to be the first move toward the NATO-approved military machine to come later.

production and after the press announcement, which would be supported by the prototype motorcycle on which the journalists would be free to have demonstration rides, the whole thing would be scrapped. The sole object of this strange exercise was to take the wind out of the sails of the great BSA Company, and no doubt Turner's presence there provided an added incentive. This move would enable the Triumph Company to go on record as the originators of this type of machine, with Turner's project making little impact when eventually it was released.

It would fill a chapter to explain in detail how we kept our work secret until the day of the press announcement for we could not make use of the services of our normal run of suppliers for obvious reasons. The cylinder, to quote one example, was a most complicated casting, and was made for us in the foundry of a firm whose **49** name is now synonymous with lawn mowers. They made a nonsense of all previous time factors connected with the production of such a component.

The first engine was running in seven weeks from the day of Mr. Sangster's 'brainwave', with the chassis and wheels ready to take the power unit. After about twelve hours of bench testing and very sketchy adjustment, Freddie Clarke had the machine on road test. A monumental effort for an exercise in futility!

The machine was very similar in appearance to that which, more than 10 years later, was to become known as the hybrid or the 5TW, which sold in substantial quantities to foreign governments and later the British War Office and was fully accepted as the standard motorcycle for NATO usage.

Press release date was 25th February 1943 and a large gathering of journalists and key figures from the industry met at Grosvenor Hotel in London, by invitation, where Sangster made the announcement with the help of lavish hospitality. And, of course, there was the one and only motorcycle which many pressmen afterwards rode. So ended what was for me a frustrating episode and we all went back to Coventry. The exercise seemed to have achieved the desired result for we quickly forgot the whole matter, but BSA were furious, and rightly so. The launch of their machine, which was made many months later, went off like a damp squib.

I was anxious that we should now get on with real design work with an eye to the future, for although we were in a position to resume production of our pre-war range, we had no follow up plans. It is strange that, although the country was having such a battering and our military achievements then were not over-encouraging, no one seemed to have any doubts about the final outcome of the war. Many of us were planning for the return to sanity and were anxious that we should not 'lose any tricks'.

I discussed with Sangster the possibility of a new machine with a four cylinder engine and he agreed that we get on with an in-line engine with traditional Triumph valve gear geometry, very similar to the triple engine which was introduced twenty years later, but of course having an additional cylinder. The power unit was of 700 cc capacity with a designed power rating of 50 bhp at 6,500 rpm and was planned with a two-stage primary drive to the gearbox. The frame was an entirely new type with a rigid triangulated backbone structure and the engine crankshaft ran transversely across the frame, with a chain drive to the rear wheel.

Nowadays this reads like the specification of many of the Japanese machines we have come to regard as normal, but in the early 1940s the rather awe-inspiring and handsome mock-up machine which we had made left most of us in no doubt that a supporting product of this sort would create a sensation.

All very nice, so far as it went, for I felt that at last we were away with a project and could take time and get things right, which would be a change to say the least. But it was not to be, for Sangster and Turner were beginning to get friendly once more, and I feel that this affected the decision to scrap the whole thing.

350 cc single cylinder ohv army machines ready for despatch at Triumph Meriden works in 1943.

The 350 cc ohv single cylinder military machine in production at Triumphs during the greater part of the war years.

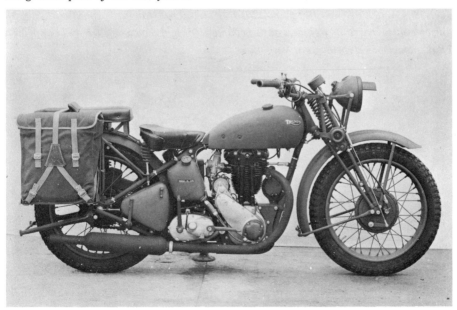

Chapter Three

Naturally I felt somewhat deflated for I was certain that the post-war world would be ready to welcome a product such as the one we had before us in design and mock-up form. Unlike the Square Four, it would have been comparatively simple, quieter and would certainly have had good performance.

Nonetheless, in spite of the disappointment, I looked back on an incredible 14 months during which we lost Turner, our Managing Director, and had managed without a replacement. Furthermore we had moved the whole manufacturing unit from Warwick to Meriden and had maintained an unbroken flow. We had designed two new motorcycles and road tested one, and had drifted for a period into another world and produced and tested the crawling attack vehicle or 'magic carpet'.

In 1943 Turner severed his connection with BSA and returned to us once more as Managing Director. It was known that the environment and discipline of the huge Small Heath complex did not suit him and he had been unhappy. It is not surprising that this unusual man, who had so successfully master-minded a small private company and literally been answerable to no one, should not take kindly to the organisation and discipline which fundamentally are necessary and usually more in evidence in a public company.

Although we were, I felt, back to square one, so far as future planning was concerned, I am certain that no one at Triumph felt guilty of having sat on their backsides during the past 14 months or so. I took great exception to Turner's first

Prototype of ultra-light version of the 500 cc sv twin cylinder machine for military use. This machine was later modified to a more standard specification with consequent increase in weight and it became the highly successful NATO-approved TRW model or 'Hybrid' as it was nicknamed.

comment on greeting me for, in his own words, he had been 'invited back to get the place organised to pull back some of the leeway'.

I am afraid that on this one occasion I was guilty of excessive rudeness in my comment 'God help BSA if you have organised any of their leeway'. We had a most shocking row and our relationship never recovered to the old basis, but hurtful as my comment was, I knew Turner well enough to realise that it had made him pause awhile to consider the content and this in itself was a little consolation.

The military authorities were beating at our door for a standardized War Department motorcycle to replace the various machines which the trade were supplying, but now the Fighting Vehicle Development Establishment had decided that ohv engines were too complicated and inflexible and in the main were unnecesssarily fast. The snappy performance figures, which the public expected, were of no interest and the new requirements were long and reliable mechanical life and a very soft performance, which would be just able to cope with marshalling and piloting duties for convoy work, together with the lightest possible weight and an ability to traverse rough terrain.

We made the decision to press on with the 500 cc side-valve twin as such a machine was already available and indeed a prototype had been standing in our Experimental Shop since the press demonstration in London some months previously. Some work needed to be done to meet the specification now laid down but the motorcycle could not be seen as Turner's own design so, inevitably, we started all over again and finished, months later, with something very similar.

Prototypes were made and eventually went away to Chobham for user trials. After much co-operative effort by military personnel, the machine was accepted. It was to become the NATO-approved military motorcycle and Triumph were to enjoy a lucrative business venture with the provision of machines and spare parts for several foreign governments as well as to secure a modest turnover with the British forces.

We were then approached by a government department to submit a design for a portable generator set capable of supplying sufficient current for starting aircraft engines. Basically the unit comprised a small air-cooled engine coupled to a 6 kW generator, with a hand or foot starting arrangement and a working speed of 4000 rpm. The unit was to be light and compact enough to enable two men to carry it from hangar to aircraft, where the set would be cranked and started then coupled to the aircraft engine so that the latter would be supplied with ample current to permit a switch start. Our pre-war 500 cc ohv Speed Twin engine was ideal for this purpose and it was used to form the power unit with the addition of a fan and cowling for cooling purposes and a governor system for maintaining constant speed with or without engine load.

There was, I remember, only one severe problem which could have been obviated immediately but our Managing Director once more had a 'bee in his **53**

The 500 cc sv twin 'Hybrid' engine.

Triumph 6 kW portable generator set made for the RAF during the war years.

The ashes of World War 2 bring a transformation of facilities

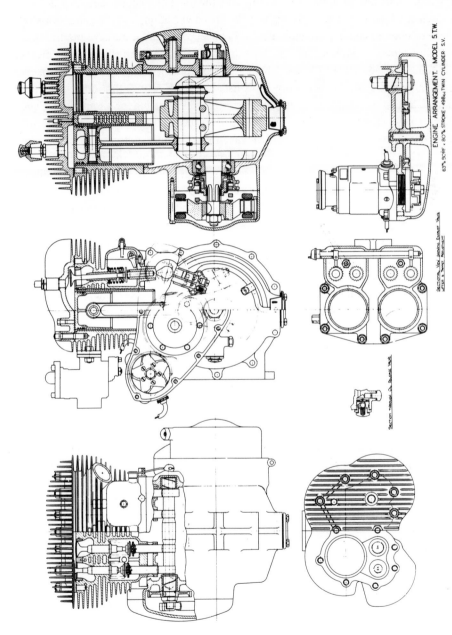

ENGINE ARRANGEMENT. MODEL 5.T.W.
63⅞ BORE × 80⅞ STROKE = 496 c.c. TWIN CYLINDER S.V.

Details of 500 cc sv twin engine used in the 'Hybrid' military model.

bonnet', and under these conditions, design and development became a wearisome thing indeed. In this case, the 'bee' was to take the form of a rubber coupling between the engine, which had inherently high cyclic speed variation, and the generator shaft which, of course, could be regarded as a flywheel for it had a massive inertia value.

The rubber coupling, which was trying to cope with these two diverse conditions, did not seem to know whether it was coming or going and we broke so many generator shafts, which were short-listed at RAF stores, that crisis point was reached. But for this I think we may have continued struggling for a long time. Faced with this new situation, our Designer was forced to capitulate and we resorted to a simple cam-type shock absorber, which was in use on most motorcycles of that day. This worked beautifully from scratch and solved all the high speed oscillation and dither. After endurance testing, the generator set was accepted and the RAF placed orders for several thousand which gave every satisfaction in use.

On the score of weight saving, the cylinder head and barrel of this engine had to be in light alloy material and because the unit was fan cooled, a sheet-metal cowling enveloped the cooling fins of the cylinder. As it was simpler to fabricate square shapes on cowlings of this type, the fins of the cylinder were square in profile, rather than the more attractive shapes which were customary on most motorcycle engines. Later, from this source came the Triumph Grand Prix engine, which was so popular with sporting motorcyclists and which could be recognised, at a glance, by its severe square finned cylinder shape.

Incidentally, an offshoot of this generator set was made by us, at the request of the RAF, in the form of a power egg. This fully enclosed version was used as a fitment inside aircraft to supply all ancillary current and the prototype was actually fitted inside the prototype Short Princess Flying Boat which was accidentally destroyed by fire while moored, shortly after its maiden flight.

We were soon to be asked by the Admiralty to help them by designing and making a target-towing winch for use in naval aircraft for gunnery practice at sea. The aircraft would carry engine-driven equipment and pay out about one mile of cable which terminated with the target in the form of a 'box kite'. This enabled naval vessels to shoot at the target without danger of damage to the towing aircraft. We designed and produced the necessary quantities of this device and were congratulated by the Admiralty for the satisfaction they gave and the short time factor involved in their production. A version of the Speed Twin engine paid out or recovered wire cable through an epicyclic reduction and drove a laying gear which laid the cable neatly coil by coil on the storage drum, with a warning device to obviate withdrawing the kite target through the aircraft.

All of these rather unusual projects were, of course, quite unconnected with motorcycles but are mentioned because they are relevant to the rapid growth which the company had made since its formation in 1936. This small private company was becoming very stable financially for we had a steady production outlet of one type

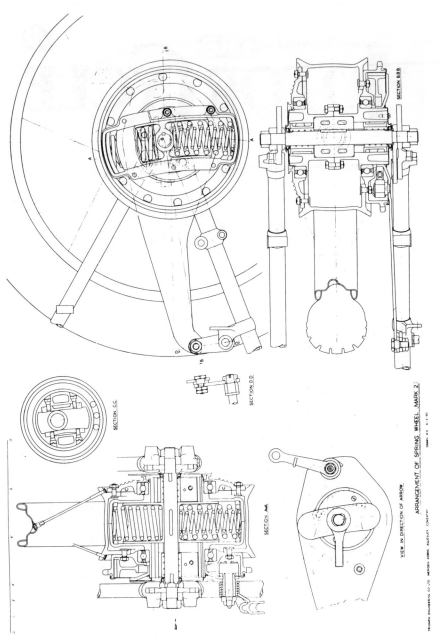

Details of the Triumph spring wheel.

THE MOTOR CYCLE

4D

SALE THREE TIMES THAT
OF ANY SIMILAR JOURNAL

FOUNDED 1903

CIRCULATES THROUGHOUT THE WORLD

No 2220   Vol 75   Thursday, October 25th, 1945

The advertisement in The Motor Cycle *of 25th October 1945 which so incensed Edward Turner.*

of motorcycle to one customer source, a dream condition for management, and various arrangements with the fighting services for design and manufacturing help on an agreed cost plus basis.

The war ended in 1945 and the company very soon reverted to production of the pre-war range of machines in the form of the Speed Twin and Tiger 100 models, with slight changes in their make-up. Very soon we replaced the girder-type front fork with an hydraulic telescopic type which greatly enhanced the appearance of the machines and their handling characteristics.

Not everyone will know that the German BMW motorcycle with its flat-twin engine, its shaft drive, its telescopic hydraulic front fork and its superb harmony of oil tight shapes, had set a standard in the motorcycle world for many years. It was considered by many as the Rolls Royce of motorcycles but it did not sell in very large quantities, probably because the price was very high. In addition, the unusual appearance of the engine produced the illusion of excessive width and bulk.

The beautifully engineered hydraulically-controlled telescopic front fork, which was fitted as standard equipment, put to shame the girder type forks which were then common to every other motorcycle. With cost considerations uppermost the industry did not as yet feel justified in making expensive changes of this sort. However,

Some of the personalities who made things tick at Triumph in the mid-1940s. Left to right: Charles Parker (secretary) Bert Coles (works manager) Alf Camwell (works director) Sid Tubb (assembly shop) J. McDonnell (material and works progress) and Jack Welton (sales manager).

Chapter Three

Associated Motor Cycles had been experimenting with a telescopic fork, which incidentally was a 'Chinese copy' of the BMW design, and had gathered much experience with this type of component. They had a valuable lead should the market seem to demand this type of fitment at some later date.

We had sufficient 'savvy' at Triumph to know that, very soon, we should be compelled to improve the front end handling characteristics of our motorcycles; power output and speeds were increasing and it was inevitable that hydraulic damping with more generous movement must replace the rather crude girder fork with all its limitations. So Edward Turner designed a front fork of telescopic construction which was unbelievably simple and very much more slim in profile than the BMW design. Always in his favour, he would rather die than be seen to copy, but unfortunately this latest 'baby' at first would spew oil from the top securing nuts in generous doses, straight into the rider's lap.

On the score of neatness, so we were told, the speedometer drive which was taken from the front wheel was also a telescopic device, which involved coping with rotary as well as generous linear motion and was an engineer's nightmare. It was some time before common sense prevailed over stubbornness and a modified form of Turner's original telescopic design went into production.

By that time AMC had their BMW type of fork available and had standardised it on certain models, but it was the trim appearance of the Triumph design that created much favourable comment in the technical press.

Within a week, Matchless advertisements took the form of full page captions which warned the motorcycling public in banner headlines that 'all is not gold that glitters' and gave an explanation of why the Matchless front suspension system was the only one that mattered. Today this sort of thing would not be given a second thought and rightly so; I never could understand why many people, important in the industry at the time, took exception to this form of advertising and why Donald Heather, then Sales Director of Matchless, was so unpopular for a time. Turner inevitably took this as a personal affront and it was some time before he fully recovered.

The Triumph front fork was later to become a standard of excellence throughout the trade and it was not unusual to see many makes of motorcycle, particularly those used in racing and other competitive events, with the Triumph component replacing the original equipment. But it was an unnecessarily long time before this was so and we were bedevilled in our Service Department with quite serious problems, mainly relative to severe oil leakage.

Turner's long leaves of absence each year left a void, for he simply would not delegate real management status and I suppose that he and Sangster thought the company was self-motivated. These periods did sometimes afford opportunities to make decisions and take action and although there was usually a row when his sunburned face reappeared, it was of no real consequence.

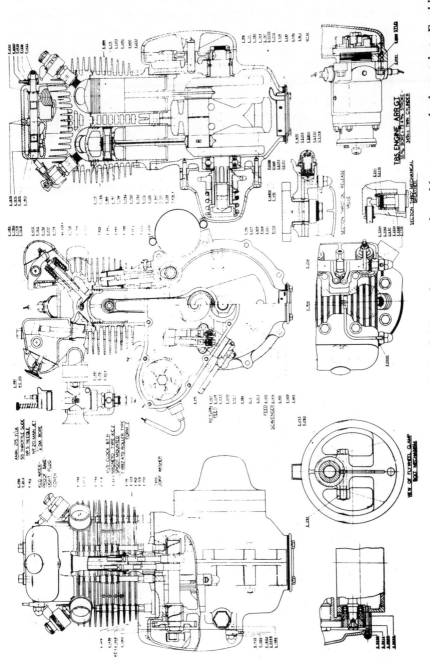

The Triumph T85 engine details. A 350 cc ohv twin; it had a flabby performance and would not respond adequately to Freddie Clarke's development magic.

Chapter Three

It was Freddie Clarke who, during one of these 'aways', hit upon the damping system which depressurised the unhappy telescopic fork legs and we made this change so that when Turner returned we were out of trouble and regaining some of our medals. One would have expected our Managing Director to be pleased, but it is difficult to please everyone!

It was also the great Freddie who was responsible for developing the Tiger 100 into the flyer which very soon became known as the Grand Prix model.

It was he who took advantage of the availability of a stock of the light alloy version of engine cylinders, left over from our aircraft generator set days, which had been developed at government expense. From this framework, like the genius he was, he very quickly achieved the reliable characteristics which made this engine so sought after in the sporting world. This involved many design changes, some insignificant but others quire substantial, and most of this work was done during Turner's absence, with Freddie personally checking each progressive advance in power.

Finally, in September 1946, Ernie Lyons rode one of these prototypes, to win the Manx Grand Prix in the Isle of Man. It topped a great work performance and gained for Triumph good publicity and a firm foothold into a rapidly emerging sporting market place.

Freddie Clarke with his record breaking Speed twin at Brooklands in 1939.

The ashes of World War 2 bring a transformation of facilities

It was unfortunate that this happened during one of Turner's lengthy absences, for on his return from the USA he realized that a new model had been created which, one would have thought, should have given pleasure. Our dealers in the USA had been clamouring for exactly such a motorcycle and in addition he had pledged, in public, that he would 'deal with this pretty soon.' However he raved at Clarke and was particularly rude to me, pointing out that my duties were to 'keep things on an even keel' while he was absent.

I was never so surprised for I am sure that this was the first occasion on which he had touched on the subject of terms of reference, much less anything so important and sweeping, for bestowing job titles was not one of his weaknesses, particularly if

The actual machine on which Ernie Lyons won the 1946 Manx Grand Prix, later to be manufactured as the 500 cc Triumph Grand Prix twin. The genius of Freddie Clarke made this development possible but earned him a shabby response from Edward Turner.

they savoured of authority. I am sure that most people on the outside regarded me as some sort of draughtsman, even if they had heard of me at all. The facts are that we had developed and produced a new machine which had been promised the public for some time and his absence had allowed us to 'cut the cackle and get to the hosses'. Eventually the whole childish internal eruption at Meriden blew over and the Grand Prix Triumph motorcycle went into production, to prove a popular and profitable addition to our range of products.

As time went on and Triumph machines gained a greater reputation from successes in races and competitive events, Turner would never listen to the many persuasive voices urging him to enter and support Grand Prix events such as the TT **63**

Details of the 500 cc Grand Prix Triumph engine of 1946. The aircraft generator set, with its light alloy engine, developed and made by Triumph during the war years, made this breakthrough possible in the short time scale. Relics of the generator set can be found in the square and uniform finning of the cylinders and the fixing bosses

for the cooling air cowling.

races. I feel now, as I did then, that this policy was absolutely right. Our strength and reputation lay with the many sporting Triumph owners who themselves entered and were successful in various competitive events throughout the world. This gave the product the publicity it needed and underlined its reliability, without having the problem of works supported race teams and their management. Furthermore, it left us free of the extreme demands which such projects would have made on the cream of our technical staff, to the possible detriment of the production programme.

Freddie Clarke and I were now beginning to feel that it was high time we parted company from Turner, whose sacking by Sangster and disciplined period with BSA had produced no change in his objectionable and hopelessly egotistical attitude. We felt that before we were driven completely into the ground, it would be nice to know whether we had any capability or were just imagining it, as the boss put it. Clearly it was time that we proved our skills in fields afresh.

I loved my job and was thoroughly steeped in Triumph matters. I also was fortunate enough to be part of a wonderful management team, each an expert in his own particular sphere. However, I had, regretfully, come to the conclusion that there were no prospects whatsoever for me, or for many others in this team, with such a sloppy set up. Why Sangster allowed such an organisation to exist I shall never know.

Of course it was highly profitable and I suppose that was all that mattered, but we lacked a smooth and continuous process of forward product design and development and I felt that a series of crash projects initiated at the whim of the Managing Director would sooner or later expose the company to dangers that would be difficult, if not impossible, to remedy in spite of its present strength. We needed to mend our ways but to do this the Chairman and Managing Director of this privately owned and successful company would have to be convinced of the hopelessness of the present situation and I am afraid that this seemed to be quite impossible. As Donald Heather had said, relative to another matter 'all is not gold that glitters' and I had a strange lack of confidence in the future. I felt that, at some time, we must pay dearly for our lack of ability to assemble ourselves as a strong and authoritative management and get some sort of sophistication in the top strata.

In 1946 Freddie Clarke resigned and joined the Associated Motor Cycle Group in London as their Chief Development Engineer. He quickly made a tremendous impression with the directors of that company, as I was to learn much later, but his promising career was all too brief and he was killed while riding a motorcycle very shortly afterwards. I am certain that, had he have lived, Freddie would have reached one of the top places in an industry he so dearly loved, for he was a master in his sphere of activity and was respected by all who knew him.

The art of the Development Engineer is to be concerned only with facts, which sounds simple and straightforward, but really it is not, and I have since met only one person, Doug Hele, whom I would place alongside Freddie in this respect. Very soon **65**

All is now forgiven. Edward Turner, happy once more, during a celebration party. Ernie Lyons, in riding leathers, is toasted after just returning from Shelsley Walsh hill climb, having trounced Raymond Mays in his highly tuned ERA car. Freddie Clarke has his back to the camera.

The ashes of World War 2 bring a transformation of facilities

A later offshoot of the Grand Prix effort, the Triumph Trophy model of 1949, which brought so many trials successes for the company.

after Freddie's death I was offered the job of Chief Designer with Norton Motors, whose Managing Director, Gilbert Smith, had learned through the grapevine that I was not too happy at Meriden. I accepted the post and commenced my new duties on April Fools Day, of all days, in 1947. So ended, I felt, an era which had linked Edward Turner and myself very closely in that part of his activity which, by now, had brought him fame as a design engineer, to be known and respected throughout the world.

Although I did not realise this at the time, it was acknowledged that our partnership was tailor-made, with Turner the inventive genius, sometimes brilliant, sometimes outrageous and I, so I was told, the rather dour catalyst who not always shared his convictions. On the numerous occasions on which we disagreed, an onlooker would have felt that the doctor was diagnosing chronic lunacy but these transgressions mostly concluded with the patient prescribing the tranquilizer. In spite of this we were, I think, as ideally paired as was possible and many years later, during one of his more expansive and generous moments, Turner admitted this to be true.

He invariably chose to regard anyone who attempted to apply the sciences at the design stage as an academic and made no bones about his opinion of such time wasters. It was difficult for him to realize, particularly in the earlier period of his career, that some of his projected ideas simply were not on. He never realized, I am sure, that my sense of humour never deserted me, otherwise I could not have coped, and I am given to believe that he regarded me somewhat as a prophet of doom. Nonetheless I am sure he realised that if fed with the right dosage this had a reasonable stabilising effect and we could get through.

Chapter Three

My career with Turner had been exhilarating and eventful and although perhaps the top strata of management of this small private company was not a model of efficiency, I felt very confident that I had a splendid background of experience and looked forward to the future.

I was sorry indeed to be leaving the Company but the decision was inevitable. Turner for his part was shocked that I had made the decision and after fruitless endeavours to bring about a change of mind, he finally made the remark, to several just within earshot, that 'he felt we were losing a limb'. Praise indeed from such a man!

Chapter Four

With Norton Motors Ltd in the late 1940's

WHEN I moved to Norton Motors in Bracebridge Street, Birmingham, as Chief Designer I was quite shocked to learn that neither Gilbert Smith, the Managing Director, nor Joe Craig, the Engineering Director, had taken the courtesy to inform the incumbent head of design that such a change was being contemplated! This man, Jack Moore, who apparently had been in charge of product design functions, was a first class engineer and a highly skilled designer, as I was later to find. We became good friends and colleagues as time went on and I forever will be indebted to him for his loyal help in the difficult times for me which were to follow.

Naturally Moore was quite angry with Gilbert Smith, who introduced me to him and without more ado said 'now I will leave you two together'. There was no office for me and Jack immediately offered to move out of his but I would have none of it and told him that it was obvious that we each needed the help of the other so we compromised by sharing his 'space'. This office, if that it may be called, was eight feet square and we managed to get two drawing stands inside, with the pair of us sitting back to back, each supporting the other, a strange set up but the only one possible.

As we got to know each other, we saw the funny side of the situation and as I intended to get down to business immediately, and indeed was expected to do so, Jack would helpfully be busy with jobs which engaged him in the workshops, leaving me to spread myself in my eight by eight cell.

Not even during the war time blitzes did I have to work under such difficult conditions; the whole Norton building was such a slummy shambles sandwiched with machines and parts, and men and vermin, in a noisy and dirty conglomeration, that a space such as mine did not seem too bad. After all, it was reasonably quiet and did not let in all that much rain!

Chapter Four

James Lansdowne Norton ('Pa' Norton) founder of the Norton Motor Cycle Company.

The first Norton motorcycle was powered by a $1\frac{3}{4}$ hp Peugeot engine.

I was told that Nortons must have a multi-cylinder machine, preferably a twin, to implement their scant range of single cylinder models, to enable them to compete in a market which had become multi-cylinder conscious. It was important that we satisfy public demand in the shortest space of time as the prospects were meagre for the very outdated range of machines which seemingly were sold to a brand of motorcyclist who simply would not consider any other make on the score of the firm's considerable achievements in the field of Grand Prix racing.

The production motorcycles on sale to the public bore no resemblance, of course, to the works racing machines, a handful of which were made each year. Yet such had been the company's racing successes, over a period of many years, that the rough, noisy and leaky production models were sold at the rate of just under 200 per week, to a long suffering, and slowly diminishing clientele.

I was horrified to find that, for more years than most could remember, the company's design engineering activity had been of the order of 90% racing and 10% product activity, so it is not surprising that the range of motorcycles on offer to the public had remained unchanged for many years while the company cavorted on the race track. I was hoping that this would soon be put into better perspective but I was to be disappointed, as will be seen later. The Managing Director did not realise, until too late, that it was commercial suicide to have racing as a first priority.

All of the motorcycles we then produced were unbelievably noisy and I remember that one of our largest dealers pleaded with Gilbert Smith not to produce a new model with a twin cylinder engine as he felt quite sure that engine noise would be doubled. The Big Four model, a 600 cc single cylinder side valve machine, and the International Model, an ohc-engined sports machine that retained a link with racing successes of the distant past, had a very small but dedicated following, who seemed to love the massive vibration of the former and the leaky clatter of the latter. The rest of the model range was nondescript but the company just managed to keep the wheels turning and make a small profit, helped along by quite substantial payments from various supplier companies in respect of the racing activity. Not always, of course, had it been like this, but the curious imbalance of engineering effort had taken its toll and I was now being told, by the Managing Director, that the time had arrived for something to be done about it.

I started the design of a 500 cc ohv twin cylinder machine immediately and my experience at Triumph of excessive cylinder head overheating problems made me determined to improve the air flow conditions. This is how the splayed configuration of the Norton valve gear came to be evolved. It enabled the cooling air to have free passage between the inlet and exhaust valve ports, a condition quite lacking in the Triumph design. Of course the overheating problems of the Triumph engines, when higher power was extracted, had been partly corrected by the use of light alloy materials on the Grand Prix model. By now, however, I was very much aware that many things which were possible with Triumph, a rich and successful company, **71**

One of the earliest examples of the ohv Nortons. A picture taken in the early 20s showing 'Pa' Norton, with Rex Judd in the saddle and D.R. O'Donovan, a tuning wizard of the day.

Rem Fowler aboard the Norton machine which made the fastest lap in the first TT race in 1907 and also won the twin-cylinder class. The engine was a French Peugeot.

would not be possible at Norton Motors, where facilities and efficiency were at an appalling low.

On the new engine I would have preferred a single-piece crankshaft rather than a three-piece built-up type like the Triumph design then in use, but I was turned away from this by the production planners on the score of some difficulty with the current and very ancient machine tools that would handle such a component. So regretfully, I designed a three-piece crankshaft, somewhat stronger than the Triumph design which, at a quick glance, infringed their patent. However, I had carefully avoided this by using a central dowel and an offset fixing flange.

With the clatter of current production motorcycles ringing in my ears, I tried to do something about the noise problem, and I used a single camshaft with a chain drive to operate the valve gear. I had a strong patent on the unusual valve gear and one also covering the crankshaft design, which Edward Turner was to dispute a little later. I had to tell him that neither his claim nor mine would hold water for I knew that Vauxhall Motors had used a very similar principle, with central flywheel and all, for their three-litre racing engine of 1922.

With an eye on the possibility of racing the new twin, I designed an ohc version which had a great deal in common with the roadster, but with an unusual arrangement of valve gear drive which was located centrally in the engine, to avoid excessive overall width. The separate gearbox of these machines was of Burman design and merely had a facelift to give somewhat cleaner lines.

An entirely new frame and associated parts were designed but the current Roadholder telescopic front fork was to be fitted and a quite new styling approach was adopted for the petrol tank, which had a bulbous to slim shape of eye-catching proportions. The combined appearance of the whole had the promise of a good looker.

It was vitally important that the engine be on the move as a first priority and after a week or two the design was complete. I passed this on to Bill Pitcher, a Design Engineer with few equals, to whom Nortons must be indebted for the master craftmanship he displayed during the following months while the draughting work was in progress. It was he who created, from my original, the engine which was to reach the production line in 18 months from conception and which was to have a production run, unaltered in basic structure, for three decades. It seems to me that, in later years, when the Norton company was on the rocks and going begging in the hands of the Official Receiver, Dennis Poore, who had the company for a song, was wrongly described by the press as the saviour of this famous marque. There is no doubt at all that there would have been no marque to be saved if Pitcher and his boys had not performed the kiss of life and enabled the company to amble along during the next twenty years into the hands of its 'saviour'.

We had few real problems with the prototype engines, thanks to the first class design help which I was privileged to have. The biggest headache turned out to be **73** the dynamometer which was used for development purposes. This equipment, which is a means of running engines under all degrees of power output, was so antiquated and worn out that during extended runs of power testing, oil and water would leak in such copious quantities that it formed a sizeable river across the shop floor and into Aston Brook Street. We had many complaints from passers-by and indeed the police were alerted but I posted a labourer outside the works at this point and he did what he could, on a continuous basis, with a large broom.

We were not short of up to date dynamometers but these were sacrosanct and locked away in the peaceful and leisurely confines of the Racing Department, presided over by Joe Craig, our Engineering Director. My suggestion, in my brave innocence, that we should have the use of one of their spare machines as a matter of urgency, met with a steely look from Joe and an appalled refusal from our Managing Director.

During the few odd times I was able to pause and think about my surroundings and the new commercial enterprise with which I was now rubbing shoulders, it seemed that I was out of the frying pan into the fire so far as long term viability was concerned. I remember considering seriously whether a career in the motorcycle industry was worthwhile in view of this further example of a very sloppy commercial set up. I was not able to do too much ruminating, however, for Joe Craig had now asked me to do urgent work on the racing side and the next twelve months or so was one of the busiest periods of my career.

Joe was a dour Irishman who strongly believed that unless silence can be improved it should, most certainly, not be broken. During our short, but close business association, our verbal deliberations would have made a very short list.

Gilbert Smith, the Managing Director, had told me on joining the company that he did not expect me to get on with Joe and he felt sure that we should have a row within a month. In his strange way, I think he was trying to be helpful but it did not happen that way and it could be that my unique experience with difficult individuals helped a great deal. As it turned out, Joe and I never seriously had a cross word. There were fundamental problems of management structure, however, which, unknown to me at the time, would prove to be the 'bete noir' of this particular part of my career.

I did not know, for instance, that Craig's contract linked his remuneration with competition successes and was a relic of the days when he was the Racing Manager. Since then however, he had been promoted to the Board and as Engineering Director he was responsible for all engineering and technical activity. But Joe's activity started and finished with racing, while the company's products were a disgrace and were likely to remain so. Who could blame the man for concentrating the whole technical resources of the company on the race track when a great part of his remuneration was linked to this activity?

The businessman who negotiated this contract, presumably Gilbert Smith, did

Norton irreparable harm, but I shall never understand why anyone with any ability at all failed to realize what was wrong. We did, however, agree that we must recruit more technical staff and it was at this stage that Doug Hele joined us from Douglas (Sales and Service) Ltd, and a partnership was started which progressed through several decades. I was to enjoy a unique friendship, unequalled in my business life.

Although I had more than enough on my plate trying to get some sense into an antiquated product line, Craig insisted on my spending much of my time advising him and helping on racing design. Although my heart was elsewhere we did manage some marginal improvements to the already highly developed 350 cc and 500 cc single cylinder racing engines. By this time Hele was helping on racing design too, but the art of developing the big singles was beginning to obey the law of decreasing returns. For instance, a complete re-design of the cylinder head and valve gear with slightly more streamlined porting and a re-design of the crankcase to embrace more rigid mainshaft bearings gave us about one half of a horse power increase in power output, a very meagre return for such a time-absorbing and costly exercise. Each year witnessed greater effort with equally miserable response and although the engines were absolutely reliable, the main key to Joe's success during this period, time was fast running out on the single cylinder racing configuration. It should have been obvious that real power increases could be achieved only with the benefits of multi-cylinder engines.

In spite of all this, Craig continued doggedly to coax and refine his beloved singles, extracting a meagre bonus of power each year but, above all, maintaining a fantastic reliability. Even against a background of rumblings from racing stables abroad, in the form of brilliant new twins and fours, he continued until 1955 to field single cylinder machines which beat most comers in Grand Prix racing.

It must be said, however, that towards the closing stages of Craig's career, when the foreign multi-cylinder racers were beginning to have a few outings, the continued Norton success was due mainly to complete reliability and the superlative skill of his team of riders. In addition to their skill, they were seen by all to be taking more risks in their efforts to match machines from the Continent that had superior speed.

Back on real production matters, I had managed to convince Gilbert Smith that our lifeline must be a more up to date and reasonably priced product range and, to this end, we started to recruit more technical personnel. Racing still took priority in all matters but at least it was a start and the balance of technical strength, at last was beginning to change.

The construction of a new Drawing Office and Development Shop, which had been commenced a little before I joined the Company, was well under way and this was a great morale booster that helped considerably in our recruiting campaign. The new building was a two-storey affair, with a ground floor Development Shop and a Drawing Office above, but because it was jammed in the centre of existing buildings, there was practically no natural light on the upper floor and none whatsoever on the **75** lower. I remember being most unpopular with both management and the builders, who at first refused to modify the building and who connived with the architect in placing every difficulty in my path. I persevered because I felt that it was not unreasonable to expect to have natural light in a Drawing Office so I sat down and re-designed the building. Although far from being an award winning design, we did have light on the top floor, albeit from rather unusual sources, and we did manage to get a degree of air and light through to the rather dungeon-like Development Shop below. So I won this silly fight and the technical staff spread itself into more workable surroundings. At last I began to feel that things were moving in the right direction, albeit somewhat slowly.

The prototype engines of the new twin cylinder machines were now being run and were giving surprisingly little trouble. Meanwhile, we were redesigning the rest of the single cylinder product range with a view to them giving more power and improved silence. I made many attempts to discuss forward policy with the Managing Director but apart from agreeing the need for twin cylinder machines he seemed to have no further concern and simply did not understand any plan for continuous forward product policy. He felt that, with the twin in production, a small company like Nortons would be 'safe' for the next ten years or so.

He did not want growth and he was very proud of the performance of the company which at that time was making a profit of about 7% before tax on its sales turnover. But a high percentage of this turnover was from products other than motorcycles and I suspected, and was later proved to be correct, that the motorcycle element was not so lucrative as the other products.

The Norton trading set-up was made up of Norton Motors and R.T. Shelley Ltd. with the two concerns being mixed as a single production unit, Shelleys making a variety of small tools and mechanical lifting gear for commercial vehicles and also some components for Norton Motors. Both units, being under the same roof, were the responsibility of a single Managing Director and it seemed to me that there was a lack of responsible management attitude towards any generative policy for either company.

The Shelley concern was, in the main, making cheap spanners and the like for the car and allied industries and we were always in danger of losing their business overnight to more efficient and better equipped specialists. Gilbert Smith seemed to talk good business sense on most occasions but, perhaps through no fault of his, no action ever took place and it had been so for many years. He appeared to go it alone almost as a dictator and there appeared to be no regular management meetings or Board meetings which could be recognised as such. Instead, it seemed to be a case of survival, leaping from crisis to crisis.

Many years later, when I became Managing Director of Norton-Shelley, I made a point of researching the Board meeting minutes and agendas of this period. I was **76** appalled to find that most took the form of a series of statements from the Managing

Director on generally trivial matters, without any apparent discussion or comment.

Far from being depressed by the squalid business expertise around me I was spurred on by my knowledge that the new twin cylinder engine was a certainty for production and that the considerable changes we made to the rest of the current range of machines hopefully would indicate to the buying public and the dealers that other things were on the move apart from racing.

I decided that perhaps I ought to put before the Board, via the Managing Director, a stage by stage product plan for the next ten years, although one would have thought that this should have been masterminded by the Engineering Director. It was at this stage of my career, in 1948, that I evolved and worked out in detail a product design plan on a modular basis.

Although this sounds a little frightening, it really is a simple straightforward means of producing a range of machines, from small to large, with as few different components as possible. Because Norton Motors would, I felt, be forced to market a more comprehensive range of motorcycles, it seemed sensibly economic and time saving to follow such a principle.

In taking this approach nothing must be sacrificed for the purpose of using similar parts for different engines. If the best and most up to date thinking and a good background of sound experience concerning such things as bore/stroke ratios, valve gear geometry etc., is used, there is no fundamental reason why a single cylinder engine and a two-cylinder engine of twice the capacity should not both perform with equally high efficiency, having a great family likeness and enjoying a considerable benefit from the use of a minimum variety of components.

Obviously a small company such as Norton Motors would not be in a position to launch a whole range of motorcycles and maybe would not need to consider so complete a product line as I was about to outline; it would need to be a model by model plan in order of importance and profit would have to be made before further new models were launched. By late 1948 I had such a plan ready, with design layouts of three engines based on a single cylinder module of 125 cc capacity. The first engine was a 125 cc single cylinder unit with ohc valve gear, the second a 250 cc twin cylinder with basic doubling up and the third was a four cylinder unit of 500 cc capacity, quadrupling the module.

To many readers it may seem strange to suggest the additional expense of overhead camshafts in a plan for a company with such painful cash problems. However, I felt that the idea had commercial soundness because the overall cost of launching would prohibit fundamental changes for many years and it was very important that we should anticipate the likely technical strength of growing world competition. Also I considered that there had been enough nonsense in struggling year by year with the big racing singles, at enormous cost, to just scrape through with the cream of the world's riders taking unnecessary risks. If we were to continue racing, and while Joe was with us we would, we must have a multi-cylinder machine **77**

The Norton Dominator motorcycle introduced in 1950.

for this purpose and I had made provision for this with the modular four by substituting the normal cylinder head for a racing version that had four valves per cylinder. A simple enough change to make to an engine with which to go racing, especially since a change in policy of this nature would have cut our enormous competition costs by 90% and enabled the whole of our enginering personnel to be engaged on what I considered to be more legitimate work.

I took it upon myself, rather foolishly as it turned out later, to advise the Managing Director on a future strategy designed to take the company through a decade and hopefully build a much more productive and viable enterprise. The initial designs were ready and discussions had been completed with production personnel to make quite sure that our production equipment could handle the new generation components.

I had done this myself without the knowledge of Gilbert or Joe for they simply were not interested at this stage. In addition to the design drawings, I had provided a written plan which explained the thinking behind the strategy, giving the likely performance and rough costs of each engine together with likely time factors agreed with production personnel. The plan strongly advised the Board to make a statement in the press that the company would pull out of racing for a period of three years and if, at the end of that period, it was felt desirable or necessary, would return with equipment which was much more up to date and competitive. This would have been a shock to the public but time was of the essence and the strategy was to achieve a viable range of products as quickly as possible, enabling the whole of our engineering strength to be concentrated solely to this end. This latter part of the plan proved to be my undoing so far as Craig was concerned, as will be seen later.

My suggested range of machines to carry us through to the early 1960s was as follows.

(1)   a 125 cc ohc single cylinder model that would be very light and fast and form an unusual supplement to the Norton range, one which I felt would be a best seller and a real money spinner. It would not have been as cheap to produce as most small machines of the day but I felt that the Norton background and the forward technical specification would enable a somewhat higher price to be asked.

(2)   a 250 cc twin cylinder model and a modular concept of the 125 cc unit. Because of its advanced specification (in those days) of ohc and basic racing strength, it would have been a model which could easily have been sold at a slight premium.

(3)   A 500 cc four cylinder model with the engine across the frame and normal chain drive to the rear wheel. It would be based, of course, on a quadrupled 125 cc unit and look somewhat similar to the racing Gilera, which later was to become the dream machine of most motorcyclists. This machine would have inbuilt strength to take it 'production racing' but a special 16 valve cylinder head had been catered for to enable a change to be made which would have added enough horse-power to an already healthy output so that the model could be raced in Grand Prix events.

On reflection, when I recollect that Doug Hele had recently joined my team at Bracebridge Street, I am sure that had the plan been understood and adopted, we should certainy have given serious consideration to a 375 cc triple cylinder model in addition. Hele was keen on the three cylinder conception even in those early days, mainly because of its relative smoothness in operation and its very compact dimensions.

Readers may be puzzled why, on the eve of the launch of a very important new machine, the twin cylinder Dominator model, I should be advising the Board to give consideration to a breakaway new generation of products. I did so because I felt that

The Norton International model of 1951.

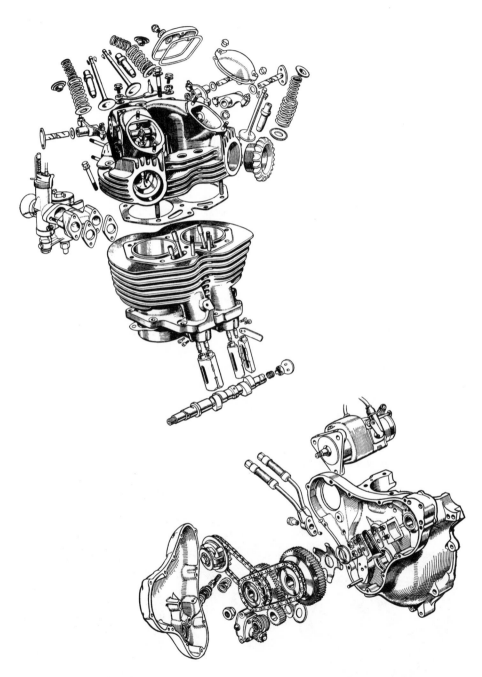

80   *The Norton Dominator engine, a 500 cc ohv twin, designed by the Author in 1947.*

the Dominator should be regarded as only a stop-gap and that a much more sophisticated range of products would be necessary if we intended seriously to compete in a market which surely would be dominated by Germany and Japan.

My reasoning, in those early days, was that Germany in particular had been so destroyed that there simply was not the wherewithal to manufacture products even if the records had remained intact. Almost everything had been destroyed and as and when they got round to competing in world trade. almost every product from motor cars to sewing machines would be freshly conceived. Having very little option they would, very shortly, be offering the world the most up to date merchandise, this process being hastened along with massive doses of Marshal Aid.

Quite frankly, I do not understand why the so-called businessmen who were then running the British motorcycle industry did not work this one out for themselves and stop fiddling with the yearly up-dating of ancient merchandise to get to grips with an obvious situation.

Gilbert Smith seemed impressed with my strategy and said that the Board would give it some consideration but whether any discussion took place at that level I shall never know. What is certain is that Joe Craig took exception to my suggestion that official works racing should cease for a three year period and from that time on, my days with Norton Motors were numbered.

I can now understand that Joe, with his contract weighted to a successful racing activity, must have felt that I was out for his blood. Of course this was not so and in any case the Board could easily have corrected the situation with a stroke of the pen. I felt that Joe's real value was entirely in racing and in my opinion he could not have done justice to any other part of engineering policy.

Craig and I did not have a row; the reason for the sudden change to a hostile attitude was never mentioned but from that time he initiated a campaign which was aimed at discrediting all I had done during my eighteen months with the company. He concentrated his attention on the new 500 cc twin cylinder Dominator machine which had been shown at Earl's Court in November 1948, which I had passed as fit for production, having satisfied myself through extensive testing that it was reliable and had a performance at least equal to that of any of our competitors in this class.

In December 1948, he decided that the new machine was short of performance and told the Board that production must be delayed to enable him to rectify the situation. Although my development work was satisfactorily finished he had not, until then, shown the slightest interest. One would have expected those at top level not to fall for this one, more particularly as dealers throughout the world were clamouring for delivery of this new machine and orders for other models in the range were negligible. The situation was serious with the strange anomaly of a cash crisis and a full order book for a model which had gone through the motions of launching but was not yet in production. I was quite disgusted and urged Gilbert Smith to give the go-ahead before the Company went bust but the sad truth was that the sugar   *81* could not be sifted from the sand. Consequently the work force was cut and short time was in operation.

Craig continued to fiddle with cam forms and inlet port shapes and although engineering personnel were keen and confident, he dilly-dallied and slowly wore me down until, at last, I wrote out my resignation. However I did not immediately hand this in to the Managing Director, probably because I would have wished to see the Dominator safely in production whilst still with the company. I carried this piece of paper around in my pocket for several weeks. The end came when Gilbert Smith told me that it was time that we parted and I agreed; it was a convenient moment to hand him the slip of paper from my pocket which I had almost forgotten.

At a much later date, when I became Norton's Managing Director, I looked up the appropriate Board Minutes which recorded the parting of the ways, for I was interested to know exactly how Gilbert Smith explained the situation to his co-directors. The entry read, and I quote 'We have today dismissed our Chief Designer on the score of economy'. A classic statement which surely questions the business acumen of the Board.

So it went on record that I had been sacked and I departed, leaving Craig in peace with his fast decaying world of Grand Prix glory. But of course it was perhaps as well that I had passed in that direction for Norton Motors had unconsciously stumbled through to the production stage with a new motorcycle which was to be their bread and butter for the next thirty years.

With me out of the way at Bracebridge Street, the Dominator went into production some weeks later and the press road test of this machine was glowing in its praise. In spite of the supposed lack of power it returned a maximum speed figure in excess of any competitive machine then in existence. Of course at a later stage I was able to ascertain what changes Craig had made to the technical specification of the engine unit and the answer was none whatsoever.

It is interesting to take note of the Managing Director's report to his co-directors at the Board Meeting which followed the production release of the new machine and I quote from the Board Minutes which I have before me. 'The machine has been well received and it is believed generally that this is the best machine that Norton has ever produced'. It seems a little strange that the poor Designer was rewarded with the sack!

I had no real plans for the future and although my heart was really in motorcycles I felt that I had received such shabby treatment from Norton Motors, who gave me not a penny compensation for the brief action-packed eighteen months or so that I had been with them, that I seriously considered whether it was worth while staying in an industry which seemed to be run by businessmen who were incapable of seeing further than their noses or, in the case of certain private companies, by people who seemed to be operating on a hobby basis. I felt enormously relieved that I was clear of the personal politics with which the Norton

Joe Craig (left) photographed here with the author.

Gilbert Smith, Managing Director of Norton Motors from 1945 to 1958.

organisation was riddled but was somewhat sad that I had not been able to convince the directors with my suggestions relative to a long overdue 'business policy'.

I had been approached by the Renold Chain Co., whose headquarters were in Manchester, with an offer of a job as assistant to their Chief Engineer and as this company was one which I have always admired, I took a trip northwards with my wife, to discuss the situation.

I am afraid that Manchester on that occasion fully justified its reputation for it rained incessantly and this, together with the somewhat dingy suburbs, set the seal on a decision which was made there and then. If we moved from the Midlands it would be towards the South Coast.

Instead we went on a long holiday in Devonshire walking the coast and slowly recuperating from a rather strenuous experience which had apparently taken much out of me. As always, it had also taken some toll on my wife, who had been aware of my frustrations in the past eighteen months or so. We toyed with the idea of buying a business on the South Coast and indeed looked several over but did not immediately take the plunge and went back home to think over the whole situation.

On my return, a message was awaiting me suggesting that I call to see James

Nortons were to become desperately unorthodox in their battle with foreign competition powered by multi-cylinder engines with their vastly superior performance. Bob Collier, an engineer with Nortons, who was the brain behind the 'kneeler' model, is shown here aboard his first mock-up.

Ray Amm with the final experimental 'kneeler' model which was discarded after an outing or two.

Chapter Four

Leek, the Managing Director of BSA. I went along to see this man, whom I had never before met, and I was impressed, taking a liking to him immediately. He was a man's man if ever there was one, for he had been trained basically as a production engineer and had reached the top by sheer guts coupled with the ability to make decisions.

He offered me a job as their Forward Product Designer, which I accepted with the proviso that I should be allowed to work, until such time as I could see some daylight, in a back room with no telephone. It was an appointment which I was beginning to feel was essential in such a neglected corner of management in the motorcycle industry that I knew.

It was highly amusing, during my meeting with Mr. Leek, that when the moment came for salary to be discussed, I suggested a very modest figure which seemed to rock him with surprise. He told me, quite sharply, that it was higher than the current salary of their Group Chief Engineer, who was literally their Engineering Director. I was equally shocked but fortunately not lost for words and I remember quite well, telling Mr. Leek that the executive in question was either NBG or in need of a very large salary increase.

I think that this approach must have been appreciated for I learned, much later, that the incumbent was immediately regraded financially, much to his surprise. It's an ill wind!

Chapter Five

Some refreshing years with the Birmingham Small Arms Company

IN MAY, 1949, I commenced working for the BSA Company at their Small Heath works in a small office deep in the bowels of the rabbit warren of Armoury Road. As agreed, I had no telephone or other distractions and I was able to work in remarkable peace and tranquility, for a fleeting time. A most enjoyable experience.

I had been briefed by Bob Fearon, a splendid Production Engineer at the top of his profession, who outlined some major engineering problems which were bedevilling the Service Department repair shops and I clearly remember my very first task being a re-design of their major gearbox, which had severe gear-shift operation problems.

I was asked to re-design the 500 cc twin cylinder engine to permit unimpeded air cooling and a more efficient combustion function. At the same time, a 650 cc version was designed, which was later to become the 'Golden Flash' power unit. Time was of the essence and as I was working without interruptions of any sort, I designed a 250 cc single cylinder engine, which had unique four valve ohc valve gear with the valves radially disposed in the cylinder head. Mr. Leek was anxious that BSA should make its impression in the sporting activity of production racing, now rapidly becoming more popular, and this small engine with its up-to-the-minute technical specification, was thought to have a future as the power unit of a super-sports motorcycle, for which the demand was fast growing.

On looking back, I can hardly believe that this work was done in about four weeks but it surely proves, beyond any doubt, that forward product design activity must be a separate function and quite removed from the day to day activities of the company.

I had been a little over three weeks in my new job when Mr. Leek told me that I had been appointed Chief Designer. He was curt and left no option. Although I

The BSA manufacturing plant suffered severe war damage and many lives were lost in this particular section of the works.

reminded him of the agreement we had reached, he was apologetic and pointed out that the incumbent was nearing retirement age, so he felt that the change was sensible and orderly. I was surprised and quite unprepared at this turn of events. At first I was not sure that I should be wise to accept, but after a little soul searching I took over from Herbert Perkins, who was in his sixties and not enjoying the best of health.

Fortunately for me, after a brief interval of guarded appraisal, Perkins and myself quickly got down to forming a partnership which we both were able to enjoy. I feel grateful and proud to have been given the opportunity of working closely and serenely with this fine man.

Herbert was a first class engineer, very practical and down to earth, and he knew thoroughly every inch of the designer's territory. The general excellence of the BSA range of products at that time was to some extent a testimony to his ability. A splendid organizer, he ran the Design Department with the discipline and expertise of a regimental sergeant-major and his men loved every minute. Salt of the earth; may his memory linger on!

A very smart BSA machine which never reached the production stage. An ohc twin cylinder prototype produced in the late 1940s.

Chapter Five

The great BSA empire straddled a group of twenty or so companies, manufacturing cycles, motorcycles, buses and armoured cars in the field of transport (the Daimler Company was then part of BSA) and a variety of other companies made machine tools, guns, alloy steel, general engineering products, etc. In the 1950s there seemed to be no cash shortage in the motorcycle activity, and indeed production figures were high and profits were good enough to support, to some extent, some of the activities such as cycles and Daimler, which at that time were in difficulty.

Sunbeam was then part of the BSA Group. Although its only product, the unusual shaft drive motorcycle, was lauded by many cranks whose writings on the subject practically filled the gossip columns of the technical press, none of these

Bert Perrigo, trials wizard and in addition a very capable business executive, shown here on a Blue Star BSA.

The immortal Jeff Smith.

admirers were anxious to own one of these wonders. Very few were sold and the activity fluttered through a year or two to a lingering death.

Having now 'inherited' the technical responsibility for this beautiful but troublesome baby, I was not sorry to see this happen. It would be true to say that the machine, throughout its few years of production, was a heavy financial burden, mainly because the problems in service were due to fundamental design faults which could not be corrected without starting afresh.

BSA production figures for motorcycles were in excess of 1000 per week and in the early 1950s output reached a figure of 75,000 units per annum. It seemed strange that, although I was now working for a large company and controlled an engineering staff of a hundred or so, I felt more remote from top management than ever before. My management colleagues were not unfriendly but it was not difficult to sense that there would be a considerable period before being either thrown out or fully accepted, to belie the traditional comment amongst the long service staff, 'We have seen them come and we have seen them go'. I felt sure that this proverb must have some sort of ending!

One must bear in mind that most of my associates had a record of twenty, thirty or even more years of service with the Company and it must have seemed like bad medicine to have imported me to fill a rather important position even though (I was told much later) I was 'very cocky'. After all, the BSA range of products was, by and large, reliable, which indicated high technical ability within the company. It is small

Harry Perrey (left centre, without hat) with a team of BSA riders on the summit of Snowdon in 1925.

Tests with a BSA and sidecar on Screw Hill, North Wales, in 1925. The slopes are so steep, with several hairpin bends, that local people used sledges rather than wheeled transport.

wonder that many should look askance and, perhaps, hope that I should not linger too long.

The visible performance of the individual is, of course, the answer to this sort of problem and I have preached this to many people who have been responsible to me, for as long as I can remember. So I really got my nose down and kept hard at it, feeling that, if I had any ability at all, someone eventually would notice and perhaps all would be forgiven.

There were some stirring moments for me during this period of my career with BSA which was to last the next seven years, but clearly in my mind I have recollections of the excellence of top management teamwork once decisions had been made. Arriving at decisions was another matter, but we were fortunate enough to have a Managing Director who was thoroughly practical as well as having good business sense. The traditional animosities and distrust between design, sales and production factions were always ironed out satisfactorily under his chairmanship and positive decisions were made, leaving no one in doubt of his responsibilities after a meeting was over.

93

An early BSA moped of the late 1930s which did not reach the production stage.

A 557 cc BSA motorcycle of 1918 vintage. Note the workmanlike rear drive enclosure.

Some refreshing years with the Birmingham Small Arms Company

The original 125 cc BSA Bantam two-stroke first produced in the late 1940s.

The facilities of this giant group of companies were most impressive. With its famous drop forge and huge press shop, together with its steel works and Group Research company, it meant that the in-house availability of these types of services invariably made possible huge savings in time during the manufacture of new components. In the case of experimental versions of new products, time factors were cut to such an extent that very rapid progress could be made.

The art of 'getting a move on' seems to have been lost forever, at least in this country. One wonders whether the giant consulting groups, who seem to be busy advising most big companies these days, have ever paused to consider why, in spite of better facilities, the time factor from conception to production of any new product lengthens as the years go by. It seems strange that in the early 1950s it was possible to conceive and mass produce a motorcycle in one year flat but nowadays a three year period is considered a rush. Yet neither the trade unions nor the current government can be blamed entirely, as some would have us think.

It is, of course, true that modern tooling and production techniques have become more complicated but can it be that sooner or later we will arrive at a stage where it will be a waste of time to consider a brand new product because it will be out of date by the time it gets to the production line? Certainly in the 1950s, under the dynamic leadership of James Leek, the BSA company did not waste much time once a decision had been made. It was providential that his intimate knowledge of production techniques and time factors greatly facilitated the correct projection of new product datelines.

Chapter Five

This was an era, in BSA history, of complete dealer confidence and it is true to say that servicing and spare parts facilities had been so organized under the able leadership of Bill Rawson, that the famous piled arms message 'service is the keyword' was never for one moment doubted. A sad contrast to a situation, which developed later, when new models were announced yet never appeared and the spare parts and servicing situation had become catastrophic.

On reflection, I find myself admiring more and more the simple but effective management technique of Jimmy Leek. He had a straightforward approach to the running of a company, and I believe that his early training as an engineer augured well in enabling him to probe through a jungle of opinion and facts to correct policy making. There is no doubt in my mind that the solid foundation of the Motorcycle Division of BSA after World War Two until the mid-1950s, was based on his ability to inject large doses of urgency and purpose into his top management team. Certainly, at a later date, when I was promoted to Chief Engineer and became part of that team, I was never in any doubt about first things being first and urgent.

Back in those Armoury Road days, top management was very much engineer orientated and I recall, with some amusement, that Mr. Leek appeared to regard executives who were other than production engineers, particularly accountants, as some sort of 'clerks'. A reflection of this is perhaps indicated in the make-up of the 'top brass' at Small Heath in the early 1950s when the team was composed of four engineers, the Buyer, the Sales Director (trained as an engineer) and the Accountant.

Quite unlike many latter day management teams, the non-engineers at this time thoroughly understood the company's products and I remember that Bill Smith, the Accountant, was always able to discuss intelligently the technicalities and prospects of any of the products, whether old or new. I recall that when I took over as Chief Engineer, I was a little upset by this man's arrogance (as I then thought) in making statements on matters which were far from his subject. He was a very fine accountant, with a most direct approach and had no time for the many catch phrases which were becoming popular in the world of finance. There never was any doubt at all, in anyone's mind, as to the company's financial position at all times.

Bill Smith had a habit of expounding at great length on other management subjects and until one knew him very well indeed, it could often prove a little painful, so that one was apt to consider him to be foolishly self-opinionated. This was far from the truth, for his brusque manner masked a highly intelligent mind. He was, in fact, able to cope with many subjects and I believe that BSA benefitted greatly from his versatility. I am afraid that it was I who nicknamed him 'Chief Engineer Smith' in a moment of annoyance but it was a nickname which he thoroughly enjoyed and as it grew to be his synonym, we became very good friends.

There were occasions, inevitably I suppose, when management meetings at Armoury Road took on the appearance of a grand council of a government department at times, when middle management were invited to be present

Some refreshing years with the Birmingham Small Arms Company

Sometimes such large meetings could be very frustrating, particularly if new concepts of products were being considered. It was invariably the case that by the time the drawings of new models had been passed round the table and commented upon, the only common ground for agreement would be that the wheels should be circular. Most other items, such as engine, frame, gearbox, etc became fogged in dispute and like the black countryman, I always had the feeling that, if we wished to go that way it would not be possible to start from here, although the wheels were always a safe bet.

Whilst working for BSA during that period, I deduced that in the early stages of conceptual design it is fatal to have discussions with too many people, no matter how capable, for there will be no agreement and it becomes virtually impossible to move from square one. It is fundamental that a small select body should make the decisions at this stage and should continue to do so until the point is reached when middle management need be involved, by which time certain irrevocable decisions will have been made. Jimmy Leek was well aware of this and although, at times, we went through the pantomime of discussing certain new projects at enormous gatherings it was only, I think, for the purpose of enabling some of the lower strata to feel more involved. I am thankful that the real and lasting decisions invariably were made during meetings where seven or eight only were present, although sometimes even this number seemed to be a crowd.

A BSA scooter which did not reach the production stage, although fully developed in the early 1940s. The picture shows Gwen Arey, then Mr. Leek's secretary, riding one of the prototypes.

Chapter Five

After all, in the motorcycle business at least, the public do not seem to know what they want until they see it. The technique of producing a winner is surely based on good business ability and on all-around awareness of the motorcycle world and the mostly youthful people who populate it.

The production planning capability of the company was phenomenal as instanced by the firm dateline fixed for the new 650 cc twin cylinder Golden Flash model. We were to have three prototypes available for testing by August 1949, and the new motorcycle would be shown at Earls Court in October of that year, with initial production quantities available in November. I had joined the company in May 1949 and had completed the design plans by the middle of June. In a matter of five months we were to make detail drawings, order prototypes, machine the prototype parts, assemble these parts, engine test and finally road test the complete motorcycles before passing them for production. From that stage on, the planning and tooling engineers were to design and produce the jigs and fixtures etc, which would be used for quantity production.

Obviously some short cuts were taken. For instance, much to my amazement, it was decided to assume that little or no design changes would be necessary during the development process and production tools were designed and ordered immediately, without waiting for any test results. Mr. Leek knew perfectly well that if serious faults were thrown up during the proving period, many of these tools may have to be scrapped and re-designed at great expense, but the decision was made in the light of extreme urgency and it was not the only time that such a calculated risk had paid off handsomely. After all, in such circumstances a good businessman will, if he is wise, balance the cost of scrapping and remaking equipment against the all-round cost of 'missing the boat', probably for a whole season in important overseas markets. 'Risk' decisions, such as this one undoubtedly was, are classified in my language as good management strategy. The important proviso is that the management team must be unanimous in agreement and must, of course, be capable of superb teamwork, particularly in emergency.

Although my intimate knowledge was necessarily scant, I was impressed and believed that we had just such a team of top personnel. Certainly I was never terribly worried. I was concerned, of course, and took steps to make certain that my 'homework' was thorough, but I realized, as did my colleagues, that the short cut was important. I felt certain that if there were any hiccups we were stong enough and capable of baling out of the situation or at the very worst reverting to a production dateline some six months in arrears.

I shudder to think what the various learned experts and consultants, who have since bedevilled the British motorcycle industry at the invitation of various chairmen, would think of a Managing Director who gave his blessing to such a travesty of the management book. I can understand why such matters would never form part of their curriculum, for after all it would be difficult to achieve a critical path of analysis

The BSA Golden Flash model A10, a 650 cc ohv parallel twin first produced during the 1951 season.

of likely validity. Even so, it was with this background that the BSA company went on to produce a product on time, which was to prove one of the most reliable and profitable best sellers of that era.

The inside story reveals a few exciting moments during this period, which are indelible in my mind, and only on one occasion did we show a slight sign of panic. We had three experimental prototypes under road test and because many more miles per machine were needed than a single rider could possibly achieve, a twenty-four hour round the clock operation was set up, with three riders per machine each having an eight hour shift of duty. By operating in this way, with nine riders, we could achieve an average of around 4000 miles per week with each machine. The machines were surprisingly free from trouble with the exception of a tendency for the offside piston to run dry and seize.

At that time BSA were manufacturing their own pistons and I would have liked to have called in an expert piston manufacturer to take the responsibility of this problem and develop a cure but, although I was instrumental in doing this at a later date, we had no alternative at the time but to soldier on. I was concerned that the solution to this problem might mean some sizeable re-design and of course the very expensive die casting equipment was already well advanced. Our Production Director, Tom Whittington, with a typical directness of approach, suggested that we put a window in the engine and take a look while it was running. This sounded the   ***99*** obvious thing to do and I suppose I could not see the wood for the trees. From a Perspex window bolted to the top of the open crankcase, we were able to observe a gross inadequacy of lubricant on the offside of the engine, which was very easy to correct. Our problem faded overnight.

I had been with my new employers a month or so when I heard from Doug Hele. He was unhappy at Norton Motors and it was agreed that he would join my design staff at Small Heath, where he settled down very rapidly and became a pillar of strength to support and advise me through more than two decades. Doug had served his engineering apprenticeship with Austin Motor Co. long before the spoilation of Leyland and I understand that he was one of the finest apprentices to be trained by this once famous company. He is an excellent engineer and the finest designer with whom I have ever been associated and his academic background ensures that he is a giant in his class. I shall always be thankful for his wonderful expertise, both on the drawing board and in the development shops, where his keen and analytical mind enabled him to be so outstanding. His extreme loyalty during some of the more difficult phases of my career can never be repaid. We became firm friends through success and difficulty and although we both are now out of the industry which meant so much to us, our friendship continues.

Some BSA management personalities during the mid-1950s. Bert Perigo (centre) was then Competition Manager and a man more steeped in the motorcycle business would be impossible to find. His business talent and alertness would have helped avoid the chaos soon to overtake us if our Board of Directors and business advisers had been aware of latent talent within the organisation.

Some refreshing years with the Birmingham Small Arms Company

It was my intention to form a separate design team and work solely on more forward projects, with the short term year to year changes and other redesigns of cosmetic nature to be dealt with by a quite separate team of engineers. I was rapidly coming to the conclusion that someone must mastermind, as I put it, a complete forward product plan for a new generation otherwise we should fiddle on with yearly face lifts and only a semi-new model from time to time.

Outstanding new machines from Germany and Italy were now making a great impact and some of these motorcycles were so new and attractive in concept and so efficient and quiet in operation, that, even at this early stage British machines were by comparison very outdated although they were thoroughly reliable.

The German motorcycle industry in particular, which a few years previously had been reduced to rubble, had set about its task with typical energy and with the help of vast injection of capital from the USA in particular were now marketing very impressive and up to the minute models. The NSU Max was one such example which boasted a superlative performance and was a handsome machine with a brilliant 250 cc engine of unusual design and a frame which was manufactured basically from two huge pressings which were flash-welded together in a matter of seconds. Many other German companies were re-entering the field and some had amazingly silent and efficient two-stroke engines. Furthermore, there was no doubt at all that the Japanese were working industriously with their eyes towards a world market which was poised for rapid growth.

What shocked and disappointed me then, and to this day leaves me with a great feeling of despondency, was the complete unawareness of the chairmen and other top executives of the British industry. They did very little to prepare for the intensive competition which was so obviously threatening to obliterate us. Almost everyone at board level seemed to be asleep and on the rare occasions when I had the opportunity of discussing the situation with people of this stature, I was upset by the self-satisfaction and feeling of lethargy which seemed to exist.

At that time the only opportunity I had for conversing with people of such importance in the industry was during the annual show at Earls Court or at various functions. I feel that Sir Bernard Docker, who was Chairman of BSA, and any of his colleagues who were in the main financiers, regarded me as some sort of bumpkin with a cause which was aggravated by the current shortage of swedes!

Even the technical press, who later were to become so pro-Jap, and were to lash the British industry for lacking business foresight, seemed quite happy with our progress. I quote from the *Motor Cycling Year Book of 1954* in which Bob Holliday, then Editor of *Motor Cycling* and who normally spared no one with well-founded criticism wrote 'There is nothing wrong whatever with the policy of improving upon a machine that has earned a sterling reputation, and it is a far better method of doing business than introducing startling novelties for novelty's sake and in the hope that they may catch on. This is an all-British policy. It may be staid and perhaps *101* exasperating for impatiently minded people but it is the way we do things and I think the 1953 Motor Cycle Show was a fine example of how well we do it. And what a wide variety our industry has to offer. No other manufacturing country can approach it.' A very surprising statement I felt, particularly when he should have been aware that nothing really new or outstanding was on the stocks.

As Chief Designer at Small Heath, I was directly responsible to Harry Faulkner, who was nearing retirement, and whose main expertise lay in the area of gun engineering. Consequently the initial planning and strategy of design projections was left in my hands. I separated the Design Department and placed two or three first class men under the control of Doug Hele and moved them away from the hurly-burly of the daily design task. Out came the 250 cc single cylinder engine

The 250 cc single cylinder BSA with a high-performance engine having four valves radially disposed, driven by ohc. Designed by the author in 1949, a somewhat modified form reached a satisfactory stage of development by 1952.

which I had sketched in my few weeks with the company and Hele worked on this, refining and redesigning parts of the unit to make it a more satisfactory production proposition and to improve its overall efficiency. It was my suggestion that a range of engines of this design should be developed to be ready and waiting to follow on, to supersede the Gold Star models which were soon to be so successful. Performance was very much a key factor and even with today's standards as a guide, it will be seen that our engine design was very up to date.

In 1953 the twin cylinder Grand Prix NSU Rennmax was developing 35 bhp and we were soon to be within striking distance of this sort of power output with an engine which had not been allocated a real development programme. The Rennmax was a works racer built in very limited numbers and was sweeping the board in

Grand Prix events all over the world. We were greatly encouraged to feel that the Gold Star brand name may, one day, be replaced by a worthy successor.

My original engine, sketched in 1949, was a radial valve unit substantially similar to the one which Hele had re-designed, with a bore and stroke of 70 mm x 64.5 mm respectively and I left the work entirely to him, knowing full well that my target of power and reliability would need all of his expertise. It may seem strange that, for a new generation of Gold Star machines, I was reaching for extremely high power per litre but I felt sure that our target must at least be the equivalent of the world beating NSU Rennmax.

Although we at BSA had no intention of entering the Grand Prix racing arena, it was essential to have such power outputs available from the basic design structure, for it is a simple matter to detune but much more difficult to reverse the procedure, particularly if the 'scantlings' are not there.

Many of my business colleagues can be excused for having difficulty in understanding my logic, for we had just re-designed the Gold Star range and were

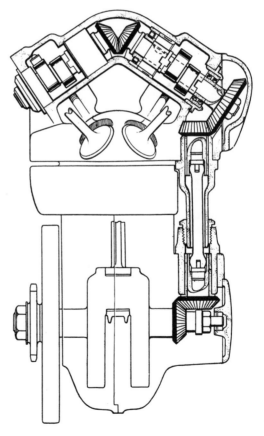

Drawing showing the radial layout of valves and the bevel-gear drive of the 250 cc BSA MC1 high speed engine.

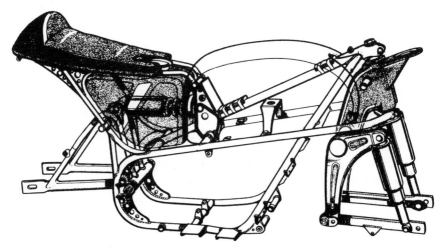

By the time the 250 cc BSA MC1 high-speed machine reached the development stage in 1952, Doug Hele had considerably modified much of the layout. The picture shows the frame and fork arrangement and a wealth of forward thinking.

about to benefit from the successes of this remarkable machine throughout the world, in all forms of two wheel sport. But it seems that sales personnel are often blind to the dangers of success for it is they who must have their eyes on the future, whilst enjoying the present, and their ears to the ground. The successful years can become the critical ones if the initiative is lost.

Of course, when the pendulum swings in the opposite direction after someone, probably with a strange foreign name, has crept up overnight and rudely shattered the peace, marketing directors will often come into their own once more with urgent projections of something which is not in the catalogue. It has always been my experience that the men who are really in control of a company, who invariably have financial or marketing background, are the last people in the world to be capable of realizing whether the company they are supposed to be running has product plans for viability.

My records show that by early 1952 three of the special 250 cc engines had been built and that straight from the drawing board 31 bhp at 9,300 rpm was achieved. A few weeks of development pushed this up to 33 bhp at 10,000 rpm, and the target was in sight. Doug Hele's ingenuity shows in the frame for the machine, which was very unorthodox, the pivoted rear fork being triangulated and controlled by a single spring and damper beneath the seat. Front suspension was also of the pivoted type. The front fork assembly pivoted round a fixed stem which was clamped top and bottom to the frame structure. The machine was very light at 248 lbs dry weight and in June 1954, the late Charlie Salt put in 130 laps at the MIRA testing ground at an average speed of 100 mph.

Some refreshing years with the Birmingham Small Arms Company

Geoff Duke had heard about the machine over the grapevine and I agreed that he should try it out for an opinion. On a windy, leaf-strewn day in December 1954, he equalled the 250 cc lap record at Oulton Park. He was so impressed that he chanced his arm and without so much as a by your leave, entered the machine as a GDS (Geoff Duke special I presume) for the following year's Lightweight TT. It was partly the publicity accruing from that tentative entry that killed off the project. I was called into the Managing Director's office to have my knuckles rapped and rightly so, for although I had no prior knowledge of this somewhat irresponsible action, there were, of course, no excuses.

Duke was a national figure and although, much to their credit, the technical press preserved a tactful silence, the fact that the GDS was really a BSA motorcycle became an open secret and the national dailies and even the BBC gave us an embarrassing time for a while.

We had a successful production racing policy plus an almost unbeatable scrambles and trials team so there was no need to plunge into Grand Prix racing, for sales were high. But, of course, we had to have the opinion of an expert and who better than the European Champion? The fact that he was a freelance and quite unconnected with the company did not help in preserving the secrecy which was desirable.

It was all much ado about nothing for I was merely carrying out tests as best I could on the first of a family of machines which I hoped would follow the Gold Stars some years hence. I can only say that our initial efforts gave me a clear indication that, management permitting, the later 1950s and early 1960s would show BSA to have strengthened its grip on the 'everyman' world of sporting motorcycles, with modern sophisticated machinery. I believe that if the attitude of top management through the past twenty years had been different, the BSA company would be leaders today, for engineering personnel have initiated viable policies throughout this period.

It is also sad to recall that throughout its history, the BSA company have a record of being first off with many projects which, for some reason, were later abandoned. One can only feel that none are so blind as those who will not see. For example, BSA had a reasonable scooter long before the Italians made them a success, and a long list of similar examples strengthens the theory that through the years, the Small Heath engineering faculty have been let down very badly.

From those glorious 1950s emerged production racing, a term used for the racing by private individuals of machines which had been made in specified quantities (or semi-mass produced). This comparatively new sport was beginning to appeal to the public and BSA were soon to dominate most of this area of activity. Nortons, with their 'Manx' models, seemed to 'fiddle' their way through in the early 1950s and the A-CU, we felt, turned a blind eye to the sometimes blatant 'bending' of the rules which stipulated the production quantity that gave eligibility. Soon BSA, *105*

Four pictures of the 250 cc BSA MC1 high speed project. The petrol tank shown, probably the ugliest ever created, was a seven gallon monster, designed to take the full TT race without a fuelling stop.

The German NSU Rennmax machine of the early 1950s. The machine on which John Surtees was all conquering in the 250 cc Grand Prix racing events. BSA sights were set on at least equalling the performance of this machine during the development of their MC1 project.

with their new breed of semi mass-produced Gold Star models of both 350 cc and 500 cc capacity became almost 100% successful. This was a fine tribute for the company, world wide, and the publicity value was such that all products enjoyed boosted sales figures and the profits of the Motorcycle Division attained new peaks.

I was fortunate enough to be given the opportunity of visiting the USA for the purpose of calling on as many BSA dealers as possible. The psychology behind sending a Design Engineer on such a mission was new enough then to cause considerable comment. Service problems were beginning to worry our two distributors and if, as is often the case, corrections in design need to be made, there can be no 'buck passing' if the engineer himself is in confrontation with angry dealers or customers. If he has any sense at all, he will get back and take action, for he may be called upon to meet the same people at a later date.

My feeling was that there was a significant lack of communication with the US dealer organization which meant that we worked in a partial vacuum at Small Heath. We were only just beginning to learn that motorcylists in the USA were very different from those back here and the user problems simply could not be compared, as was soon to be demonstrated to me.

Bert Perrigo, our Competition Manager, teamed up with me and we embarked on a tour which was made by road, in company with our distributors. It took us from North to South on the Eastern and Western seaboards, with an opportunity of visitng Daytona Beach in Florida to witness the classic Daytona races of that year. This visit gave on-the-spot evidence of user problems and the very different usage to which our machines were being subject, as well as the vastness and variety of savage terrain which permitted much of this. Sometimes the going was tough indeed, for we were seeking trouble and almost exclusively meeting very angry people. We soon learned that listening, showing willing, and more important, seeking suggestions, often took the heat from the discussion and was half the battle. I had, even then, decided that I could never face these people again if I failed to show some results and it was not long after this trip that the primary drive chain of the Golden Flash was upgraded to the triple strand type, although we at home were never able to break the duplex type, even with the most brutal treatment.

My biggest surprise and shock came with a demonstration, at the Daytona races, of the unreliability of the 500 cc Gold Star machine. No less then 36 were entered in the 200 mile classic, yet every machine broke down and to my horror I saw gearboxes broken so completely that the 'innards' were exposed. Not a single engine was free from serious valve and rocker gear trouble. In retrospect, this trip paid handsome dividends for results were not long in forthcoming. The pedigree was vastly improved and the impact of the performance and reliability of BSA products has never been bettered. I suppose the crowning achievement came a year or two later in 1954, with BSA winning the Daytona 200 mile classic race, the blue ribband of motorcycle racing in the USA, with 5 machines in the first 6 places.

We had sent three twins and three singles and when these machines were unpacked at Daytona beach, they were so obviously workmanlike and well prepared that the American Motorcycle Association, who organize the races, threatened to disqualify them on the grounds of rule-breaking. They were being pushed by the Harley-Davidson racing personnel and had no option, but Hap Alzina, our West Coast Distributor, threatened to delay the race with an injunction until such time as it could be proven that no rules had been broken. In addition he would organize the dismantling of the motorcycles, piece by piece, under the spotlights on stage at the local theatre with the public invited to attend and see for themselves. This was too much and the race was run on time, with the threats of disqualification retracted.

I am afraid that back at Small Heath, with other things to occupy my mind, I had forgotten about the exact date of this race, and one Monday morning in March I was sent for by Mr. Leek who handed me a cable, just in from the USA, which indicated that we had won the classic with 5 in the first 6 places. I do not know to this day whether he was serious but he seemed irritated about the 'other machine' *109* and wanted to know 'what the hell had happened to it!' It is difficult to please everyone, but the sixth entry was in collision at the first corner, otherwise even my Managing Director might have been satisfied.

It was during my trip to the USA in 1951 that the Triumph Motor Cycle Company changed ownership and was sold to BSA but for a year or two there seemed to be no intention on the part of the new owners to interfere at Meriden. It was not until several years later that the merging of the two companies had any effect at Small Heath or Meriden, although Mr. Sangster had now become a member of the parent board.

By 1953 I had been promoted to the position of Chief Engineer of the Small Heath group and by this time, the Golden Flash and its 500 cc counterpart were selling well. The single cylinder range, although getting a little long in the tooth, were in brisk demand, mainly because the price was reasonable and they were very reliable machines indeed. The baby of the range, the 125 cc two-stroke Bantam, had its origins in Germany where the design drawings had been handed over to BSA lock, stock and barrel, as part of war reparations. This was a short-cut indeed to the manufacture of a very reliable motorcycle, for the original had already had a successful production run in Germany and therefore needed little or no development. The BSA Bantam went into production in 1948, to become a most successful machine and a good profit earner for two decades.

The Gold Star range of sporting machines had been re-designed and developed to a degree that almost every sporting event, whether production racing, trials, or scrambles, was dominated by motorcycles of BSA manufacture. Our Managing Director had given instructions to see to it that BSA products were second to none in these three forms of motorcycle sport and certainly by 1954, with the tremendous success of the Daytona exercise, it could be seen that these instructions had been well and truly carried out.

The American market had grown to a healthy, ever-expanding proportion of our export market and now a far cry from those tenuous early days in 1945 when Mr. Leek came to an agreement with Alf Child. He was an American who had come over from the USA, without invitation, for the purpose of 'soliciting the agency for the 48 states of the USA' as he put it. Jimmy Leek realized the vast potential and immediately the agreement had been signed, several thousand prospective dealers were circularized direct from Small Heath.

With a 5 year agreement in his pocket, Alf Child sailed back to the USA from Fowey in Cornwall in a Liberty ship laden with china clay, which sank after colliding with an oil tanker off the US coast. Fortunately for BSA, Child was hauled from the sea and typical of the man, was, next day, setting up office in New York. He started operating from a small hotel room but he quickly went on to build a huge and efficient dealer structure which, by 1949, was operating smoothly from 2 distributor *110* centres. The Rich Child Cycle Corp. in New Jersey served the eastern states and

Hap Alzina Co. in San Francisco covered the western part of the operation.

Alf Child is a huge man with a vast source of energy, a born leader and much respected by most, if not exactly liked by all. He is never lost for words and his sense of humour is prolific. The dedication of his effort and that of Alzina built a foundation on which BSA could and should have erected an enduring and ever growing edifice. To use Child's own words, 'Trees die from their topmost branches down to their roots and it is the same with business.'

Now that I was occupying the Chief Engineer's seat I was to make an effort which was determined enough to make me unpopular at times, to arrive at agreed strategy. It would have enough detail to enable management to be more unanimous about likely trends in the technical make-up of future motorcycles and more happy and united about our action so far as long term time factors were concerned.

We had a short term plan to take BSA through the next four or five years, with a new 250 cc single cylinder machine to replace the long outdated C11, the new engine being basically half of the 500 cc twin cylinder A7 unit. The twins were modern and trouble-free enough to survive a time factor of this sort and the rest of the single cylinder range would have mainly cosmetic changes during this period and would survive as value for money products. This work was being left entirely in the hands of a normal design department. The more forward, new generation, work was being dealt with by another team of engineers led by Doug Hele.

The new 250 cc looked smart, had a superlative performance and was extremely quiet in operation. These parameters alone should have spurred our Board into some sort of action but in addition, the machine had several interesting features and included an option for rear chain enclosure which was very simple and smart. The engine unit had a great number of twin cylinder components in its make up and we had three prototypes, two of which had completed in excess of 30,000 trouble-free miles. As a final test I decided to run one of the machines into the ground with flat-out endurance runs at Montlhéry track, near Paris.

M. Rabuteau, our French distributor, was very impressed with this machine and was interested enough to be at the track to see the motorcycle, in standard trim with all normal road equipment, lap the track steadily at speeds in excess of 90 mph. The motorcycle seemed unbreakable and after three days Billy Nicholson, who was with us, took the model round the track at a speed marginally short of 100 mph. We decided to return to Small Heath thoroughly convinced that we had a very reliable and worthy successor to the old C11 model. But back at home the local board, now more numerous but diluted with several tiers of so-called financial expertise, decided that it would be foolish to replace a model which was, they said, holding its own in the market.

As responsible management they should have known that Continental manufacturers were bearing down on us with models which would make some of our products seem pitiful. Thus an opportunity was missed to market not only an *111*

The BSA Parent Board at the Annual General Meeting in December 1955 in the showroom at Small Heath. Sir Bernard Docker is seen addressing the meeting and Jack Sangster is on far left, with Jimmy Leek seated next to him.

extremely up-to-date machine before our competitors did likewise but also to take advantage of a more sensible production approach by maximising commonality of component parts and their production tooling.

With its performance, appearance and reliability I am sure that the new 250 would have had a successful production run of many years. It would have obviated all of the aches and pains associated with the small capacity 4 stroke machines which the firm later produced and were to prove so troublesome during a period when performance and reliability were being underlined by the first class products of foreign manufacturers.

M. Rabuteau was horrified by the decision to put the machine in cold storage, fully knowing what this really meant. He pleaded with the BSA Board to be given

The 250 cc single cylinder BSA prototype which was designed to replace the ageing C11 model in the early 1950s. The engine was basically half of the 500 cc A7 twin and in this trim this motorcycle finished several days of gruelling tests at Montlhéry track by lapping at 100 mph.

the right to set up a works near Paris and manufacture the motorcycle for sale on the Continent, but, for some reason, his request was turned down and so yet another opportunity was missed. There seemed to be no excuse for this rather stupid decision, for the financial situation was good and the weakest part of our marketing strategy was the small capacity class of machine which was being catered for by a model twenty years old.

But by now I was familiar with the peculiar business logic which seemed to have penetrated the board rooms of much of our industry and it seemed that we were doomed to a too little, too late policy. The tragedy is that at this period of time, in 1955, the industry on the whole was strong and healthy and well placed to update **113**

The 250 cc single cylinder BSA (half an A7 twin) prototype which, in this form, was planned to be introduced as a lightweight machine to augment the Sunbeam range.

and regenerate its product lines, yet the growing menace of foreign competition, with brilliant new machines, did not seem to affect the serene tempo of the industrialists of the British motorcycle business.

This sort of business thinking seemed to make nonsense of my intention of designing a range of new generation products from small to large capacity, but we pressed on with the investigation of a group of power and transmission units based on a single cylinder module and a variation of multiples. The term modular seems to frighten many people and I have found that it is a painfully absorbing task to get the logic across to those with an accountancy background, with the exception of Charles Parker, late of Triumph, David Probert, who was much later to become one of my colleagues, and Alec Skinner with whom I was soon to work at AMC.

However, it does not matter what the concept is labelled. It seems to me now, as always, that a loud and clear mandate should be that a range of products, such as that envisaged, should have a maximum commonality of parts and tooling. No one will disagree, I am sure, when it is put in this way and that is exactly what the modular approach is all about.

Unfortunately during the mid-1950s, Mr. Leek became seriously ill and the operation which resulted left him very weak for some time. His absence from business began to take its toll, for I am sure that until then, the extent of his personal effort was not realised. It is not surprising that Sir Bernard Docker, the Chairman, began to exert pressure to correct the situation by suggesting that forthwith there should be an understudy or Deputy Managing Director.

The occupants of our remote London Board Room looked to their pie in the sky

A 500 cc BSA Gold Star in road race trim for Daytona 1956.

A flat track 500 cc BSA Gold Star with rigid frame.

and after a time newcomers began to appear on the scene to fill positions, having job titles which stood out like sore thumbs. The thought never, for one moment, occurred to any of our directors that any single person who was part of our management team at Small Heath was worthy of promotion to the top. It was too much to expect a board such as this not to fall for the 'whizz kid' type of management sophistication soon to become so popular, and so the creeping paralysis was set firmly on its course.

A racing version of the 500 cc BSA Shooting Star twin of the mid-1950s.

A picture taken in the Isle of Man in 1952 after Eric Houseley (22) and Bob McIntyre (76) finished first and second respectively on BSA Gold Stars in the Junior Clubmans TT race. Also in the picture are several BSA management personnel with Bill Rawson (5th from left), the author (6th from left) Bert Perrigo (4th from right) and S. Digby (3rd from right).

117

Chapter Five

Exactly how much Mr. Leek could have done, had he been fit, to avert the chaos which followed, one will never know. The change in management attitude was quite dramatic and I regard this period as the point of real downturn in the fortunes of the BSA Motorcycle Division. One would have thought that we had all before us for we now embraced the BSA, Sunbeam, Ariel and Triumph marques. There is no doubt whatsoever that the specialized management expertise and technique within the group could and should have positioned us for mastering the expanding markets throughout the world.

Mr. James Leek, CBE, Managing Director of BSA, with Alistair King (left), winner of the 1954 Senior Clubmans TT race and Philip Palmer winner of the Junior race, photographed in the Isle of Man.

I must confess that the real impact of this critical period in the history of BSA management had little effect on me for a while and I had no time to be concerned about the firm's future prospects because plans were under way for our new generation products. At no time did I doubt that, by the early 1960s, we should be in production with a range of modern motorcycles from 200 cc to 800 cc capacity, which would take the company through to the 1970s.

I was, however, concerned that very little of the considerable profit being made was being ploughed back and I expressed my concern, many times, at management

Bill Nicholson, the famous competitions star of the 1950s, helping with tests at Montlhéry in France.

An unusual shot of the versatile BSA Bantam earning its keep on a sheep farm in Australia.

M. Rabuteau, the BSA distributor in France (4th from left) outlining strategy during French police tests of BSA machines near Paris. Charlie Salt, well known BSA racer, is astride the 650 cc Golden Flash, and Arthur Lupton of the BSA Technical Department, staunch linchpin through several decades at Small Heath, is seen third from left.

The Sunbeam S7 500 cc ohv twin which went out of production in the late 1950s.

A happy picture of Ted Crabtree, Managing Director of the Ariel Works in the mid-1950s, standing third from left.

The Triumph 'Terrier' in its original form in the 1950s. This machine was equipped with a 150 cc ohv engine and 4-speed gearbox.

Details of Triumph Terrier engine of 150 cc capacity

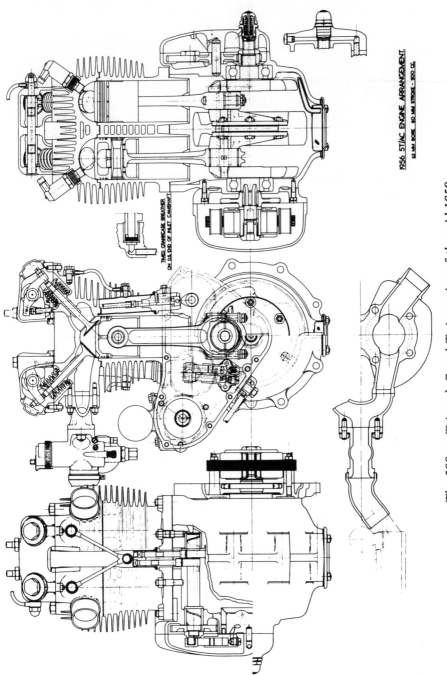

1956 ST/AC ENGINE ARRANGEMENT

63 MM. BORE 80 MM STROKE - 500 CC

TIMED CRANKCASE BREATHER ON D/S END OF INLET CAMSHAFT

The 500 cc Triumph Speed Twin engine of the mid-1950s

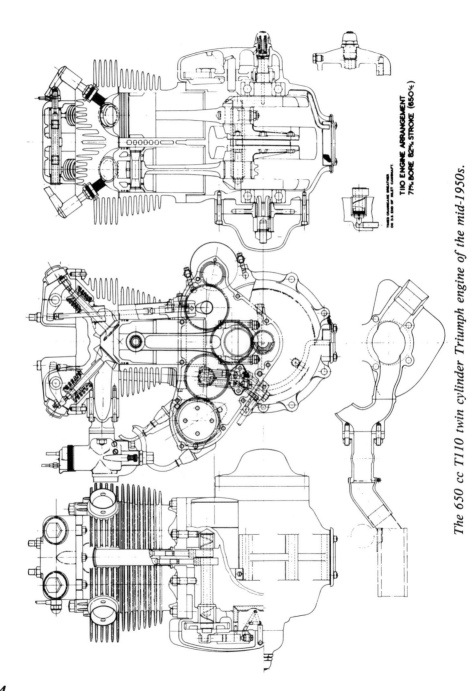

TIIO ENGINE ARRANGEMENT
71% BORE 82% STROKE (650 %)

THIS CRANKCASE BREATHER
ON D.S. END OF INLET CAMSHAFT.

The 650 cc T110 twin cylinder Triumph engine of the mid-1950s.

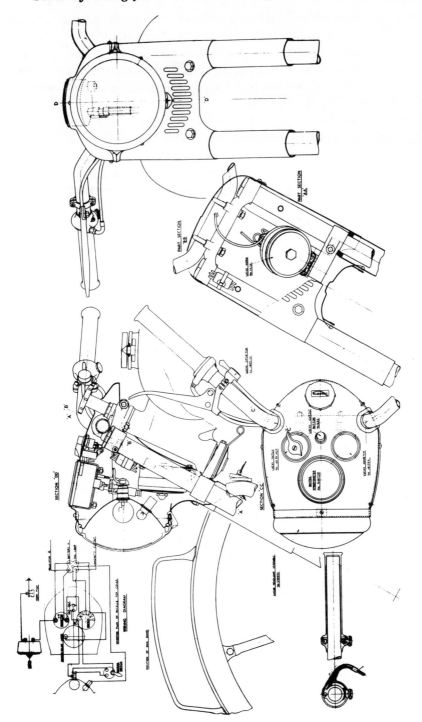

Details of the Triumph headlamp nacelle, a fashion-setting breakthrough from the late 1940s.

meetings. It was too obvious that most of our machinery was so old as to be almost antique and it should have been equally obvious to the financial brains in the business that future products must have more sophisticated specifications which could only be achieved if labour costs were cut by automation. I must say that I found accountants and the like to be very tiresome people on the whole, for whenever this important subject was discussed, it seems that I was regarded as an expensive lunatic with a social bent to improve the working conditions on the shop floor. But I did not lose too much sleep on this score for it was early days to be worrying unduly and I knew that, if a new generation plan such as this was accepted, it would have to be backed by a massive injection of capital. Sufficient unto the day for I felt reasonably confident that, when the time arrived, management would have heard the projected funding costs so often that it would not be too severe a douche.

Whether other industries are as shy to plough back the right percentage of profits as were the motorcycle companies for whom I had worked, I do not know, but this is poor management and the whole of the British motorcycle business seemed tarred with the same brush.

Johnny Allen set a World Record for two-wheelers of 193.72 mph at Bonneville Salt Flats in USA. The machine was equipped with an unsupercharged 650 cc Triumph twin cylinder engine.

Johnny Allen, second from right, at Fort Dunlop, after breaking the World Speed Record for two-wheelers. Bill Johnson, Triumph US distributor, is at the extreme right, and Edward Turner third from right.

With the Triumph Company within the group and Jack Sangster and Edward Turner as members of the BSA Board of Directors, one would have hoped that this would have strengthened the company significantly by providing a more balanced body of businessmen at this level. It did not work out like this, however, and the Triumph company seemed still to run as a private company, with Turner at the helm and refusing to allow interchange at middle management level. Consequently Meriden seemed to be a closed shop with the mixture as before. One would have thought that the £2m or so which BSA paid for this merger should have earned the shareholders a better management deal but the earnings at Meriden were very good indeed and this of course was the saving grace, albeit a somewhat short-sighted one.

The grand sounding phraseology of the take-over expert must have been a great comfort to the shareholders of BSA who felt, not unreasonably, that their company was capable of dealing adequately with a changing market situation which was building up throughout the world.   *127*

The Ariel 'manufacturing unit' was efficient, if spartan, even through the 1950s, and this picture gives some indication of tight packed activity and the simplest of assembly methods.

A situation developed, slowly at first, but gathering strength very rapidly, in which the BSA and Triumph operations became so separatist and opposed that it was difficult to believe that the two companies were part of the same group. The two units were soaked with antagonism and continued to go their separate ways, with not the slightest attempt being made, so far as I could see, to bring the situation back onto the rails. This state of affairs sprang directly from top management level and Edward Turner, in particular, made it no secret that Triumph territory was sacrosanct. He flatly refused to allow any movement towards inter-company management collaboration and it is not surprising that, given this sort of encouragement, a barrier of mistrust grew which was, much later, almost impossible to remove.

Perhaps this is the correct method of running a group of companies each manufacturing a similar product for, after all, British Leyland have not had much success with the strength that groups are supposed to generate. Theirs is an example, it would seem, of reasonable inter-company collaboration.

However, one must assume that when the BSA Board took over Ariel and Triumph, they really did feel that 'specialist management strength' would be **128** tremendously improved and that the resources now available to the group would enable it to meet the future with much more confidence. But it is sad and deplorable that no one, at that exalted level, seemed to take the reins and give the poor shareholders some indication that their money had not been entirely wasted.

Reverting to my own particular problems, two new products had recently reached prototype stage, and our diluted management felt they should be marketed as quickly as possible and certainly long before any real work had been carried out to assess their acceptability.

The first was the Dandy, a 75 cc machine with a two-stroke engine of BSA design and an open frame and smallish wheels which allowed a low saddle height and inspired a feeling of confidence and safety. It had a semi-automatic, two-speed gear and this extremely simple machine, which was provided with some degree of weather protection, was to be marketed at a very competitive price. It was aimed at a market which was growing rapidly and now catered for by the foreign 50 cc mopeds being imported in large quantities. The second was a scooter named the Beesa, a handsome machine with a 198 cc, four-stroke engine and equipped with electric starting.

The prototype of these two new machines had been completed only a few weeks before the opening of the 1955 Earls Court show and, rather foolishly I thought, it was decided that they should be exhibited. The problems and worries associated with

Part of the Ariel works in the 1950s. The Engine Test Department.

Another view of the Ariel works, showing the final inspection bay with subsidiary operations being carried out in the gallery.

a formidable design and engineering activity, now being condensed to near impossible time factors at this important stage, were beginning to have some impact on my general health and enthusiasm. This and a new type of rat race together with a most depressing espionage system, which seemed to have descended on us, forced me to seriously consider my resignation.

Arrangements were being made to rush the Dandy and Beesa into production for their reception had been good, but although there had been no development engineering time at all spent on these machines we seemed hell bent, at all costs, to 'get in while it was hot'. Getting away with this sort of thing, as we had with the Golden Flash several years earlier, was all very well, but once is enough for the strongest and it was tending to become a very bad habit. It is questionable procedure even when the management team is capable and unanimous and right now, we were far from being in that happy state.

I cannot be sure whether the Dandy was in production before I left to take up a new appointment, but no one ever succeeded me as Chief Engineer. Edward Turner was soon to be the new Chief Executive and I would have been surprised had it been otherwise for he had told me, so many times in the past, that such titles were luxuries and unnecessary in a company finding itself fortunate enough to be powered by his

The Beeza scooter introduced at the 1955 Earls Court Show and later abandoned. It was equipped with electric and manual start, a 198 cc four-stroke engine, shaft drive and interchangeable wheels.

all embracing personality. I had left the company by the time he was appointed. He had overall responsibility for the BSA, Triumph and Ariel operation as Managing Director of the Midland group.

My feeling has always been that this important management change was borne of very doubtful reasoning, for Turner had always been open and voiceful in declaring Triumph territory as inviolate with BSA, an unworthy associate. This, from Parent Board level, had greatly encouraged the animosity between the three operations. It was now too late for any blandishments on his part for the opportunity had been missed long ago and, contrary to taking an active part in the management of each separate unit, he seemed to hibernate at Meriden with rare visits indeed to Selly Oak and Small Heath.

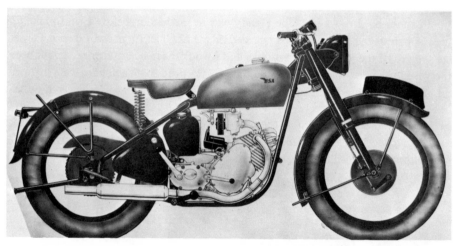

A BSA machine, intended for military usage, equipped with the 198 cc engine designed for use in the BSA Beeza scooter. This machine did not reach the production stage.

Having ousted Sir Bernard Docker in 1956, the Board had appointed Jack Sangster to the chairmanship, a change which was welcomed by many. It seems, however, that Mr. Sangster had indicated that he was willing to take this office for a short period only, which was unfortunate. It tended to generate an atmosphere of instability, however slight.

Soon after Doug Hele and I had departed from the BSA empire, almost everyone who was not an engineer had a pencil behind their ear. The Dandy, in particular, suffered the loving care of a dozen or so 'chief engineers' most of whom were obviously out of their depth. Problems still persisted until, eventually, the model *132* was withdrawn from production.

The 70 cc BSA Dandy which was priced at £60 plus purchase tax and was introduced at the 1955 Earls Court Show. It was equipped with a simple two-speed, pre-selector gearchange, controlled from the handlebars and the all-aluminium engine had a hard chromed cylinder bore.

Another picture of the 1955 BSA Dandy.

133

Chapter Five

One example of ineptitude was the substitution of cast iron for the light alloy specified for the engine cylinder material, a move which proved fatal as it was vital, with this power unit layout, that the heat dissipating properties of aluminium be available. The cost saving probably gained a medal momentarily for someone and provided, I would think, a happy release from the relentless battle I had been waging with certain boffins to get moving and show some of the old BSA spirit. In particular I nagged away for years in the hope that we should develop a mass production process for coating light alloy cylinder bores with a hard chrome surface but, to the last, I was fobbed off. It did not seem to be too much to ask, for the German NSU company seemed to have no difficulty in doing just this and obviously very cheaply, for they were flooding the world with their *Quickly* moped, so equipped. Ironically, we had within our group a small company which had done much to pioneer this process.

The Beesa scooter did not go into production and although a variant model with automatic transmission was under construction, it was not completed and the whole project was scrapped.

Not surprisingly the new boss indicated that the product 'goings on' at Small Heath were not his 'cup of tea', to use his own words to me at a later date. Needless to say, unless someone in top management is behind a project, it is a waste of time to continue.

It must be remembered that top management had become very much Triumph orientated and it was about now that Mr. Leek went into retirement. The re-formed board can, I supose, be excused for making the picture at Small Heath look as bleak as possible, with the usual trick of writing off, forthwith, much of the work carried out by their supposedly clueless predecessors. It is surprising to me how readily this can be done, particularly as was the case at that time. If the cash position will allow it, and sometimes even if it will not, it has the advantage of indicating to the hapless shareholders how fortunate they are that the new management arrived just in time!

Fortunately I was off the scene before this debacle and as I tendered my resignation to Mr. Leek, I felt a great deal of nostalgia. Most of my seven years with him had been happy and fruitful and although he was, at all times, a tough and determined master, one always knew where one stood. It was sad for me to sever my connections with one of a rapidly declining type of business executive.

It had, apparently, been obvious to outsiders that things at Small Heath were not what they should be and Donald Heather, the Managing Director of Associated Motor Cycles, had been in touch with me. He suggested that I join their organization and I accepted, to commence my new job in April, 1955.

Chapter Six

With the Associated Motor Cycle Group through the late 1950's

MY NEW employers manufactured Matchless, AJS, James, Francis Barnett and Norton motorcycles from four separate units, with Matchless and AJS at Woolwich, James and Norton at Tyseley and Aston in Birmingham, and Francis Barnett at Coventry.

It was agreed that I become a Director of Norton Motors and R.T.Shelley Ltd. and should be located at Bracebridge Street. From the very start, Mr. Heather was most anxious that I should not become too bogged down with design engineering, although this part of management should be my first responsibility. The terms of reference were that I should be appointed 'an Executive Director of our subsidiaries Norton Motors and R.T.Shelley Ltd. with full executive control of the works including production, engineering and product design'.

Gilbert Smith was still the Managing Director of Nortons, but Joe Craig had gone and at the time of my appointment Alec Skinner, the company secretary, was promoted to the Board. Alec was a Chartered Accountant then around 40 years of age, who had great ability and was very similar in character to Charles Parker, that worthy veteran of Meriden. Like him, he was able to fully understand and appreciate the more practical problems of the business and with his feet firmly on the ground, his financial control was simple and easy to understand. He and I became firm friends from the outset and we worked together with a smoothness which many regarded as quite remarkable.

At a later date, when I was to become the company's Managing Director, I was thankful indeed to be fortunate enough to have such a colleague who kept me updated weekly with financial projections, so vital in the daily running of the company. I cannot think that there is a more certain recipe for commercial success *135* than the smooth dovetailing of engineer and accountant and certainly this made my job easier and much more pleasurable.

Gilbert Smith, the Managing Director, at first presented me with a somewhat different problem, for it must be remembered that the outcome of my last conversation with him, some seven years previously, had concerned my getting the sack! Fortunately, as I was to discover later, he was genuinely glad that I had been invited to fill the appointment and things turned out to be less difficult than I had expected. I did not beat about the bush and told him that I was not interested in the past. Starting from now, I had a job to do under his jurisdiction and he could expect my loyalty at all times. Furthermore, I would always be looking for his help and advice. Gilbert, I think, was rather surprised and relieved by my very direct approach and we went on, from that point, to work together in great harmony until his retirement two years later. I shall always feel glad about this for there is no doubt that he found the bondage of his new bosses more than a little irksome. My presence was catalytic when Woolwich and Bracebridge Street were directly involved with each other and I settled in very happily in a rewarding team atmosphere, which was underlined each time the three directors sat down at a meeting.

The 'bogey' was our parent company, although as yet I did not fully appreciate this. Since Associated Motor Cycles had taken over Norton Motors in 1952, Gilbert Smith had become opposed to their policy (if one could call it that). He had previously been completely unfettered and was quite understandably finding it very irksone to be shoved around by acquaintances for whom he previously had very little time. I felt sorry for him but took pains to point out that there was some compensation in being some 100 miles distant from the source of his trouble and that it would make good sense if he would stop banging his head against the wall and face the facts of life. Unfortunately he never disguised what appeared to be total dislike and opposition to all connections with Associated Motor Cycles. Although I was not with the company at the time of the take-over, I understand that his feelings were obvious from the very first day of the partnership and it is no small surprise that the Woolwich Board had themselves become somewhat disenchanted. But more of this anon.

It was most unfortunate that on the very day that I took up my new duties with Norton Motors, a strike began over the dismissal of 26 redundant workers. Since all of the men had been found jobs in their own trade at comparable wages it was difficult to appreciate what more could be done.

The true situation was obviously clear to the strikers themselves for there was steadily diminishing support, notwithstanding the dispute now being declared official). Although, through the rest of the year, we had all the workers we needed, the official trade union attitude was to fight for any cause, whether worthy or not. Although broken in the main by the workforce itself, the strike dragged on for six months or so and whereas the wheels continued to turn, the various disruptions

The Norton model 99 of 1955 with a 600 cc version of the Dominator engine.

caused by officially-backed trouble makers made severe inroads into a cash situation already aggravated by a current economic downturn.

I am thankful that the Managing Director took all of the load in this dispute but he insisted that I should be present at every meeting on the subject. Not only did I witness my senior colleague dealing with every situation with commendable expertise, but also I learned a great deal in a very short time about industrial relations.

My terms of reference were to involve me in a situation quite different from hitherto for in addition to engineering and production matters I had also been instructed, by Mr. Heather, 'to involve myself on the commercial side'. At first, Gilbert did not relish this but, after a time, he seemed to realize that it made nonsense for him to continue going it alone and I am thankful that there was never a cross word so that we settled down and progressed on a new basis. However, he did at first simply fail to comprehend just how 'a designer by trade', as he put it, could possibly rise to the occasion and least of all, help in the complexities of commerce and finance and the like. It was obvious that I was willing to start learning and as we got to know each other, as colleagues, I got as near to friendship as was possible with this rather dour individual.

Norton Motors were not, at this stage, seriously inhibited financially by being part of a group of companies. Although this may seem an illogical statement, the sequence of events through the years followed the all too common pattern in organizations of this type by reducing the level of the best manufacturing units to the lowest common denominator.

The strike caused a severe loss during the 1955/6 financial year and with the economic climate tending to worsen, the excellent financial forecasting by Alec **137**

Chapter Six

Skinner provided a sound early warning system. It was not long before I insisted on trimming further the workforce figure to a level which left us 'lean and hungry'.

Shelley production was made up of sub-contract work and spanners of various types together with a small range of mechanical lifting jacks for commercial vehicles. All in all, a business which could disappear overnight, for any of these items could be made and sold by almost any workshop throughout the land and we were already feeling the effect of this by having to cut our prices to ridiculous levels in order to retain business. If Shelleys were to survive and prosper, we surely needed a branded range of our own particular products and, when I first mentioned this to the Managing Director, he did not agree. Later it was decided that I should draw up a plan on this basis for comparison with the alternative of merging out the Shelley manufacturing activity and concentrating on increased motorcycle turnover.

It is a pity that by the time I was able to positively identify the situation and have a detailed plan of action, Gilbert Smith had left the company. Although much of the new Shelley product plan cut across certain of his principles, such as not entering the private car original equipment market, I feel sure that he would have come round to endorsing the strategy we finally adopted.

The motorcycle range consisted of the 500 cc and 600 cc Dominator twins which, by now, had graduated to frames similar to those of the racing 'featherbed' type. Throughout the year we produced eighty or so 'Manx' racing machines in 350 cc and 500 cc capacity, which were sold to racing 'privateers'.

The Dominator engine, I found, was identical in all respects to the design released by me for production some eight years previously and the camshaft and cylinder head drawings were of pristine 1948 vintage completely untouched and

The 1955 Manx Norton racing machine

bearing my original signature. So much for the validity of the 1949 communique which delayed initial production of this model 'to allow Mr. Craig to carry out improvements to cam forms and inlet port shapes to improve performance'.

Production figures of 200 motorcycles per week could be achieved under favourable occasions but it was quite impossible to achieve anything better from this small dilapidated factory which was a relic of a different era and needed new machinery and, more important, some space and light to give the shop floor a break from the unbelievably slummy conditions. There was great potential for expanding our sales, especially in the USA where our distributor took four or five machines annually and seemed to be more interested in buying and selling local motorcycle hardware than vigorously pursuing the Norton franchise and building up a dealer organisation. I felt that we should dispense with his services forthwith but found that he held a contract which was still valid for a year or two and which seemed to have been drawn up by an amateur. It was a ridiculous situation and one which I was determined to remedy, but in the event, it was not until four years later that it was possible to make any change.

The pattern of trade at this time was quite spasmodic but, in spite of the seasonal demand at home, there seemed to be little reason why we should not do better if we tried hard enough. Now that selling had become part of my interest, I spent many hours analysing and searching for reasons why we, as manufacturers of no small repute, should be so bedevilled by such huge market variations when a busy period would be followed by almost complete stagnation.

The reasons, of course, were not difficult to find for we were operating with a product range of one basic machine which was selling at a price considerably in excess of similar competitive machines such as the BSA and Triumph twins. I felt that Norton products should command a slight premium, mainly because of our racing activity and the accruing publicity, but we were way out relative to other makes and it was obvious that one of my first jobs was to get our costs down. Another serious shortcoming was the weakness of our export business and with no USA activity whatsoever, we were not able to spread our production more evenly thoughout the year and take advantage of varying seasons of demand.

Added to these problems, I noticed that very rarely did our dealers at home display our products, partly because they were, as often as not, out of stock. It is difficult to image how any brand of motorcycle can be marketed successfully unless it is available on the showroom floor.

The Board agreed that we take steps to enlarge our range and we decided to pursue the 250 cc capacity class. To lay plans for an entirely new machine, quite out of character with the traditional large motorcycles which had been a feature for so long, was a sobering experience. Intensified by a worsening financial situation, the decision gave rise to doubts as to whether such a venture would ever become viable. However, logic said that our range must be enlarged and the design teams bent over *139*

Geoff Duke, who did so much to retain Norton race leadership in the early 1950s, pictured here during the 1952 Senior TT race.

backwards in their efforts, so in a very short span of time we were considering plans which gave us options of two small machines with a minimum of capital expenditure and a simplicity of approach which I have yet to see bettered.

We were projecting a choice of two engines, which could have been produced with a capital outlay of 15% more than that required for the production of one engine size only. There was a 90% commonality of parts, although one power unit had twice the capacity of the other. These designs were simple indeed but a reasonably high power output had been catered for and a feature of some significance was a one piece cylinder head, barrel and rocker box which obviated a number of joint faces and potential leakages. More important, it cut the cost significantly. The smaller engine was a 125 cc capacity single cylinder unit capable of being bored out, if need be, to 150 cc, and the larger unit was a 250 cc twin cylinder, with options of 300 cc capacity.

It was not intended that Norton Motors should be contemplating the manufacture of both these units for this was beyond our reach as our facilities were

The Norton Assembly Shop, photographed from, what I termed, 'the musicians gallery'.

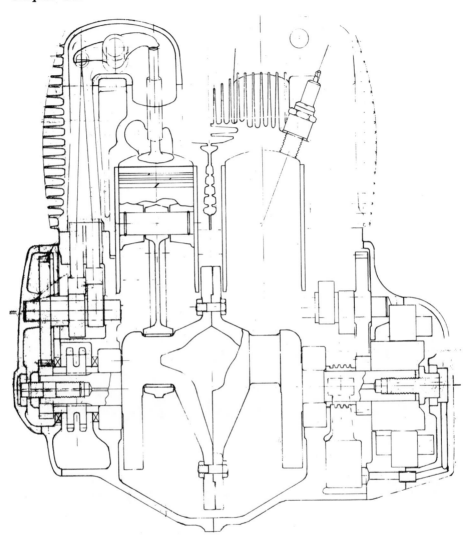

My first sketch of the original 250 cc twin cylinder Norton engine. This would have been a more suitable engine for Norton than the Jubilee, but this scheme was vetoed by Mr. Heather during 1957.

unlikely to enable us to expand to this extent for a considerable time. Yet, in reality, a very small motor cycle of 125 cc or 150 cc capacity was an essential product for any motorcycle manufacturer who intended to stay in business.

British manufacturers were shy of entering the market with a small capacity machine, which always commanded a good slice of total sales and seemed, to me, to be a type of motorcycle which would always be in steady demand if only because **142** most parents were more happy to facilitate the graduation of their youngsters to mechanical propulsion with this 'safe' size of engine. The excuse made for not marketing machines of this type was always the stereotyped one that the financial reward would be meagre from products such as this, which must sell at low prices, but I felt that we had made very little real effort to redress this problem. While it is true that value engineering becomes more difficult in relation to products with small returns, it is also true that somewhat less demanding usage factors give the designer more scope for unusual cost cutting approaches than with the large, fast type of motorcycles. I feel sure that if our industry had seriously tackled the problem of producing the 'baby' machine in viable form to take advantage of its vast share of the total motorcycle market, it would have been almost impossible for events to submerge us in total surrender to the Japanese.

To be fair, one could say that the BSA Bantam and the Triumph Cub were outstanding examples of this type of machine and indeed they were, but it must be remembered that there would not have been a Bantam if Germany had not designed and developed it for us. Both this machine and the Triumph suffered the same fate borne of short-sighted and dilatory development, which caused them to linger on and become extinct.

Naturally, while designing the 250 cc Norton twin, I had eyes for the possibilities of an easy way through for a simple machine of half this size and I make no excuse for embracing, with negligible extra cost, the smaller unit, which the market needed so badly. In any case, had I not been instructed to interest myself in sales and marketing matters? I was big headed enough to feel that I was performing a service to the group and that maybe, at some future date, one of our associated companies would care to consider this projected 'baby' as an addition to its range.

It did not occur to me, for one moment, that I was breaking any rule of management in giving extra thought of this sort while applying myself to a Norton problem. I am, to this day, unaware that the management book says that one must not indulge in this sort of 'caper'. For 'caper' it was, in Donald Heather's own words and it was a shock to me that, when he learned of our first brief outlines, he became most scathing. To him it was unthinkable that a director of Nortons should be concerning himself with Group strategy. I departed with a sizeable flea in my ear and I am puzzled to this day as to what I really did to cause such an upheaval. Neither he nor any one else at Woolwich seemed interested. Furthermore, to add insult to injury, when it was discovered that we hoped to go ahead with the unusual one-piece cylinder unit design, he forbade this approach with the remarkable statement that 'most motorcyclists love to spend their Sunday mornings taking off the cylinder head and re-seating the valves'. Poor hapless little souls. No wonder they decided to 'go Japanese'.

With top brass in the industry going on like this it is not surprising that we were soon to become a sorry mess indeed. With this, my first taste of AMC management strategy, I had a strong feeling, once more, that I was wasting my time. The horizons *143* of most of my superiors seemed to be very limited indeed. So a much more orthodox and, for Nortons, a less suitable engine unit, was designed, and we proceeded through the initial stages with the motorcycle which was later to become the Jubilee. We took care, in passing, that there was facility for enlarging to 350 cc capacity at some future date and, of course, laid the foundation of the Navigator.

Fortunately the disgust which I was beginning to feel for our parents at Woolwich was not serious enough at this point in time to affect my total thinking or the strategy with which Gilbert Smith and I bombarded Head Office almost weekly. Once agreement had been reached by us at Bracebridge Street, it had been Gilbert's practice to use all of his persuasive talent but it was soon to be obvious that Norton Motors would never break through a barrier such as this.

It was obvious, even to outsiders, that there was great jealousy at Woolwich of any Norton successes. Inter-group strategy, if one could call it by that name, seemed to resolve itself into any activity that would directly benefit the AJS and Matchless marques.

It is difficult to understand why AMC bothered to expand and absorb Norton, James and Francis Barnett, for the new empire seemed to be far too much of a nuisance in a somnolent organization which took exception to and vetoed any form of planning which was likely to further the business interests of any of the companies which had been absorbed. Jock West, the AMC Sales Director, was ever the exception, for he was a fighting force of great ability and could, I believe, have played a great part in straightening out the mess of thinking. Sadly, the balance of power was never in his favour and as a consequence his vital personality and his fund of experience was never harnessed to bring about the change in direction which the company so badly needed.

Back at Norton Motors we battled on producing around 180 Dominators per week, sometimes with waiting lists and sometimes with severe stocking problems. So variable was demand that rarely were we able to achieve a steady production run of more than a week or two and since the company was not permitted a bank overdraft, it needed all the management dexterity we could muster to steer us through some difficult periods.

It was then that Gilbert Smith told me that his service agreement would shortly expire and he felt that Woolwich would not wish to retain his services. I was shocked; Norton Motors without Gilbert seemed unthinkable as the man was synonymous with the company with which he had grown up since his boyhood. He loved everything about the Norton name and its long and successful tradition. He was obviously very distressed and seemed to be seeking some help or advice from me, although, as always, he was far too proud a man for me to be sure.

At that time I think that Gilbert was just over 60 years of age and still had much to offer, with his vast experience and his entré to the trade as a whole. Whereas we **144** did not always, at first, see eye to eye, we were slowly forging a link of mutual respect and were working harmoniously towards the formation of a much more forward-looking company outlook. We had gone a long way in discussing and formulating detailed plans for a phased transition, over a set period, to a new generation of products for both Nortons and Shelleys, and he had half agreed to some drastic marketing changes which I had in mind. I knew I would miss him very much indeed and that a new managing director would be unnecessary, for although he never seemed to try to get along with his bosses, they certainly never gave him any encouragement whatsoever. So I made a point of arranging a personal visit to Woolwich immediately, for the purpose of airing my point of view.

From the moment of broaching the subject at Head Office I felt that they had already decided that Gilbert should not be offered any renewal of contract but I pressed on with all the persuasive power that I could muster. I queried the advisability, at this stage, of forcing Gilbert to leave a company which, throughout his life, he had helped to make famous. He had still many years to offer us and indeed the top management trio at Norton Motors were working in close harmony and eyeing the future with great confidence. I did not, of course, mention that this was notwithstanding our being chained to an organisation such as AMC. My plea to invite Gilbert to remain with us until his retirement was rudely scotched and I was asked 'which side are you working for?'.

On my long and miserable drive back to Birmingham I had plenty of time to consider this futile question which had been put to me in all seriousness by an eminent business man. I was forced to wonder whether he felt that the tactics of guerilla warfare were right and proper in our code of management strategy. It would have been too much to expect these business giants to have discussed the matter, much less to have sunk personal animosities and made a decision of benefit to the industry as a whole, so Gilbert Smith went unceremoniously.

I believe that the sadness associated with this enforced relinquishment of all his life long interests in this famous old firm, shortened his life by many years. He died, shortly after retirement, at the early age of 62.

We continued to operate without a managing director for Alec Skinner and myself had been asked to share the additional responsibility until such time as a new appointment was made. One might have expected a situation like this to have had its pitfalls but, in fact, during the ensuing months Alec and I became close partners. As a result we benefitted greatly and a new dimension soon spread through the organisation and became manifest in the creation of a unique team spirit.

Whether the labour force, as a whole, felt that we two directors were 'orphans of the storm' suddenly cast into a cruel business world, or whether they realized that their two bosses, each of vastly differing professions, were working harder than ever, getting on well, and enjoying it, I shall never know. Probably they detected a little of both and as a result we began to realize that the whole organization was completely behind us and waiting for the word.

Chapter Six

The company was not permitted to operate with a bank overdraft and, because of this, Alec had devised a system which enabled the Board to be alerted, on a weekly basis, to ongoing accounting details and the updated production and labour force figures etc. I was thankful that I was always aware of the current bank balance and also, in a crude way, of imbalance in material stock, which enabled action to be taken immediately.

Alec was quite different from most financial experts with whom I had rubbed shoulders elsewhere in the industry, for his was such a pure, simple approach that even a poor engineer was able to understand, at all times, his language and documentation. Unlike many of his more flowery counterparts that I had met, his expertise was something of a keystone of our forward strategy rather than the millstone which seemed to be more normal and which had usually had a great bearing on the strangulation, at birth, of many a bright plan.

It is, on reflection, amusing that Alec's simple little sheet of paper, which gave management such vital information, was to appear, once more, in the year 1971 as a sort of new invention or whatever term is used in the financial world. It happened during the period when the Managing Director of the mighty BSA empire was at his wits end when data relating to stocks, wage bills, production and scrap allowances, to mention just a few, were each chasing one another in all directions, in spite of a mighty army of accountants and the cream of the financial world occupying the Board Room. In what must have been a small piping voice, I ventured to suggest some of Alec Skinner's vintage logic and although the shower of financial expertise could barely disguise the disgust for the simple-minded sophisticated mechanic who had said something, a Chinese copy of Alec's weekly 'state of the art' was soon in evidence. It came to be regarded as a 'breakthrough in communication', to use the exact term.

It would be foolish to suppose that the Norton-Shelley enterprise could be left too long without a chief executive. It was bad management on the part of the AMC Board for Skinner and I had quite enough detail problems without having to act as Joint Managing Directors in addition. Fortunately our friendship and the extreme urgency of management business in our separate spheres seemed to cement a bond between the financial and the industrial elements and I feel sure that this was the key to the slowly improving business and the emergence of the remarkable sense of purpose and team spirit with the staff and the shop floor.

Nonetheless it was an unnecessary situation and as the months went by I made a mental note that very soon the Board must be requested to put us out of our misery. Fortunately in 1958 Donald Heather made one of his rare journeys to Birmingham for the purpose of installing me as the new Managing Director. This came as a great surprise to me and I felt that Alec may have been a little disappointed although outwardly he seemed very pleased and relieved that a newcomer would not be filling the job.

With the Associated Motor Cycle Group through the late 1950's

I imagine that no one except Donald Heather and I know that when I was given the news I refused the appointment. I felt that the approach was slap-dash and lacking in any detailed discussion and was more in keeping with the appointment of an office boy. I pointed out that if a chief executive was required, it was worthy of more thought and a more businesslike approach and on this we had a slightly heated exchange. Nothing was further from my mind than occupying the managing director's chair.

I was surprised when I was re-approached in a matter of hours in a manner which pleased me a little more, so I accepted the appointment. I felt that, by being fussy in matters such as this, I had given my boss the opportunity of thinking again, even to the point of sacking me. More important, the job had been given slightly more perspective.

From the moment I was installed in the 'Holy of Holies' at Bracebridge Street, a largish gloomy room but imposing in a dismal and forbidding sort of way, I felt a great sense of loneliness and a little of the isolated friendlessness which the top job in an organisation usually generates. I was naturally very proud to be heading a company such as this but I knew that mine was to be a baptism by fire if only because of the pitiful state of group affairs.

Hope springs eternal and in truth I felt that soon the shareholders would demand the appointment of some directors who would stop the rot at Woolwich and introduce a more businesslike approach to our affairs. Our group trading results were deteriorating and although the three subsidiaries, James, Francis Barnett and Norton were profitable, the main giant in London seemed all set on a crash course. Any cash generated by us was, of course, absorbed. Consequently the possibility of financing new products was becoming more remote. It would not have been too bad if the cash we generated was used to some purpose by the rapidly deteriorating parent unit, but there seemed to be no sense of awareness or urgency and no attempts were being made to set right the appalling wastefulness which was plainly evident to many visitors to Woolwich.

One outstanding example of wastage was the production control system, appearing first at Woolwich and later to be installed at the subsidiary plants. It was, I would think, designed to operate with a giant such as ICI in mind. The massive complications which were the heart of this method of controlling the flow of parts and production through the works needed something like a university course to master and it required a massive staff of non-producers to operate. All of this was, I understand, a relic of wartime production, when the demand was for one type of machine only and in large quantities on a cost-plus basis.

It would not have been very difficult to set right the many inefficiencies at Woolwich and to have made the company viable and alive. Like many other firms in the industry, where a seasonal demand created problems, it should have been possible to plan reasonably steady production and one would have thought that it **147** was a first duty to trim the economy to suit. It may seem that I over-simplify but AMC had no more problems to cope with than any other successful motorcycle manufacturer and most would agree that the company's products, at the time, were excellent and beautifully made. The range included single cylinder machines of outstanding quality which were remarkably silent and smooth in operation and were often regarded as a yardstick by their competitors.

One of my first priorities at Bracebridge Street was to discard the ridiculous production control system which had been installed by our masters on taking over the company. This enabled a saving of £5,000 per annum to be made on notepaper costs and the balance between productive to non-productive employees, always a major consideration, began to seem more sensible.

The 250 cc twin cylinder model was now well on the way and nearing the end of its development programme. Meanwhile, the decision had been made that Shelley's must continue as a unit, for, as yet, we needed many more outlets for our motorcycles before increased production figures were possible in order to absorb the Shelley workforce. John Thompson, Shelley's Sales Manager, in his inimitable and most persuasive style, was instrumental in providing us with a rapidly filling order book on this side of our business, and we launched our first branded product in the form of the Shelley Rollalift jack for private cars. Before very long we were enjoying all of the Austin original equipment business for their Mini.

With the Dominator twins proving very reliable machines, giving us no after-sales problems and the range shortly to be strengthened by a small capacity newcomer, things seemed to be much brighter. However, our motorcycles were more pricey than those of our competitors and we needed a much more sophisticated selling policy. Even more important, we needed outlets abroad, particularly in the growing USA market, where our turnover was practically nil.

My personal survey of our various dealers in this country had shown that rarely was a Norton motorcycle to be seen on the showroom floors and indeed rarely was one to be found in the stockrooms. I went back to my magnificent office and brooded for a while among the hundred or so silver TT replicas which had been won, through the years, by our famous racing men. The collection of racing goodies which I had around me, each one radiating a success story of past and glorious years, helped me to form a plan which would get Norton machines on show, at least for a while.

There was a much more fruitful way of displaying this unique and famous collection which most motorcyclists would travel far to inspect, so I insured the whole lot and offered each dealer the loan of them for one week. I also supplied giant photographic reproductions of famous TT race scenes large enough to fill a normal showroom and most of the floor. This presentation enabled us to get other makes out of the showroom windows in the case of many of our dealers.

We made the most of it and we were handsomely rewarded, for none but **148** Nortons could boast that successful racing improved the breed. Amongst other

The Norton collection of TT race trophies was loaned to various dealers on condition that their showroom window was generously decorated with Norton motorcycles. The picture shows the trophy collection in the window of the Colmore Depot, Birmingham, with Albert Moule, a well-known racer then an executive of the Colmore Depot is on the extreme right and Bill Smith, Sales Manager of Nortons, is next to him.

149

things, the featherbed frame, now fitted to all our Dominator twins came directly from this source.

I was delighted to learn that our masters at Woolwich were working on a plan to form a Group distributing organization for the lucrative US market which was to be based on the eastern seaboard of the USA. The new arrangement was, I think, partly linked with the Royal Enfield distributing unit but would be re-formed to create a dealer organization, with coverage suitable for floor planning AMC products throughout the USA.

In my innocence, I had assumed that all of the Group's products would be embraced in the new arrangement and I think that any normal person, knowing something of costs and staffing problems involved, would have thought the same. I felt relieved indeed that, at last, Nortons would share a sophisticated franchise arrangement for this vast market.

I was utterly disgusted to find that we should not be allowed to export our goods or enjoy the trading arrangements of this new source and I shall never forget the temper which Mr. Heather displayed when he learned of my assumption. I was told that the new arrangement was solely for the benefit of the parent company; exporting Norton motorcycles to the USA was entirely my problem.

Having underlined my problem in this way, it seems strange that he appeared to be somewhat displeased when, a few months later, I was fortunate enough to be alerted, by a friend, that Joe Berliner, the Ducati distributor for the USA, might be my man. After much thought I decided that he was and I hunted him to ground in a Frankfurt hotel and offered him the Norton distributorship.

The Norton 600 cc Manxman designed for the US market. The engine was later upgraded to 650 cc.

We got on very well from the start and although it may not have been the ideal arrangement, I simply could not fiddle any longer with our present set up. The Berliner Corporation had a ready-made dealer organization already in business and I was most pleased when Joe and I finally reached agreement and we were under contract. In a few months our machines were being sold in the USA and after a joint advertising promotion for the introduction of the 650 cc Manxman model, a very much re-vamped Dominator with cosmetic treatment aimed at the US motorcyclist, we were definitely in business. Admittedly not on the scale of giants like Triumph and BSA but rewarding enough to enable us to plan.

So far as I am aware, Joe Berliner never met our Chairman, for on the occasion that a meeting had been arranged I took Joe, by car, to the depths of Plumstead Road, Woolwich. The Chairman did not turn up, so we were left high and dry, literally on the doorstep of that unimposing building without welcome or courtesy from a soul. I felt ashamed and embarrassed but I admired Joe a great deal for he did not bat an eyelid and said, 'I've always yearned to see Plumstead Road, Woolwich. Now we will recuperate by having lunch at the Ritz'. I took him at his word and our friendship endured through a generation.

It was important that I should shed some of my previous work load and among the promotions from within was the appointment of Doug Hele to the position of Chief Engineer. It was a position he, first of all, did not relish, probably because of his modesty and perfectionism, but, in the months to follow, he rapidly settled down and more than justified our faith in him.

We were still making racing machines in the form of an annual eighty or so Manx models, but our works-sponsored racing team had long since gone. Each of these machines was sold at a profit, but in certain circumstances we would loan, to selected riders, our experimental racing prototypes of the previous year, if we felt that information to be gained under Grand Prix racing conditions was necessary.

We were paid something approaching £20,000 per annum by various suppliers for the advertising value of our racing achievements since our Manx machines still were quite successful, even when raced by privately sponsored riders. This sum compensated us adequately for the rather meagre racing development programme which formed part of the annual budget. Even so, we were careful to link this special development activity with production engineering, as much as possible, and our successes and tribulations on the race track during this period were to guide us with many later designs.

We were able, at last, to understand a great deal more about the ideal bores and strokes for various cylinder capacities and also the most desirable connecting rod and crank ratios to satisfy certain parameters. We learned much about desmodromic valve operation and whether this was to be worthwhile, for we did much work on the test bench with our own special design. We were able, once and for all, to arrive at some basic formula which transformed the handling characteristics of the single *151*

A batch of Norton machines, with Watsonian sidecars, about to be delivered for RAC patrol usage.

track vehicle and which were later to be used in endowing certain British machines with a standard of roadholding and stability which was the envy of motorcycle manufacturers throughout the world.

Alec Skinner was encouraged to take a much wider detailed interest in the production and marketing functions and this was beginning to pay dividends in the form of much improved communication and more rapid decision making.

I made a point of walking through the works on at least one day each week and by this means generated, by actual contact, an intimate acquaintance of many of the workforce. I was pleasantly surprised with the relaxed and friendly atmosphere on the shop floor as the next three years were to provide a period of complete industrial peace for which I was more than grateful. This enabled us to concentrate, without pettyfogging problems, on the real job of planning for profit.

We now had a surplus of £300,000 at the bank which, for such a tiny company, with a gross turnover of less than £2m, was something of an achievement. Today this seems to be 'small beer' but the year was 1958 and the effect of the abortive industrial strike of 1956 had left us in debt with the parent company who, of course, expected us to be a help rather than a hindrance and who, by now, had very real financial problems of their own.

Much of Shelley capacity was occupied in the manufacture of motorcycle components for AMC. Gilbert Smith had been given no option in taking on this work, which was an embarrassment, for the prices had been fixed at Woolwich. They bore no relationship to our costs, with the consequence that we were supplying at a heavy loss. An unbelievably puerile form of Group business and one which I had earmarked to throw overboard, if possible, in favour of work which would bring some return and satisfaction. It was useless attempting to discuss matters of this sort for if one were fortunate enough to run to ground the Chief Executive, who normally arrived very late and mostly claimed to be 'too busy', the conversation would rarely be allowed to have any bearing on decision making. In consequence my many long pilgrimages to Woolwich were to become more of a trial.

I ceased to mention matters of this sort after the day I had a letter from Head Office, inviting me to a meeting for the purpose of discussions relative to costs of inter-company trading. I was full of hope, but should have known better, for there was, as usual, no discussion. I was told that I must reduce the cost of the clutch to them by 15%. We manufactured all the large clutches used by both Norton and AMC and were supplying Woolwich with these items at considerably below cost. I played hell but worse was to come, for I was told that the saving must be retrospective to the beginning of the financial year.

Alec Skinner told me, long afterwards, that he had an awful job to 'stroke me down' and get my signature on a cheque for a fairly considerable sum. Frustration was beginning to take its toll and I now knew, without any doubt, that a clearout at Woolwich was essential if we were to survive.

153

Jock West was exceptional and was outstandingly energetic but none of his vitality seemed to rub off on his colleagues. I felt sorry indeed for it seemed that 'one voice logic', however zestful, would not bring to life to this Board or set into motion any plan to ensure survival.

AMC continued to market their big single cylinder Matchless and AJS machines, which were almost identical, in mediocre quantities. Their 500 cc twin cylinder model never seemed to create a strong impression with the buying public although it was the only twin available which boasted an engine with a three bearing crankshaft. However, in spite of this feature, it was much more vibration prone than the simpler Norton, BSA and Triumph engines, each of which had only two crankshaft bearings. The cost penalty of this feature became an added detraction and although the machine was attractive in appearance and had reasonably good performance, this motorcycle never became very popular.

The author (right) discusses the 250 cc Norton Jubilee model at the 1958 Earls **154** *Court Show.*

With the Associated Motor Cycle Group through the late 1950's

AMC had decided to manufacture two-stroke engines of their own design and discard the Villiers power units which had long been the standard power unit equipment for James and Francis Barnett machines. As a result, an Italian consultant was engaged to design the new range of engines. The first power unit, a 250 cc single cylinder two-stroke of conventional layout, never really made the grade and the costly upheaval of this fundamental change in commercial tactics, which neither improved the products nor reduced costs, was, I feel, the beginning of the end.

It seems that most company chairmen must be permitted at least one 'pie in the sky' and ours was no exception, so that convincing new voices from outside sources had an easy sell. Within the group at that time were some of the finest design brains in the industry and it is a pity that a persuasive and powerful spokesman, preferably with slightly foreign accent, could not have been employed for the purpose of outlining group design plans to the parent board. It would, I feel sure, have been a walk-over and if I could have the opportunity of re-living my past, I would certainly 'engineer' such a situation.

I may have a bee in my bonnet but I am certain that the genius responsible for the future product should be in permanent residence and not free to do the disappearing act at the first sign of trouble. It is true that the responsibility of staying with it is a sobering one for it has served to remind many an adventurous design engineer that his feet must be firmly on the ground.

About this time the parent company went into production with a new 350 cc single cylinder motorcycle in Matchless and AJS form which was to prove a reasonable performer and, after the usual spate of early teething problems, to settle down as a reliable machine. However, the 350 cc capacity market was, at that time, the most difficult and least rewarding of all, mainly because the potential buyer expected to pay very much less for a machine which, for economic and safety reasons, was invariably equipped with wheels, brakes and general cycle parts which were similar or identical to those employed on the larger and more expensive models in the range.

Although this new machine was not exactly a flop it did not become popular and consequently the effect of this, together with the chaos created by the decision to switch to Woolwich manufactured two-stroke engines for supply to James and Francis Barnett, had the effect of causing several severe crises at Woolwich. It also provoked the near stoppage of production at James and Francis Barnett, both of whom relied on the two-stroke units for their entire production. A badly organised situation, to say the least, and one which reverberated throughout the Group, although we at Norton were not, as yet, directly affected.

But, of course, our fortunes would be governed by the success, or otherwise, of our parent. After having discussions with the late Eric Barnett, who was then in charge of Francis Barnett, and Charles Somerton, the Managing Director of James, it was agreed that I should make a further attempt to discuss the possibility of a more *155* businesslike policy which would embrace the whole group of companies. It was getting a little late in the day for this sort of thing but we three were agreed that unless something was done to halt the fragmentary planning and get real 'pep' into a group approach whereby we harnessed the wealth of talent and experience which we had around us, we should not be in business very much longer.

Perhaps I was the least suitable person to tackle this job for I realize that, by now, I must have been something of a pain in the neck to my friends at Woolwich after so many attempts to force intelligent discussion on policy matters. Nonetheless my two colleagues were anxious that I should once more make an attempt to interest our Parent Board in what, by now, was a very detailed plan to rationalize and cover our likely market requirements in a range of model capacities from 125 cc up to 650 cc.

I am sorry to say that the net result of all our trouble was a very rude response for 'did I not know that AMC were on the way with a much enlarged range of machines and their own two-stroke engine units to boot?' I finally gave up and went back to Bracebridge Street having decided to make Nortons so successful and prosperous that in the likely event of the Group going bust, here would be an outstandingly viable enterprise. Maybe, out of the rubble, we would inherit a new approach.

By 1958 Norton Motors had been established for 60 years, a Golden Jubilee of progress, and we launched the 250 cc twin cylinder machine. Naturally it was named the Jubilee model. The engine was not my first choice of design, as I have explained earlier, but 'needs must as the devil drives' and we were now set to expand our sales with this small capacity machine. The engine was modern in design and attractive in apearance and was 'beefy' enough to expand to 350 cc capacity if this were desirable at some later date. Much of the rest of the machine had a strong family relationship with the Francis Barnett products and by this means we managed to minimise tooling and production costs which helped to shorten development time factors.

At the Earls Court Show that year we had a model on the stand on which all the metal parts were gold plated, an extravagance which cost £1000, but the publicity and interest it created, was well worth this reminder to the public that this was the firm's Golden Jubilee year.

We had our teething troubles with this model, in spite of some of the most rigorous testing I had known a motorcycle to be given. To finalise the proving we took the first three production models to Wales. By putting them over a very varied course of rough and smooth, slow and fast, and flat and hilly, we subjected them to many thousand miles of mixed riding and very little happened which caused any concern.

It is strange that expert testers often fail to unearth some of the more obscure weaknesses of a new design so that the problems emerge after mass production models are in the hands of the public. The Jubilee model was no exception.

Prototype testing Norton Jubilee machines on rough terrain in North Wales.

Chapter Six

At first we were bedevilled with broken crankshafts but a material change cured this problem once and for all and within a short space of time we settled down to trouble-free production. This experience convinced me that a more sophisticated system of prototype testing was needed and such a system was designed and installed, with the BSA organisation, at a much later date.

Some would argue that less sophistication is needed and indeed the final part of a test programme prior to the production release of a scooter, many years later, was to enlist all the mechanical simpletons, whose actions to the experts may be unbelievably stupid, and let them loose for several thousand miles on the first dozen machines off the production track. The difficulty, of course, was the degree and quality of diplomacy which was expended in mustering this gallant force and releasing them on an exercise which paid off handsomely.

At Bracebridge Street, Doug Hele's efforts were now reflected in the marginal power improvements of each new batch of Manx models and although they were no match against the highly sophisticated foreign purpose-built machines which dominated the Grand Prix race scene, these Nortons, together with the AJS 7R racers, were far from disgracing the British industry. Indeed it is worth while

Mr. Marples, then the Minister of Transport, discussing the gold-plated Jubilee model on the Norton stand at the 1958 Earls Court Show.

remembering that as they were the only machines reasonably suitable for Grand Prix work which were being manufactured in modest quantities, their availability made it possible for the sport to continue.

It is of some interest to recall that our Woolwich masters regarded this pseudo racing as a very serious matter indeed and I was frequently drawn into hot and excited discussions on racing strategy. With the knowledge that there was no possibility of our succeeding against the Grand Prix giants, who made their machines in batches of two or three each year at phenomenal cost, I simply could not bring myself to get hot and bothered.

The Manx Norton machines were much more successful than the equivalent AJS models, although the reverse should have been the case, for the Woolwich power curves tended to make ours look somewhat seedy. I thought that, in the interests of science, it would be right and proper to have an AJS engine at Bracebridge Street to check on this phenomena, but this was firmly disallowed. One was left to assume that our horses were of a somewhat different breed!

There is no doubt that our activities in this field and the excellence of the Manx models, were a source of great irritation to certain elements at Head Office, but how silly can one be? Donald Heather need only have instructed me to cease the production of the Manx Norton which would have pleased me greatly, and enabled me to concentrate important personnel on very urgent work in a more realistic field.

By the Spring of 1960 it was becoming obvious that our premises were hopelessly inadequate if we were to be realistic as regards the growing production potential of the combined Norton/Shelley enterprise and we engaged a local surveyor and estate agent to give advice. The extra punch of our sales promotion was beginning to bear fruit and of course, we were now shipping modest quantities of Norton machines to the USA through the Berliner Corporation.

I attribute much of the success, which was slowly emerging, to the remarkable team which I was fortunate enough to have and to the loyalty and purpose which was ready to be tapped. Right through the organisation one could sense a solid potential and I felt that mine would be the easy job if we were allowed to plan our destiny. Our turnover had been around £2m for the year and our profit, before tax, was about 7% of this figure. Although Skinner and I were not jumping up and down with excitement, we were moving so much better and had made substantial cost savings such that we were projecting a 10% return for the current year. So far, the indications were that this would be achieved.

After inspecting many premises we were alerted that a comparatively modern factory was shortly for sale and on inspection we found that the place could not have been more suitable if it had been designed for our purpose. It semed ideal, particularly as it was located within half a mile of Bracebridge Street, a factor that was greatly in our favour as most of our employees lived locally. The whole of the management were unanimous in agreeing that the premises fitted into our plan of *159*

Rem Fowler, astride the machine on which it is alleged he won the twin cylinder class of the 1907 TT race. The author is aboard a modern Manx Norton machine.

expansion and modernisation, so I lost no time in agreeing with the vendor that we should purchase at a price of £250,000. The contract was drawn up and Skinner and I felt vastly relieved that facilities more in keeping with out future plans, were now safely on the way.

We had, of course, the approval of the Parent Board for such a move and indeed they were, at all times, closely informed of all negotiations and projected plans which had been fully agreed. But in the event it turned out that we need not have bothered for, on the verge of my signing the contract, I was called to Head Office to be told that a 'minor cash crisis' had arisen and it would not be possible for Nortons to go ahead with the purchase of the new premises. We had to send a cheque for £250,000 to Woolwich and as the rest of our cash balance was needed I had to call the deal off.

My first reaction was to resign and have done with all this sort of nonsense, but I was enjoying my job and in spite of this latest setback, it struck me as sound commonsense to continue with the determination that the Norton enterprise should become the 'jewel in the crown', come what may. Once again I reasoned that our

160

production and profit projections were being achieved and we must surely be allowed to continue in business even if the Group went bust. Of course our profits were Group profits and such cash was generated for group purposes but I knew that Woolwich was beyond help and finance of this sort, whether it be in large or small doses, which was not the medium to correct the situation.

By now some shareholders were becoming a little restive and several came to see me to ask me to express their concern to Mr. Heather. One of these people was a well known motorcycle dealer, who had a considerable shareholding in AMC. Frankly, I was puzzled by their attitude as none of them attended shareholders meetings and had no intention of doing so in the future. I could only point out to them that I was merely a local director employed by Woolwich and if they had

Our Fraternity

A MOVING ceremony was performed in Birmingham last week—a ceremony that is eloquent testimony of the spirit that binds motor cyclists together today—has done so, indeed, for a half a century and more. As recounted on page 348 H. Rem Fowler, winner of the twin-cylinder class of the first-ever Isle of Man T.T. Race in 1907, was lured to what purported to be a brains trust so that, without prior knowledge, he could be presented with a specially made T.T. replica to mark his success. No replica had been given on that historic occasion 52 years ago. And no method of making up for that omission could have provided a more dramatically vivid mark of the esteem in which today's riders hold yesterday's; of the way in which a generation so often said to be lacking in all the graces should have come up trumps.

The presentation was made by the managing director of Nortons, makers of the machine used by Rem Fowler, and in that modest club room in a Birmingham suburb were gathered together other representatives of the industry as well as clubmen—enthusiasts all. Surely no other sport or pastime can display such camaraderie. Grumble we may about each other's faults and shortcomings— and right loudly when occasion demands—but to be a member of the close-knit fraternity of motor cyclists is something for which we can all be grateful.

Editorial comment in The Motor Cycle *of 12th March 1959 relative to the presentation to Rem Fowler.*

something to say, they must approach the Chairman direct or, failing that, attend the AGM and air their views. Like most shareholders, who seem oblivious of danger until their investments do the disappearing act, this was all too much trouble for them and they let the matter slide.

In the meantime, to add to our problems, the Board announced that in its first year of trading, the Indian company, which was the trade name of the newly-formed AMC American subsidiary, had made a loss of £80,000. I was glad indeed that Norton machines were being shipped at a profit for sale through an American owned distributor network.

By late 1960, a Shareholders Committee had been formed and was begining to probe the reasons for the Group's decline. The AGM of that year was somewhat *161* stormy, with Donald Heather skillfully parrying some leading questions largely by blaming the economic climate. The warning signs of slumping profits and share-holders dissatisfaction made little difference and Woolwich dribbled on with no attempt, so far as I could see, to slash the crippling costs of an appallingly mismanaged manufacturing unit. Surely there was need to get round the table with the wealth of management brains which we had in the Group, to generate a survival plan while there was still time.

The Group scooter, which was assembled by the James Company and powered by the new 250 cc two-stroke engine, now in production at Woolwich, was proving somthing of a flop. It was obvious that the tooling costs would never be regained for it had come on to the market much too late and its specification did not begin to match that of our Italian competitors. It must be said that Jock West, the AMC Sales Director, was never in favour of marketing this product. I well remember being present when Donald Heather and Jock had an awful row after the poor man indicated that the machine was a non-starter and would only add to our problems if we were foolish enough to put it into production. It would be difficult to imagine a situation generating more commercial nonsense than having the production taps turned on after the top sales executive had declared, quite categorically, that the product would be an abject flop!

So it was that our parent company went from bad to worse and on reflection, although there was no up and coming plan for future products, the immediate sickness was due to sheer bad management. Apart from the James scooter and the new venture two-stroke engine exercise, the products being offered by AMC were good, reliable and well manufactured. Indeed I have yet to hear a 500 cc engine running which is more silent that the AJS/Matchless single cylinder unit of that time.

Back at Nortons we now introduced a new machine exclusively for the American market and it was most heartening that Joe Berliner, our US distributor, had spent much of his time with me during the initial stages of development. His presence was a great fillip to morale at Bracebridge Street and helped, more than a little, in furthering a speedy development programme and early introduction of the machine. By November 1960 it was rolling off our assembly line, after a launching ceremony by the US Consul.

The new model had a twin cylinder Dominator engine which had been upgraded from 600 cc to 650 cc and, at Joe Berliner's request, had been named the Manxman. We had fairly substantial orders and I felt proud and relieved that, in spite of being left out in the cold by the Indian Sales Corporation, we had overcome a serious difficulty 'under our own steam'. Indeed we had been fortunate enough to button up a distributorship which was a ready-made and thriving enterprise catering for 28 states in the USA.

As events turned out, the AMC American subsidiary never got off the ground, nor indeed to me did it seem likely to for, like the parent, it was loaded with

Rem Fowler astride the 1907 TT race winning machine. On this occasion at Beaulieu, Lord Montague had been presented with the original telegram which brought the good news from the Isle of Man to Bracebridge St and he is seen here, extreme right, holding the telegram. In the picture also, left to right, are Alec Bennett the famous rider who won five TT races during the 1920s, the author, and Graham Walker, the great sporting commentator and one time editor of Motor Cycling.

management and the selling process seemed to be of secondary importance.

We, on the other hand, had no stake in the Berliner Corporation, who merely purchased motorcycles from us under an arrangement whereby we were paid on the dot. Although we had no share of the distributor's profit (or loss) we were more than satisfied to have made such progress in such a short space of time. Our export performance was further boosted by sales behind the Iron Curtain and we were proud that Norton machines had been chosen by Czechoslovakia as the only British motorcycles to be imported. Our first order from them had been worth over £20,000.

By the end of 1960 it was obvious, to outside sources, that the parent company operation was being propped up by its three small subsidiaries. Although the Group trading profit was £421,121, about half of this figure had been earned by Nortons, whilst Francis Barnett were responsible for a goodly portion of the rest.

At the 1960 AGM the Shareholders Committee became very vocal and it was obvious that there was a persistent and reasonably well organized attempt by certain **163** shareholders to force changes in the AMC Board. At about this time Donald Heather outlined a grand new plan to move the AMC premises from Woolwich to a brand new factory to be constructed at Sheerness, Isle of Sheppey, and I think that this must have been the last straw for me. The Board had completely lost sight of its objective and was now preparing to be off on another grand gallop, which was quite foolish and unnecessary at this point of time. The Woolwich premises were a palace in comparison with those of the subsidiary companies and were adequate for the foreseeable future. What is more, if a profit could not be generated in Plumstead Road, it was obvious that the same management would not generate one elsewhere.

I welcome a fight only if there is a chance of winning, but I had no doubt by now that the Group was so seriously mismanaged that not a single company would be left within twelve months or so. Added to this, and much to my annoyance, I was being contacted from time to time by members of the Shareholders Committee. I had no wish to be involved and felt that the right and proper thing to do, under these circumstances, was to resign.

For the next week or two I was caught up in a whirl of sales matters which kept me busy and it is strange that during this precise period, very early in 1961, that Edward Turner, now Managing Director of the giant BSA group, called on me personally at my office in Bracebridge Street to invite me to return to the Triumph Company at Meriden. He told me that he would be phasing out over the next year,

The James scooter, powered by the new 250 cc AMC two-stroke engine, was not a marketing success and the tooling costs were never regained.

The US Consul, at right, with the author, at the time of the launch of the new Norton Manxman designed for the American market.

for he was now 64 years of age and would be retiring. He needed a General Manager of my calibre.

He was to tell me later that I was almost rude in my reply, and I do remember telling him that I had never heard such nonsense. I was sure he had no intention, ever, of retiring and what is more I could not believe from past experience that he would ever bring himself to allow his General Manager generally to manage. I told him to go home and sleep on it and he would feel better in the morning!

He must have done just this and perhaps my rather harsh words, which were meant to be constructive and helpful, touched a sore spot for he persisted. Much to my annoyance, he rang up my wife and asked her to 'work on me'.

What I did not know then, but learned a few weeks later, was that Edward Turner was a sick man and was being pressed, by his Board, to install a deputy as General Manager in the shortest possible space of time. I was approached once more by the AMC shareholders committee to meet them, but I refused to do so for obvious reasons. It was not until well after my resignation that I did, at their request, attend **165**

REQUISITION

To Associated Motor Cycles Limited and to the Directors and Secretary thereof.

DEAR SIRS,

Under the provisions of Section 132 of the Companies Act 1948 I/we hereby requisition you forthwith to proceed duly to convene an Extraordinary General Meeting of the Company for the purpose of considering and, if thought fit, passing as Ordinary Resolutions the RESOLUTIONS set forth below, of which we give you Special Notice in accordance with Sections 142 and 184 of the said Act.

RESOLUTIONS

1. That under the provisions of Section 184 of the Companies Act 1948 Mr. Donald Spencer Heather be removed from the Board.

2. That under the provisions of Section 184 of the Companies Act 1948 Mr. John Francis Kelleher be removed from the Board.

3. That under the provisions of Section 184 of the Companies Act 1948 Mr. Alfred Arthur Sugar be removed from the Board.

4. That Mr. Cyril Alfred William Bird be and he is hereby appointed an additional Director of the Company.

5. That Lt.-Col. William Henry Gardiner be and he is hereby appointed an additional Director of the Company.

6. That Mr. William Oliver Smedley, M.C., F.C.A., be and he is hereby appointed an additional Director of the Company.

Dated.., 1961. *Signed*..

....

....

Notes: 1. If the shareholder is a Company, this Requisition must be given under its Common Seal.

2. In the case of joint holdings, all shareholders must sign.

The two notices which were circulated to AMC stockholders by the Shareholders Committee, asking for removal from the Board of three Directors and calling for support at the Extraordinary General Meeting early in 1961. Their motion was only **166** *marginally defeated.*

THIS IS AN IMPORTANT DOCUMENT

ASSOCIATED MOTOR CYCLES SHAREHOLDERS' COMMITTEE

Secretaries: INVESTMENT AND GENERAL MANAGEMENT SERVICES LIMITED

24 AUSTIN FRIARS,
LONDON, E.C.2.
17th May, 1961.

TO THE SHAREHOLDERS OF ASSOCIATED MOTOR CYCLES LIMITED
DEAR SIR (*or* MADAM),

Mr. Herbert Hopwood, Managing Director of Norton and R. T. Shelley, two of our finest companies, has resigned. This is a terrible blow to Associated Motor Cycles as Mr. Hopwood was possibly one of the few men within the Group with the ability to restore its fortunes.

Shareholders have become increasingly uneasy as to the well-being of your Company and at the last two Annual Meetings voiced their anxiety in no uncertain terms. Mr. Hopwood's resignation at this stage provides conclusive evidence that their suspicions were well founded. It is a tragedy that Mr. Hopwood's services were not secured for the benefit of the Group by an agreement similar to the seven-year agreements recently given to the joint Managing Directors.

Trading profits have been very disappointing at a time when our main competitors have been able to issue reports of brilliant achievement. This has resulted in a fall in the price of your shares from 29/- in 1954 to their present price of about 5/-. In some years dividends paid have not been covered by earnings. Fuller details of the extent of the extremely ineffectual way in which your Company's affairs have been conducted are given in the Appendix overleaf from which you will see the recent substantial fall in trading profits and the very generous remuneration which the Directors have received despite the poor results.

The Board's failure cannot be better illustrated than by the purchase in 1959 of the Indian Company. Its results for the year ended 31st August 1960 showed that a loss of £51,857 had been made. Furthermore, the trading loss is shown before charging expenses amounting to £27,579 for the initial period of 4 months ended 31st December 1959. The total loss was therefore in the neighbourhood of £80,000, and our information is that this American Subsidiary is still making substantial losses. More than £250,000 of your money has already been "invested" in this venture.

The purpose of this Company was to form a distributing agency for the products of the Group, and we were told that this was a good stroke of business. In addition to the disclosure of the losses the incredible fact has come to light that the American Subsidiary does not act for Nortons, who have had to appoint their own agent in America.

You will recollect that a Shareholders' Committee was formed in 1960 when it became apparent that the Company's fortunes were rapidly declining at a time when those of its chief rival, the B.S.A. Group, were making spectacular advances. This Committee has been forced to the conclusion, after much deliberation and taking the best available advice, that only a radical change of management can now save your Company from disaster. To this end it is proposed that the Chairman, Mr. Heather, and the two Managing Directors, Mr. Sugar and Mr. Kelleher, who unquestionably must bear the main responsibility for the present lamentable situation, should be removed from the Board forthwith and that the following be appointed Directors in their place:—

Mr. Cyril A. W. Bird.
Lt.-Colonel W. H. Gardiner.
Mr. William Oliver Smedley, M.C., F.C.A.

These proposed new Directors do not require fees or remuneration and are prepared to offer their resignations as soon as Executives of proved ability have been appointed to your Board. They would, however, expect that the Company should ultimately recompense them for the expenses incurred by them on behalf of the Shareholders' Committee. Further particulars as to the proposed new Directors are also given in the Appendix overleaf.

It is proposed that the other Directors should remain, at least for the time being, to provide continuity and to help the new Directors to take whatever steps may be necessary to re-establish your Company's fortunes before it is too late. It is expected that the proposed new Directors will be able to draw upon the services of some of the most brilliant technical brains in the motor-cycle industry and will enjoy the sympathetic support of the industry as a whole. An important appointment should be possible immediately the preliminary Board changes have taken place.

In order to implement these proposals it is necessary to requisition an Extraordinary General Meeting of the Shareholders under Section 132 of the Companies Act 1948 and **for you accordingly to complete, sign and return in the accompanying envelope the two forms of Requisition and Proxy enclosed herewith.** You are advised not to sign any other Form of Proxy you may receive subsequently.

It is often said that Shareholders deserve to lose their money through their own apathy and indifference: this is an opportunity to prove that this need not always be the case.

Yours sincerely,
W. H. GARDINER, LT.-COL.,
Chairman,
SHAREHOLDERS' COMMITTEE.

168 *A picture of Doug Hele taken in the Isle of Man during 1961, with a racing Norton.*

a meeting at which I was able for the first time to meet Oliver Smedley, the Committee Chairman. He struck me as a forceful character with much common sense and I feel sure that he could have injected the AMC board with a sense of urgency, to say the least.

It is a pity that an Extraordinary General Meeting, called by the AMC Board on 31st June, 1961, at which the Shareholders Committee made great capital of my resignation, Mr. Smedley just missed being elected to the AMC Board by the narrow margin between 1.48m and 1.33m votes.

My resignation was tendered in April, 1961, and I was quite surprised that the Board took it rather badly, as I felt that, by now, they would be sick to death of a colleague who always seemed to be nagging. I was asked to think on it for another week, which I did, but I could see no alternative. My resignation accepted, I began the task of leaving my affairs as tidy as possible. It was a sad time for me for I had enjoyed my job and there is no doubt that much headway was being made. I simply felt that my time was wasted, which is why I had taken the decision not to linger on to the bitter end.

A conversation between the author (right) and Edward Turner in early 1961, before my return to the Triumph Engineering Company. I do not appear to be over-convinced!

Chapter Six

One of my most prized possessions is a silver tankard which the Shop Stewards presented to me on my departure. Today, when I drink from it, I recall with a great deal of nostalgia what were, perhaps, the happiest days of my working career and the tremendous effort which was gladly being made by everyone. What limitless success could have been the reward had we been our own masters.

Although Edward Turner was keeping up the pressure, I had not made a final decision for I required to know much more of his real intentions before giving him an answer. I learned that he was now diabetic and seemed genuinely anxious to retire at 65. Indeed, it appeared that the BSA Board was expecting this and from what I gathered, were pressing him very hard to choose an executive who would first of all be General Manager at Triumph and later, I was led to believe, would become Managing Director.

I knew Edward Turner much too well to doubt that there would ever by any basic change in his outlook, but two things had happened since I last worked with him. These were that firstly, he no longer ran a private company but was answerable to shareholders through a Board of Directors, and secondly, he was very near to forced retirement and seemed resigned to this.

I realized that he was just as self-opinionated as he had ever been, but this failing, if failing it be, never really mattered to anyone with a sense of humour. I must say that I never believed it possible that I should experience such persistent approaches with the culminating final revealing statement that I quote, he 'could not afford to make a mistake in this important matter' and had 'come to the conclusion that I was the only man with the experience and background to support him during the transition and carry on with the job after his retirement'.

This was quite a new experience for me, for compliments of any description from this source were a rarity to be cherished. I do admit that I was so pleasantly surprised that this seemed to be the decisive factor and I agreed to join the Triumph Board in May, 1961, as Director and General Manager.

Chapter Seven

Back at BSA Edward Turner bows out

MY DECISION to accept Edward Turner's offer did not mean that I was to become a member of the Parent Board of the BSA company on which he had a seat carrying the responsibilities of Chief Executive of the Automotive Division. Although, at a very much later date, I was invited to join this Board, I have vivid recollections that this body of businessmen seemed very remote indeed from the business of motorcycle production for the BSA organization embraced a group of twenty or so companies of great variety. These included such names as Jessops alloy steels, BSA tools, Churchill machine tools and the gun manufacturing division, the Daimler company having recently been sold to Jaguar Cars. The motorcycle entity represented a sizeable slice of the total capital involved in this huge group and as time went on and various subsidiaries were parted with, for one reason or another, the motorcycle side became the giant when, of course, its profit performance was much more vital.

This is the factor which I feel bedevilled the BSA organization and finally ditched the company for, through the 1960s, we became more and more dependent on the performance of the Motorcycle Division. Unfortunately, as this grew in relative importance, its top management, never at any time strong, deteriorated to such a degree that there was not a soul on the Parent Board who knew the first thing about single track vehicles.

To many academics this may have seemed an ideal business set up. Indeed in the early 1960s the Chief Executive of a world famous group of management consultants tried hard to convince me that it is ideal that top level management executives should have as little knowledge as possible relative to the product. This great man really believed that this qualification enabled them to deal efficiently with all business matters in a detached and uninhibited way but we came such a cropper *171*

The Triumph Bonneville updated in the early 1960s.

The Triumph Tiger 100 of the 1960s.

after a series of management restructures based on this theory that it surprises me that some universities do not take note and prepare some of their graduates destined for industrial management with a somewhat different approach.

I purposely digress because at this stage in the history of BSA, the early 1960s, this huge slice of the total British motorcycle industry was busy embarking on a madness of management consultancy, rather than getting on with the real job of work. It was this disaster of academic business thinking that finally crucified a British industry which was respected throughout the world. I would think that the great and highly successful Japanese motorcycle industry looked on and studied our capers with unbelieving eyes.

I felt very much at home on joining Triumph but it is understandable, I suppose, that Charles Parker, the Financial Director, looked somewhat askance at my appointment. After all, he was a very capable businessman and I am sure he would have made an excellent General Manager. However, I understand the Board insisted that the new man should have an engineering background.

I am pleased to say that, after a while, Parker settled down to the idea. We worked together so well and became such close business friends that I look back on our years of association with a great deal of nostalgia. In the period to follow we were to find ourselves forming the linchpin of what, for long periods, appeared to be a rudderless management complex.

Jack Sangster had recently resigned the Chairmanship of BSA in favour of Eric Turner, a newcomer from the aircraft industry. With the management gap now filled at the Meriden Works, this should have enabled Edward Turner to phase out comfortably. Although he now had a great deal of time which could have been devoted purely to commercial strategy, there was a strong general feeling that the Board was anxious that our future inspiration for the Motorcycle Division would come from the new executive structure now being outlined by a horde of management consultants, who had been occupying the time of many of us for some months.

BSA were making an extensive range of motorcycles, from the small two stroke Bantam through to the 650 cc twin-cylinder machine. Although the latter had been re-vamped as the A65 model, most of the products were becoming seriously dated. Nonetheless, good business was, for the moment, being done.

Ariel Motors were relying on their unusual two-stroke twin Leader model. In spite of its early success the yearly sales curve was on the decline and Ken Whistance, the Ariel boss, was busy developing a slenderised version. It was hoped this would revitalise the product and create a wider spread of demand.

Triumph had a range of four basic models, the baby of which was the 200 cc single cylinder Cub. This machine had now become very outdated and was giving quite serious service troubles due, in the main, to increasing the capacity of the original engine design by 33% using the good old bore and stroke trick. *173*

Chapter Seven

Unfortunately, little thought had been given to most of the main working parts, which hopefully were supposed to cope with this huge increase in capacity. The three other models were, of course, the twins of 350 cc, 500 cc and 650 cc capacity, the former having been introduced in 1958, but many times updated. The large machine was a somewhat cross-pollinated version of its 500 cc brother.

When I joined the company, I was told quite seriously by Edward Turner that I was a lucky man to have come in at this stage, 'having missed all the worry and hard work', and to have my job so very much simplified by a ready made and long awaited newcomer to the Triumph range of products. I ought to have known better, although he had mellowed a great deal and much water had gone under the bridge since I had last been at grips with projects from this source. The Tina scooter to which he referred, was soon to cause me such anxiety and despair that, at one particular stage, I seriously contemplated making a run for it and buying a small business!

Although our Managing Director had the three motorcycle marques as his responsibility and acted as the direct link with his co-directors at main board level, he regarded Meriden as his home and often told me so. He was very rarely seen at either Small Heath or Selly Oak, the latter where Ariel motorcycles were made. The comparatively peaceful operation of the huge Small Heath complex speaks volumes of the leadership of Bob Fearon, the popular General Manager at that time, but I feel that Edward Turner's failure to move himself and act his part as Chief Executive in a more positive manner made Fearon's job a thankless one indeed.

At Triumph I had been reintroduced to some of the key figures of the wonderful team who were the force behind the genius of the Managing Director, but I was shocked to find that certain middle management was non-existent. Initially I imported several designers and draughtsmen to bring up to strength a department which had reached an unbelievably meagre level. The Works Manager, who was almost at retiring age, admitted that he had no understudy who, in his opinion, was capable of succeeding him. This situation remedied by the appointment of a young deputy works manager, I also advertised for a development engineer and when Doug Hele applied for the job, he got it.

I sniffed out, fortunately very rapidly, that there was a restive concern among the Shop Stewards. Without showing myself, at this stage, I learned that they felt uncertain about management intentions now that some important changes were being made. There had never been industrial strife at Meriden and oddly enough Edward Turner had never met his Shop Stewards, so this was remedied on the pretext of my official introduction to them by Turner himself. This, I felt, would benefit the Managing Director as well as the shop floor and it was an experience for both. Once Turner got the bit between his teeth he talked, like the master he was, on the subject most dear to him, the Triumph Engineering Company. They enjoyed every minute of it and went off happy and satisfied.

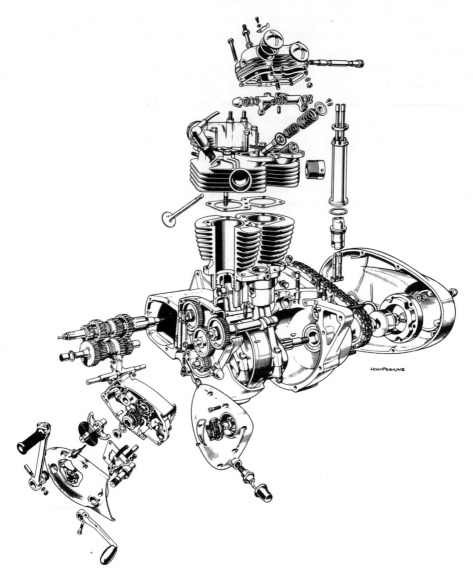

The re-designed Triumph 650 cc engine in unit-construction form.

One or two sales and dealer problems reared their heads and I urged him to make personal visits to these sources but he refused so that I had to deal with these matters instead. It provoked many grumbles from him, for he seemed to think that I ought never to stir from the confines of the manufacturing plant. He told me, long afterwards, that my reports to him and the actions suggested or already being taken, came in such quick succession that, for a time, he was not certain that it had been **175** a wise move to 'get me back into the fold', to use his own words. Later he expressed his gratitude, which pleased me more than a little, for this revealed in him a new attitude which I would appreciate more than most.

Edward had designed and had made prototypes of a new 650 cc power unit, to replace the ageing Bonneville engine. We studied these together and decided not to continue with the project because the power unit was slightly more costly, it was heavier and, in spite of a theoretical valve gear advantage, it did not produce any more power than its predecessor. Also, it was a more noisy engine and we spent some time together to make the decision, in complete agreement, which resulted in the creation of the Bonneville power unit as it is known today. We worked well together and within a matter of weeks the designs were well under way. The transition was a fairly simple one of converting the old design to a unit-construction engine and building into the new unit the improvements which we both knew, from experience, were necessary. The net result was an engine, more modern in appearance, slightly lighter and cheaper to manufacture and more powerful and reliable. This was achieved with a minimum of unknowns because the basic geometry and structural features remained unaltered.

I would have preferred the new engine to have been endowed with an oil pump which would have obviated the problems associated with that sometimes temperamental horror which is a feature of all Triumphs, but Turner dug in his heels. I had many other problems on my hands, so without more ado it was not long before we had prototypes running on test and were planning production for September, just eight months from the point of conceptual design. However, once the new engine was fitted into the frame, which was also of new design, it proved to be a real shaker. Time was not in our favour, yet our development team, then headed by the great Frank Baker, managed to compromise with a passable degree of roughness which we knew that the public would accept.

In those days, balancing devices such as those which several Japanese manufacturers now standardise on some of their engines, had not been considered. Indeed, I was told by several of our most prominent dealers in the USA that a smooth running Triumph would lose its appeal as a 'man's' machine. It was a typical Americanism which I took with a pinch of salt, for this type of comment is normally reserved to exert delivery pressure in a seller's market. At a later date, when Triumph were grossly over-producing and buyers were very much less in evidence, the very same dealers declared that enough was enough and that sales resistance had built up mainly because it was so well known that all Triumph motorcycles 'beat the living daylights' out of the rider.

The new Bonneville range was a complete success from the start. Having a sparkling performance, these machines, already very sleek in appearance, were updated technically and altogether more 'with it'. The 1962 Earls Court Show indicated that we would be set fine for the coming trading year.

This exercise, which enabled Triumph to retain a high level of profitability for the next few years, was masterminded and organised by two men who not only were responsible for the total commercial performance of the company, but also knew a great deal about the products which the company made. I wonder whether this sort of management performance was felt to be some sort of freak phenomena by the consultants who were being retained by the company and who were preaching the academic approach and the detached uninhibited executive nonsense to the parent board?

Alongside the Bonneville activity, the new Tina scooter was being prepared for production and Edward Turner had set a date in early 1962 for the official launching of this new model at Meriden. Most of our dealers had been invited for the ceremony

The Triumph Tina scooter, a 100 cc machine with automatic transmission, first produced in early 1962.

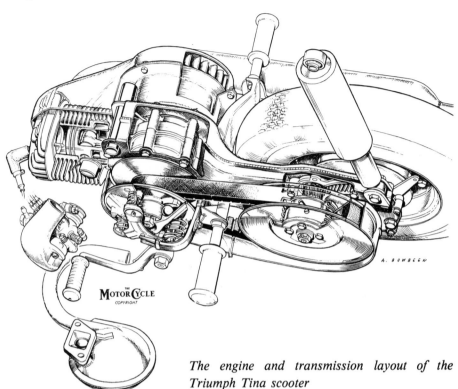

The engine and transmission layout of the Triumph Tina scooter

The massive pressed steel frame of the Triumph Tina scooter

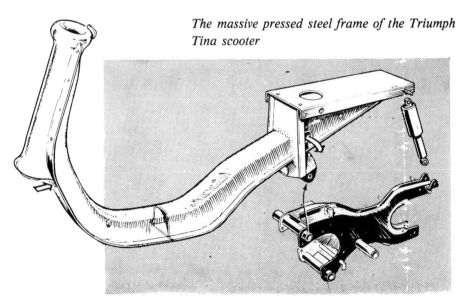

which was to be followed by a buffet luncheon in a great marquee erected on the front lawn at the works.

Quite frankly, I was horrified about the future for this new baby as, believe it or not, there had been virtually no prototype testing of any sort. Frank Baker, our Development Engineer, was equally concerned. There had been very little road testing on one prototype whilst much of the proving had been accomplished by means of workshop rig tests, mainly on the automatic gear change device, which operated by means of a vee belt drive across expanding pulleys. There had not been a working prototype available to the Experimental Department, for after such a negligible test mileage, the only complete model which the company possessed had been withdrawn from the Development Department for styling and catalogue purposes. This had left poor Frank and his team of engineers without any means of proving the design.

I played hell with Turner and I remember well his shocked expression, for really I had cold feet and this I think added much punch to my diatribe. I immediately gave instructions for three prototypes to be made, regardless of cost. I was left in a foul mood of fretting and snapping for I knew that many weeks must elapse before we would be able to commence any real testing.

What now strikes me as being most odd is that the Board of Directors should have been happy with a huge capital outlay on a quite new departure, without one or two of its members probing here and there and discovering that a new product was about to be launched for which a running prototype did not exist. This must seem unbelievable to many readers, particularly as the capital involved was, at that time, considerable. Not only did the design embrace many unusual features such as the frame, which involved huge tooling costs, but a new wing had been built at Meriden which housed a semi-automatic assembly line, designed to be capable of weekly production figures well in excess of 1000 units.

The whole thing was a management mess and the dealer convention should have been called off, but the notices had been posted and it was much too late. Frustration was added to my nagging concern when, just one day before the launching ceremony, Edward Turner told me that he was off to California and asked me to take charge of the operation in his absence. I felt very tempted to take a week or so off but I fought off this pleasant prospect and decided that I had much homework to do in acquainting myself much more intimately with the Tina design, hopefully in order that I might make a reasonably clear presentation in about 12 hours time.

Fortunately we now had two or three scooters available but although the test mileage was extremely limited, minor faults only had so far been registered. This enabled me to feel just a shade less guilty in taking the floor at the dealer convention and, in some detail, revealing our new product which was brilliant in conception but which, as time would tell, left much to be desired in basic engineering.

Chapter Seven

Tina scooters began to flow from our new production line and almost immediately serious faults became evident; frames were bending and engines were almost impossible to start. By far the most serious customer problem and one which caused an oversize headache, was a condition which caused the automatic transmission to jam solid. This caused the machine to become a laughing stock for it had no normal neutral gear. When the sticking problem occurred, mostly without warning, the scooter could not be wheeled and had to be lifted bodily off the highway for attention.

It took hours to convince Turner that the centrifugally energised balls, which opened or closed the driving pulley under variations of engine speed, did not and could not roll along the incline which operated the pulley. It was purely a sliding motion and in great exasperation, I suggested that a ball was not the ideal shape to cope with sliding motion. It would have been far better to use weights of wedge formation, which had generous areas of contact to cope with the sliding loads. By

Bob Currie of Motor Cycle Weekly *aboard a three wheel variant of the Triumph Tina scooter, which did not reach the production stage.*

Another interesting prototype variant of the Triumph Tina scooter. A four wheeled, two seater vehicle made up by bolting two scooters together via simple metal members. It went quite well but did not reach the production stage. In the early Tina days, this project was nicknamed 'double trouble'.

this time problems were coming in thick and fast and the most drastic management action was needed immediately in this crisis situation. I threatened to throw in the towel if I could not be left to cope with the trouble in my own way for I had no intention of spending any more of my time arguing about design and basic fundamental principles of engineering.

Out of this shambles I was left the thankless and uphill task of righting the problems which bedevilled us, a task which involved the redesign of almost every major item in the machine's specification. Had we not had a management team which was outstandingly capable, this would not have been remotely possible. The result of this painful exercise was a scooter which was completely trouble free but this achievement is of academic interest only, for during this period we had been invaded by hordes of management consultants. When these experts had doctored the industry, the large volume scooter market had disappeared.

I could only hope that our misdemeanours would not have too much effect on our general trading operation. Perhaps because the rest of the Triumph range was so good and in rather short supply in the home market, we seemed to be grudgingly forgiven by most of our dealers and their long suffering Tina owners.

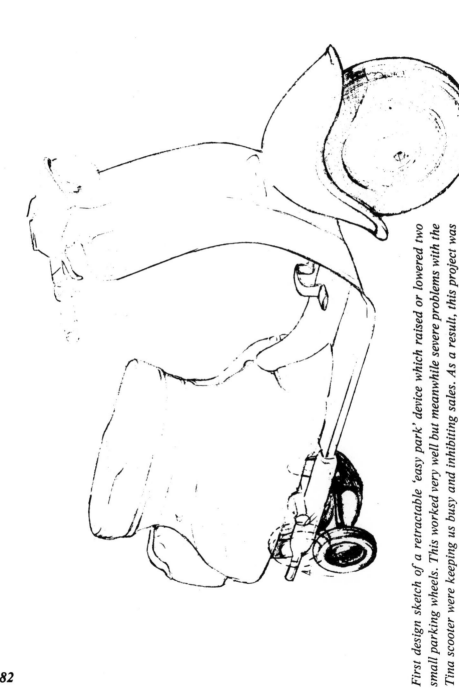

First design sketch of a retractable 'easy park' device which raised or lowered two small parking wheels. This worked very well but meanwhile severe problems with the Tina scooter were keeping us busy and inhibiting sales. As a result, this project was not pursued.

John Nelson, our Service Manager at the time, demonstrated his ability and expertise in a remarkable way and Stan Truslove, who was our direct link with the angry mob who were, in most cases, demanding their money back, was perhaps the only man on call who could rescue us from the firing line, so to speak. Truslove, a highly skilled engineer but, more than that, a man of impeccable appearance who had an unfailing ability to calm and charm the most irate of either sex, deserves a medal for his work in this crash rescue operation which did so much to readjust our reputation.

By the early 1960s first Honda and then other Japanese manufacturers, having dominated world motorcycle markets in the small capacity classes, were adjusting their sights and marketing excellent machines of medium capacity. I shall never understand the business thinking of Sangster and Edward Turner, who at that time were two of the top names in the industry and naturally were sought after by the press for their reactions to the growing strength of our Japanese competitors. Turner made statements, not once but many times, that the British motorcycle industry could count itself as fortunate in having the Japs making and selling large numbers of very small machines for they were training young riders, many of whom would graduate to the large machines which we made so well and formed a lucrative market that had become the backbone of our industry. He went on to say that there could be no profit for us in very small motorcycles and there was no point in our entering that section of the market.

A photo of Stan Truslove whose personality and engineering ability helped soldier us through our early Tina problems. He is seen loading one of the culprits into the works estate car.

The 1962 Triumph Tigress scooter in Sunbeam guise.

All of this might have been a trifle more digestible if some provision had been made to ensure that our large machines, excellent though many of them were, would stand the test of time.

I am more than amazed that one television personality, who put the question, let him get away with this hypothesis. It must have sounded feasible to most but I cannot imagine a person such as Robin Day missing the opportunity to query whether it might be possible that our Japanese friends were grateful of our attitude in making this provision for them (albeit with largely outdated designs) against the time when, at their convenience, they could cast their eyes on this so called lucrative sector of the market and enlarge their range to cater for the profitable goodies as well as the so-called financial baddies from which they had built a financially sound industry. I had bitter arguments with Turner, who would not budge, but I do not understand why members of the Board did not challenge statements like this which were the forerunners of the 'foggy' product thinking which would eventually plunge us to the depths.

Even at this comparatively late hour we had time enough, if we were at all serious and determined, to fight back and take our share of a fast growing world market. My feelings were then, as they are now, that a total range of products from small to large capacities was the right way to handle the situation, for without this, **184** our dealer strength would slowly be eroded. Naturally such a change of thinking would necessitate heavy capital outlay to cope with very high production figures which would be necessary. This is exactly what Japanese industry was facing up to and it seemed to me that we must sooner or later throw in the towel if the Board were unable to think this out and very soon get moving.

It was Edward Turner's job to produce a master plan and I feel that had he been young and hungry, he might have done it, for it seemed to me that now he seemed to have little of his old energy and did not appear to relish the hard grind which would be necessary to master mind a plan such as was plainly necessary. He often reminded me that as sales were satisfactory and profits were equally so, he felt that I was over-pessimistic. However, I knew him very well and had a strong feeling that maybe he did not feel quite so sure of the future and indeed was beginning to realise the dangers of our slap-dash policies.

Here were three motor cycle companies in a group, with each company trying to pursue separate product policies, sometimes at the whim of an individual, but at no time under co-ordinated direction. Perhaps this is how it should be for, after all, competition is healthy. But co-ordination is surely a must in the management policy of a group of similar companies. I hasten to add that the empire building and the obsessions of certain businessmen which have led to the formation of large groups have, more often than not, resulted in remotely controlled and unmanageable giants. Since we were in the unfortunate position of being a group of companies, the least that we could do, I felt, was to mobilize our total group technique and manpower, utilise our group financial strength and by sheer weight of numbers and finance speed up and vitalize such agreed plans we had. Instead, each company wandered on its separate course with our management divided and weakened and our technical manpower diluted, pursuing policies some of which were semi-agreed and some 'half-baked'. Ultimately, Ariel Motors petered out and BSA and Triumph were left fighting each other almost to the bitter end.

In the early 1960s the BSA group had the financial strength to lay the foundation for an operation to match many of its Japanese competitors and I am sure that we should have settled in right at the top in the growing world markets. But first of all it would have meant disposing of two or three top executives who were so complacent and preaching the futility of taking on the Japanese in the small capacity classes which they had made so popular. This would have meant a Board clear out to obtain a change in attitude, but this did not happen and we finally capitulated.

It seemed to me that the Board regarded it as unfortunate, to say the least, that the Motorcycle Division represented a large slice of the total Group capital and I had a strong feeling that this was regarded as a cross to bear. The acquisition of new companies and the possible growth of others in the Group was used to take the spotlight off the vexing problem of the British motorcycle industry's miserable and diminishing share of the total world market.

I recollect the take over, by BSA, of the Churchill Grinding Machine Co. for **185** a figure of around £6m, (a company which was to be almost given away at a later date). I was puzzled that any financial genius involved in this new move could be unaware that regenerative financial strategy was urgent for the good old bread and butter companies already in the Group so that this should have taken precedence. Six million pounds is small beer in today's financial atmosphere but, in the early 1960s,

Details of the Triumph Tigress scooter engine/transmission package.

this figure would have been sufficient to enable British motorcycles to survive and compete if it had been injected into the BSA Motorcycle Division together with a 'no nonsense' management.

Many of our top executives had cold feet and thought that the Japanese had some supernatural talent against which it was useless to compete, but they had

The BSA Ladybird three-wheeler prototype designed at Meriden with a 250 cc twin Tigress scooter engine/transmission unit. The project was not pursued to production.

nothing which we did not have in equal strength for they had no cheaper source of material and our technical and engineering ability was at least equal.

It must be admitted that productivity is much higher in Japan and our rather poor figures were due to a disease stimulated by trade union activity, which affects all types of industry here. It seems logical to suppose that, had BSA used its brains and cash resources wisely, we in its Motorcycle Division would have coped with the trade union problem just as other industries seem so far to have done.

Both Ariel Motors and BSA were anxious to get on with a lightweight machine and Ken Whistance, at Ariel Motors seemed to be going it alone, for Edward Turner did not seem to be fully aware of what was cooking in the Selly Oak Design Department. They had made rapid strides with a 100 cc baby machine and at the other end of the scale, projected a 750 cc monster with a four cylinder engine. I fully sympathised with Whistance, who saw the urgency for something new, but these projects had not been discussed, much less agreed at the appropriate level, so that they did not feature in any combined approach which the lumping of the three motorcycle companies was supposed to make possible. These two models did not make it to the production stage and of course a substantial slice of technical effort had been thrown away due to our slap dash tripartite product engineering set up.

Edward Turner took a great deal of interest in the BSA lightweight machine **187**

The BSA 75 cc Beagle model which was introduced at the 1962 Earls Court Show but enjoyed only a limited production run.

The Ariel Pixie, an ultra-lightweight machine introduced at the 1962 Earls Court Show. It was not successful and was made only in limited quantities.

and, I remember, personally laid down the basic design of the engine and much of the cycle structure which later was to appear on the market in the guise of the BSA Beagle. The same basic engine formed the power unit fitted to the Ariel Pixie, which had a different frame and several other variations of a cosmetic nature. Both of these new machines appeared at the 1962 Earls Court Show.

These motorcycles were poor indeed by comparison with their Japanese counterparts and dealer reaction was somewhat scathing. The design and development work had been done 'at the double' and the engine, in particular, which was described by our Managing Director as a miniaturised version of the Triumph Cub, was later dubbed by one or two of our top BSA dealers as 'a first class example of Mickey Mouse engineering'. I am sorry to say that both machines were a disaster. Production target dates simply could not be met and when the new models did, at last, trickle through, they gave so much trouble in the field that orders dried up and both models were withdrawn.

Business flourished reasonably well, however, with our other models, the exception being the Ariel Leader, an excellent trouble-free model which had been designed with cleanliness and enclosure well in mind. The demand was rapidly declining and this was causing a great deal of concern. The buying public did not

The ever-popular Percy Tait of Triumphs taking the island at Meriden during one of his daily test rides.

Chapter Seven

Breaking the World Speed Record was becoming something of a habit with Triumphs. Here we see Bob Leppan in Gyronaut, *powered by two 650 cc engines, at Utah salt flats in 1966 when the record was re-set at 245.6 mph.*

seem to be at all interested in enclosed and semi-enclosed types of motorcycles and our tactics were to revert to the normal or "naked" designs. The Ariel Arrow was on the way and Triumph were busy discarding much of the coverage which had characterised the 350 cc twins.

Doug Hele, who was in charge of development engineering at Meriden, was making his mark; the handling qualities of the Triumph machines were greatly improved and much enthusiastic comment was forthcoming as a result. Also, engine performance was improving under his dedicated and meticulous attention and a landmark was registered when a Triumph machine won the Daytona 200 mile Classic race in the USA in 1962. This was the first-ever victory for a Triumph in this great event, a strange fact when one considers the almost exclusive attention which had been lavished on this market by the Managing Director. His attentions were, of course, hailed as a great morale booster although, I must say, I often wonder why. Triumph machines were always in short supply.

The policy, at this stage, was one of not seeking to increase production by expansion. The turnover at Meriden was steady at around 350 unit per week and seemed all set to continue at this figure, come what may. This represented a rather timid marketing approach, for the home and other markets were often starved of Triumph products.

By the early 1960s, the spare parts situation at BSA was in a shocking state for, as is usual with a production hungry management, almost every type of component was in short supply. As a result, loss of prestige and dealer abuse was growing

Triumphs enjoyed most of the police force business and here we see a batch of machines outside Meriden works, being handed over for use during the investiture of the Prince of Wales at Carnaervon.

191

rapidly. Gone was the proud BSA slogan 'Service is the Keyword', an unquestioned reality in the late 1940s and early 1950s. At one of the Triumph Board meetings our Chairman had waxed long and bitter on the ever growing multiplicity of components with which we had to cope (many of which looked identical but, unfortunately, were not) and the 'criminal recklessness' of our design engineers 'who had been stupid enough to let their whims and fancies get the better of their business sense'.

I have a very vivid recollection of this occasion, partly because I was shocked and surprised that he seemed to feel that the Board was powerless to make themselves heard and to correct this sort of thing. It registered most, however, because it seemed to be little short of a comical situation when both the Chairman and our Managing Director turned to me and awaited my comment. The occasion was in fact, quite solemn but I must say that I could not help feeling amused as a first reaction. It flashed through my mind that I had been unanimously elected, the omnipotent design mind from afar, who could well have created this situation!

I should have been very annoyed for these two gentlemen should have been addressing the problem to themselves. However, I indicated that I was glad that, at last, this point was being discussed at this level for there was a simple answer to this nonsense. I outlined in principle what I felt to be the right approach to a future product range for the group, which had a clear mandate of maximum commonality

Much earlier machines in use by the Metropolitan Police. The occasion was President Eisenhower's visit and here he is seen seated in a Rolls Royce with Prime Minister McMillan.

Foreign police business from Triumphs. Here we see General de Gaulle with an escort of Triumph machines.

of component parts and production tooling. This would only be possible for us if, firstly, we agreed to make provision for producing vastly larger quantities of motorcycles and to compete directly against the Japanese and secondly that we have plans to embrace a range of machines from small to large and so dispense with our past bad habits of sporadic product changes which were now being labelled as near criminal behaviour on the part of the Engineering Department. Edward Turner was very rude and fobbed off a direct answer with the comment that this was my hobby horse. And so we passed on to the next item on the agenda. Edward seemed to feel that I had let the side down and said that he felt that I would never stop talking about 'irrelevant matters'. Certainly it was true that I had given my 'hobby horse' so much thought in the past year or two that I suppose I must have been word perfect.

I reassured him with the comment that my mini-lecture had, I was sure, fallen on stony ground and so it had, for we went on to manage our affairs in our usual smug self-satisfied manner. We did practically nothing except to make some cosmetic changes. It was not until 1965, when it was much too late, that Edward Turner grudgingly admitted that there might be something in my suggestions. By then shareholders had been brainwashed with the beautiful clear text-book strategy of hordes of management consultants backed up by a succession of chief executives, each of whom had a different business approach.

Some famous personalities of the trials world. Here we see Bob Haines on the extreme left with, next to him, Ray Sayer and Ken Heanes. Seated on the machine are Roy Peplow and Sammy Miller and Johnny Giles is standing second from right. Henry Vale, the wizard engineer of Triumph trials machinery, is standing third from right and Stan Truslove is seen standing fifth from left.

The occasion was a celebratory lunch at the 1966 Earls Court Show, during which year six machines gained six gold metals and two manufacturers team awards during the International Six Days Trial.

Some time later the Board asked me to elaborate on what I then termed the 'maximum commonality of parts and tools approach' to a forward range of products. I made it clear that it would be a waste of time unless we were prepared to go for a much more significant share of the world market and also to consider a range of products rather than the piecemeal approach of the past. It did not mean that we would be forced to tool up and manufacture a whole family of machines at once but it did mean that, if our marketing homework was correct, we should be well placed to introduce the first new motorcycle with a lead time that was fundamentally sound, with others to follow at planned intervals.

For a time I banished the word modular from my vocabulary, for I felt that the rash of badly designed bedroom furniture which, at this precise moment of time, was flooding the shops and labelled modular, would cause suspicion and distrust in non-engineering minds. I explained that nothing whatsoever must be sacrificed technically for the purpose of making components common in the range. It was essential the **194** single cylinder engine module or unit embraced the most up to date thinking in ohc

A fine action shot of Johnny Giles riding a 500 cc Triumph twin during a Scottish Six Days Trial.

195

valve gear operation and had the best possible geometry based on our combined expertise and experience so that it should develop relatively high power output. The technique could be extended through a range of four engine units by a multiplication of the module design and, by so doing, we would achieve a family of single, twin, three and four cylinder power units with capabilities relative to the number of cylinders and with a minimum variety of components, without impairing efficiency.

The total cost of tooling such a project would, of course, be substantial but because of the common approach, would be minimised when considered in total. The commonality of components would provide a real meaning to quantity production and enable such cost reductions as to make all our previous achievements seem pitiful.

The fundamentals involved were as I had explained previously. Firstly, we would have to abandon our past habits of waiting for a near crisis danger signal and then feverishly designing and developing each new project, often a little too late and always resulting in unreliability, sometimes of calamitous proportions. Secondly, a heavy financial investment would be necessary and agreement to pursue a changed policy of high mass production.

I did not give a damn what the concept was labelled or who engineered it and it need not, if the Board felt otherwise, be based on a modular approach. However, if the Chairman had really meant what he had said about past criminal recklessness in the unnecessary creation of a multiplicity of components, it would have been better to seriously consider this proposition or 'belt up' and cease moaning forthwith. In short I felt that the time was rapidly approaching, indeed it may have overtaken us, when we should say 'enough' to applying yearly cosmetics to a range of motorcycles mostly conceived twenty years past. Whilst we had the strength, we should put such a plan into motion and do the job thoroughly and unhurriedly, to emerge, after three years, with the British challenge.

I was accused of over-simplifying the difficulties and that such a scheme would need huge financial support and in any case, our products were doing very well. How many times have I heard the last comment and how many good prototypes have been laid to rest because of it? I had the feeling that several of our top executives were too comfortable in their jobs and meant to keep it that way; they were not hungry in any way and would wake up in surprise and panic looking for a scapegoat, which the engineering profession usually supplies.

On the question of over-simplifying the difficulties, none of these were of insurmountable proportion at that time. We were brimming over with experience and technique and provided that we were not expected to attempt a 'marathon' and shorten sensible time factors, none of the difficulties would have been very different from those with which we had been dealing for a generation or so. The finance needed for such a programme should readily have been forthcoming, for the Group

196 was enjoying reasonably good trading results. They did not seem to have too much difficulty in raising large sums of money, such as that for the Churchill acquisition.

The Board seemed to be very suspicious of my approach, although at that point in time I had discarded the term modular. I was asked to carry out a very quick study, based on one of our present single cylinder engines, to indicate how much of the make-up of this unit could be common to a twin cylinder engine of double the capacity.

I chose the then brand new 50 cc Pixie single cylinder engine as the module and designed a 100 cc twin cylinder unit on similar lines. I then completed a simple folder which contained a cross-section of each engine side by side with the common components coloured red on both pictures. The exercise took only a few days and although the Pixie project was to turn out such a flop, it represented our most modern engine unit. As such, it should have been new in the minds of the Board members and I felt that this would prove a great advantage. The written information, which my folder provided, indicated that excluding items such as electrical equipment and chains etc., the design of the single cylinder unit had 63 different components whilst that of the twin cylinder unit had 70, and it was clear that 49 of these components would be common to both engines.

I did not need to be reminded, as I was by Edward Turner, that items such as crankcases and crankshafts would not be common equipment. This is irrelevant, for a 70% factor of component commonality is impressive and would enable real quantity production of those items which are normally in demand and are stocked in the dealers parts stores.

I was most surprised to have the folder returned to me with the comment that it was not clear, for I had gone to great pains to make it clear to the non-engineering fraternity. I did not pursue the matter further for I felt incapable of coping with the mysteries of the accountancy mind. It did occur to me that I may be a developing 'nut case' but this fear soon passed off. At a much later date I was grateful to be reassured by my nephew, by then 13 years old and mad about motorcycles, who came across this very folder which had been lying on my table. From the intelligent discussion which followed I gathered that there was no mystery so far as he was concerned and I was greatly encouraged, although by this time, the brokers were almost with us. So I gave up the battle and went back to my job for, after all, a General Manager has other little odds and sods to fill in his working time.

With the rumblings, at least to my unsophisticated ears, of the Japanese onslaught into the bigger capacity market I could not resist asking Edward Turner what plans we had to meet the invasion and I got little or no reaction. He was, of course, on the verge of retirement but this was no reason why we should delay and I suggested that we might, very suddenly, need a larger than 650 cc motorcycle (our largest capacity machine at that time). I even ventured to suggest that it would be wise to add another cylinder to our 500 cc twin unit and have a 750 cc triple under development forthwith.

197

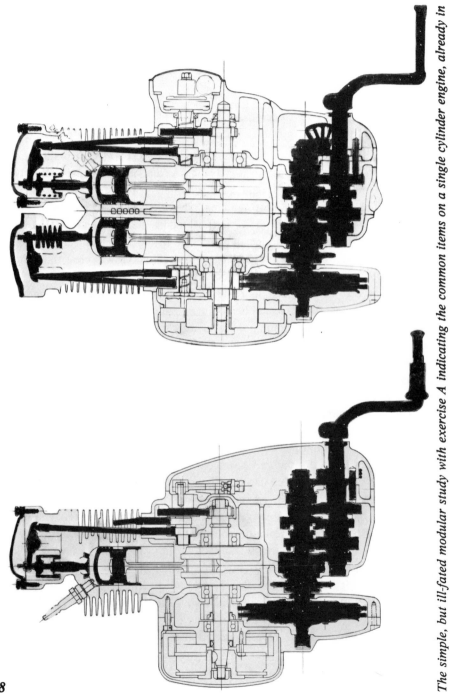

The simple, but ill-fated modular study with exercise A indicating the common items on a single cylinder engine, already in production (left) and two cylinder engine, of twice that capacity (right).

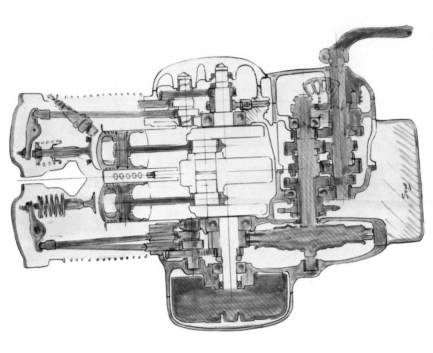

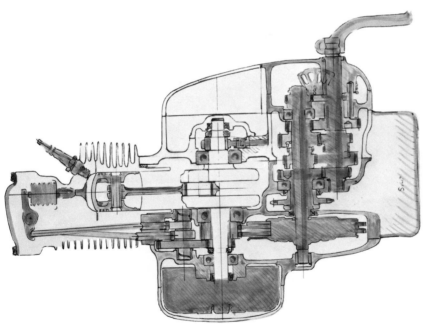

The simple modular study carried a stage further in exercise B, with a newly designed single cylinder power unit (left) and a two cylinder engine of twice that capacity (right).

199

The 250 cc Ariel Leader, a revolutionary machine introduced in the late 1950s. A very reliable motorcycle which, for a time, was in brisk demand, but sales steadily declined and a slenderised, more sporting version in the form of the Arrow was introduced.

Turner and I had known each other a very long time and neither of us minced matters on the subject of engineering design. It was not exactly surprising to me that he told me how 'potty' I was, although he seemed to have no logical reason to support his statement. As far as I could gather, he simply felt that 'three was potty'.

I persisted and pointed out that a motorcar which had a three cylinder engine had won the Monte Carlo Rally twice running; that the works tractor, fitted with a three cylinder engine, was performing very smoothly on the lawn outside his office window and that, if we were too lazy to embark on a real product range for the future, such a power unit might help the firm to last just a few years longer. There was not a chance of convincing Turner on this subject and I gave up, for the conversation was tending to become bitter. To prolong it would simply have wasted time.

Doug Hele had been nagging at me for years to give consideration to a three cylinder engine design for larger capacity units for, as he so rightly pointed out, the engine should be reasonably smooth and would be comparatively narrow and thus ideal for a large motorcycle. One evening late in 1963, after everyone had gone home, we sat in his office and to amuse ourselves we laid out the basic outline of

A picture taken at Earls Court Show in 1958 showing Mr. Harold Watkinson, then the Minster of Transport and now Lord Watkinson, centre, discussing the new Ariel Leader machine with Edward Turner (left) and Ken Whistance, Ariel's General Manager (right).

what later became the 750 cc three cylinder Trident. We thought that the result was very encouraging indeed, but in view of the rather abortive conversation which I had already had with the Managing Director, this drawing was filed away as a memento.

During 1964, the Board called in McKinseys, the US Management Consultants, and the usual activity associated with exercises of this kind saturated the whole Motorcycle Division and did a lot of damage to morale. It was during the early stages of this activity that Edward Turner announced his retirement as an Executive Director of the company, although he was to retain a seat on the Board, for the time being, in a non-executive capacity.

This left us without a rudder and sluggish though we may have been in our past direction finding, it was a serious gap. Comment and speculation was rife both inside and outside the company. I had the top job at Meriden and hoped that my title would now be changed to Managing Director, but I was realistic enough to know that this was most unlikely. It would not fit in with Divisional policy and I knew that McKinseys would advise against such a move.

A little later we heard, through the grapevine, that our Chairman was considering the appointment of a newcomer to the industry as our chief executive. The divisional directors were very cross indeed and we met to discuss the matter at length. We tabled a letter to the Chairman which indicated our very strong feelings and suggested that he should consider filling the vacancy from within the Company.

Both Charles Parker, who was Triumph's financial director, and myself, objected most strongly to suggestions that executive talent was not readily available on the spot. Both of us had come through the hard way, often propping up superiors who had much to learn about fundamental management. We were determined that the Chairman should be reminded that these facts may have escaped the notice of the Board. We were unanimous in our attitude for, as top ranking executives with years of specialist experience in our individual professions of finance, marketing, production and engineering, we felt very confident that we were capable of committing ourselves to the forward strategy which was so badly needed.

The Chairman took great exception to our letter and said that it was inevitable that we should have a newcomer in charge, making the rather lame excuse that if one of us were appointed Chief Executive the others would take such exception that it would break up the team. Rather peculiar management logic, I thought, but at least it was nice of him not to say that none of us was capable of filling the top job.

I wonder whether this had been the subject of discussion at Board level but, from information which I have since gleaned, it seems that the appointment of our new Chief Executive was a fait accompli. Once more our Board demonstrated their belief that it was unthinkable that there was executive talent with which they sometimes rubbed shoulders.

Chapter Eight

The age of the sophisticated organisation chart

IN MID-1964 Harry Sturgeon was appointed Chief Executive of the BSA Motorcycle Division, which at least had an immediate settling effect on the torn and uneasy atmosphere which had spread throughout the organization.

Harry had held a high executive position in the aircraft industry but had, until now, been Managing Director of the Churchill Grinding Machine Company, a subsidiary of BSA, and I suppose that one could say that this was promotion from within, although the average mind lacked the elasticity to grasp this point. He had the reputation of being a super-salesman and was certainly one of Nature's gentlemen. From the moment that I was introduced to him, we seemed to lock together into a business relationship which, although unfortunately short lived, I look back on with many pleasant memories.

In the meantime McKinseys, the consultants, were actively building up a management dossier and by July 1964 their recommendations were made known. The Board were quick to respond by making drastic changes in the management structure.

The BSA and Triumph companies were to be integrated into a single division with four directors and a single management structure, rather than the separate ones which now existed. The demand for Ariel motorcycles was now a mere trickle, with the result that the Selly Oak plant had been closed and the production facilities transferred to Small Heath Works.

I was appointed Engineering Director and Deputy Managing Director, whilst Charles Parker, my Triumph colleague, was elevated to Divisional Financial Director. Although we were to have a Marketing Director and a Manufacturing Director, these posts were left vacant for the time being and Harry Sturgeon assumed line responsibility for these functions until further notice.

203

Chapter Eight

This left three former executives unplaced and I was most disappointed for, if there must be a single division of management, there was very good reason why our splendid team of experienced executives should not be broken up and demoralized.

Bob Fearon, the General Manager at Small Heath, had unfortunately chosen early retirement. This, to me, was a tragedy, for he had been doing a first class job in spite of the many problems which had been greatly magnified by the policy of our former Chief Executive. Bob was, in my opinion, much too young and valuable to retire, for whatever reason, and it was a severe loss to the company. His background was one of production engineering and I felt sure that we should rue the day we were foolish enough to allow such an experienced executive to slip away as such people were very rare in our particular business.

Bill Rawson, the erstwhile Sales Director at Small Heath, had good reason to take the changes very badly, for, not only had his directorship become null and void, but he had been demoted and asked to carry on as a Sales Manager. It is true that Bill was nearing retiring age but he had a vast knowledge and had piloted several successful enterprises. There could be no doubt that our dealers, at home and abroad, respected him and knew exactly where they stood.

Our Board, together with McKinseys, seemed to think that a new horizon, a sort of Aurora Borealis, had now been created around the term marketing. Bill, who like myself did not feel too happy that the good old term 'selling' had been struck from our new vocabulary, felt that the cart was before the horse once more. Our advisors showed little awareness that it is difficult to market antiques to a new generation whose appetite had been whetted by the goodies being offered from the Far East.

How sensible it would have been to have offered Bill the vacant job of Marketing Director, on the understanding that he engaged an able deputy forthwith, and how right and proper it would have been to have promoted him in recognition of his lifelong and dedicated service to a company, whose name he helped to build up and make famous. Most of us were ready to give guarantees that the Board would never have regretted the move and also, with the team we had, we would have been much more likely to live up to much of the snappy marketing and management jargon with which McKinseys had showered us.

Ken Whistance, until recently Managing Director of the Ariel Works, was a made-to-measure Divisional Manufacturing Director and should have been transferred to the vacant seat. Instead, he suffered the indignity of demotion to the position of Quality Control Manager at Small Heath. This was a job which badly needed to be filled, for BSA products were suffering on a mounting scale from extremely bad quality, which was becoming a disease in most industries. There wasn't a person within the organization who was more ideally suited and it was utterly foolish of the Board not to have upgraded this man, for they must have known that a man of Whistance's temperament would

One of the few pictures available of Harry Sturgeon, here seen at the head of the table on the occasion of the retirement of George Savage, Home Sales Manager at BSA and a man much respected by the trade. Here George is seen on Sturgeon's left and sitting next to Bert Perrigo, with the author on Sturgeon's right.

not tolerate demotion of this sort.

I tried very hard indeed to delay any departure plans which I knew Ken must be making and even convinced Harry Sturgeon that we should re-adjust our sights. But I knew that I was fighting a losing battle and almost immediately Ken handed in his resignation. I believe that Ken would, rapidly, have put to bed most of the problems which were now bedevilling the product line at BSA in particular, and which had now been emptied into my lap. Had he stayed with us, we should have made rapid incursions into what was soon to become an increasingly worrying situation.

Harry Sturgeon was headquartered at the Small Heath Works and, for the time being, he assumed line responsibility of the marketing and manufacturing functions until two new directors were found. It was agreed that I should be located mainly at Meriden works and would, in addition, be responsible for management there.

I was just a little uncertain about the 'Deputy Managing Director' part of my new position for, although outwardly it might seem that I got on reasonably well with our Chairman, I had no illusions as to my acceptability to him as a top executive. I sensed from his attitude a firm non-acceptance of practising engineers, for he never could bring himself to believe that such people could have any business gumption. In any case I had noticed that the 'gift of the gab' was a must and this was something which, to my deep regret, I was never endowed. So, before I accepted my new **205** assignment, I asked Sturgeon what exactly was meant by the deputy part of my new title. He replied immediately 'It means that if I die, you become the Chief Executive'.

We had a good laugh about this for the giddy heights of the Parent Board were unthinkable for me and I was most anxious that Harry should stay alive. With hindsight, I feel that I missed an opportunity in not pressing this point at Chairman level, if only to have sampled the high logic of the situation which he had created.

By now we were contemplating buying out Hap Alzina, the BSA distributor for the Western States of the USA. With Triumph Baltimore, Triumph Los Angeles and BSA New Jersey, this would complete a well organised distributing organization and strong dealer network throughout the USA which was fully owned by our company. After several visits to the States, Harry Sturgeon realized that a greatly increased turnover could be achieved if the goods could be on the showroom floors during the peak selling months of spring and early summer.

He was a dynamic man, gifted with the ability to inspire confidence and energy, and it was not long before manpower was increased and the production lines at Small Heath and Meriden were responding with significantly higher output. It is interesting to note that the turnover of the motorcycle group increased by something like 40% between the years 1964 and 1966.

Harry was, most certainly, a super-salesman and I was at first alarmed but later amused to hear him always referring to our products as consumer durables. It was however, difficult, for many of our dealers to be happy with the new language which was developing. They would, I am sure, have felt more reassured if the consumer was more happy about the durability but however, this part of our 'McKinseyisation' was harmless enough, provided that we soon got to grips with a strategy that would make our new paper philosophy practical and worthwhile.

Sturgeon was a good listener and a wonderful, off the cuff, after-dinner speaker. With a wealth of interest and knowledge, he was quick to grasp many problems in the total situation which now confronted him, and we tackled these with the most unusual approach.

I had a tremendous admiration for him, both as a man and as a business executive, and I feel that had he been spared to have carried out the task he had been set, he may have developed the expertise and packed the punch and energy which the Board needed to lead them to the promised land. I think it would have depended on his ability to generate an all-embracing product policy and I think that this may have been possible, for he seemed to understand the urgency of the situation far more clearly than any of his Board colleagues. We were rapidly arriving at a stage where both he and I were more hopeful and confident about the future.

We were agreed on the need for sensible integrated effort which would embrace the three group names without too much of what we termed badge engineering. We were also in agreement that a long term design and product planning department should be formed immediately. In addition, Sturgeon suggested, believe it or not, that we should aim at some sort of modular approach in our overall tactics, to minimise tooling costs and the creation of new components, and he was very keen indeed that we should pursue this at all times, unless a basic utility model was ever considered. My long suggested mandate that all new engine designs should be capable of high power extraction was well received. This did not mean that all new engines would be racing units, but simply that the scantlings should be provided in the basic design to enable us to maximise our sports specifications without resorting to too much re-design. This would have enabled us to deal with the ever-growing popularity of production racing in the best possible way, while at the same time marketing standard models in a fully-competitive form.

It would be quite wrong of me to give the impression that Harry Sturgeon and I were locked together in complete agreement as this was not true. He was obsessed with the achievement of more production at any cost and preached this on every fitting occasion. This philosophy aggravated me beyond measure until it reached such a pitch that he would not, if possible, mention this matter in my presence.

I took him to task many times, expressing surprise and disappointment that a man endowed with his intelligence should take this view, but he was clear in his mind that it mattered little what was demanded in return for vastly increased turnover and greatly transformed profits.

There is no doubt that he was responsible for the alarming acceleration of a spiral which took the Triumph wage structure way out and beyond the very high Coventry wage rates and the shop floor was quick to grasp the significance of this extra strength in their so-called collective bargaining. Neither did it help when sometimes he would enter into the negotiating procedure and settle a new wage demand on the spot. This had a devastating effect on our Works Manager and his colleagues and I had to ask Harry to leave them free to do their job until such time as it was felt to be desirable or necessary that he or I were called upon. This did not mean that we should be ignorant of what went on until crisis time, for our Works Manager always discussed wage problems which were now confronting us daily, so that we could agree the general strategy.

This intolerable situation came to a head when Harry barged into a delicate negotiating round, quite without brief, and took the Chair. He suggested a settlement figure far in excess of our agreed last resort maxima, and believe it or not, a figure which was in excess of the demand being made by the shop floor. I had departed for a holiday the previous day and was telephoned by a shocked and despondent Works Manager. It was difficult to visualise how this intolerable situation could have been reconciled.

A few months after this particular incident it was evident to all that Harry Sturgeon was a sick man and shortly afterwards he was to undergo surgery for the removal of a brain tumour. He was absent for a very long spell, a tragedy, for here at last there appeared to be a Chief Executive who understood that our future **207** depended almost exclusively on the marketing viability of our product and intended to make this a first priority. We were rapidly arriving at conclusions which I am sure would have enabled us to plan forward without interference, with our current effort to improve quality and increase turnover.

We had agreed that a new engineering department be formed and that this should be located preferably, though not essentially, at a point other than within the Small Heath or Meriden plants. This matter was delayed as my work load had greatly increased with additional responsibility, particularly at Small Heath, where the product range was passing through a bad spell. It was many months before we were able to solve some of the problems which were now causing serious difficulties, particularly in the USA.

I think that I could be excused for wondering what the many excursions to the States by our previous Chief Executive had been about and why the now bitter and exasperated BSA dealers never got through to him. It may have been that his name was so identified with Triumph that they never gave it a thought that one of the enemy (as the BSA dealers regarded the Triumph camp) had line responsibilities at Small Heath as well as Meriden.

The greatest headache, which kept us occupied for a long time, was a piston seizure problem with the twin cylinder machines. It was not until a great deal of damage had been done to the BSA reputation that the problem was solved and we were able to give the machines a clean bill of health. Pete Colman, our Technical Director in the USA, contributed a great deal towards the clearing of the trouble which was caused, in the main, by a 'rogue' spark which roved and re-ignited the mixture, causing over-heating and consequent piston seizure. This did not happen with every machine but nonetheless the problem was serious enough to warrant substantial payments to dealers for the purpose of fitting new parts to every machine sold or in the warehouse. This represented a total cost to the company in excess of £80,000.

The panic at certain top level meetings had to be seen to be believed! I am ashamed that on one occasion I was blamed for the whole of BSAs unfortunate product mishaps, a strange but disgusting statement to make and one which was an indication of the internal bickering that was going on.

Fortunately, by this stage of my career, I had become case-hardened against this sort of treatment. Someone had to keep their cool, and by making use of the rolling road equipment which had been designed and installed by Triumph a year or so previously, we were able to simulate user conditions. I think that history was being made in a small way, at last, in combining the resources of both factories. This equipment was the Triumph answer to rusting problems, which were becoming a curse and were costing the company large sums of money in compensating dealers abroad for their expenses in coping with the problem which was evident at the unpacking stage. We had installed eight test cubicles in which complete motorcycles could be tested with the rear wheel driving rollers which registered engine power, road speed and braking characteristics, etc. This was programmed to a reasonable simulation of rider usage and we were able to discontinue road testing with its attendant fouling problems, particularly those caused by salt-laden roads during the winter months. From then on, Triumph machines were put straight into their packing cases, clean and dry.

Harry Sturgeon was keen to reintroduce the Tina scooter, which had now been re-engineered and was proving reliable after the most stringent development testing and the release of fifty pre-production machines on loan to a mixed group of users with the help of our dealers. However, he was anxious that the scooter should have a new look, a mistake I think, for the provision of a more shapely appearance and other cosmetic changes proved very costly. This did little to boost sales in a receding market and eventually the production of this machine was allowed to trickle out.

It is a great pity that the revised version of this scooter came too late for I am sure that had the design engineering been sound when it was first introduced in 1962, the market was ready for this delightfully simple machine. Triumphs certainly would have benefitted from a money spinner.

The company was bedevilled with the problem of so-called loyalties and a partisan attitude existed at most levels in the organization which had made Sturgeon's task a difficult one indeed. Much of this nonsense, which had resulted in dispersion of effort in the tug-of-war tactics within the two companies, should have been dealt with at the beginning by our former Chief Executive. Unfortunately, his own attitude, as Mr. Triumph, had established the pattern to be followed at a high level, and a sizeable headache had developed.

I suppose that it is inevitable that some strong loyalties would exist and now that two Triumph men had the top jobs, the situation was not exactly a happy one at Small Heath. I was, I felt, more fortunate than Charles Parker, for I had operated as Chief Engineer with BSA some years previously and knew most of the key figures at Small Heath which, I hoped, would enable me to be more readily accepted.

I must say that there seems to be no ready answer to these inter group problems. McKinseys must have been tongue in cheek when recommending a new management set-up which retained all the personal antagonisms. This happened in spite of the handsome text books with which we had been issued and from which we gathered we were now one big happy family.

It seems that three reasonably healthy companies like BSA, Triumph and Ariel had run into sizeable problems on becoming part of a group and Ariel Motors had to put up the shutters. The friendly rivalry and healthy competition which existed between the individual companies had been replaced by internal feuds and a sizeable problem for a Board such as ours was arriving at any viable projection of a plan of action which would meet with the approval of all three companies, each of which was in business to sell motorcycles.

209

Chapter Eight

The long absence of Harry Sturgeon imposed a high workload on us and although our Chairman was now available on a day to day basis, the management structure had several important gaps. Charles Parker and myself had to rise to the occasion and, as I reflect on this period, I realize what a fine business brain Parker had. I simply do not comprehend why he had not been invited to join our Parent Board long ago. He had an outstanding grasp of industrial management and besides being an unusually practical Chartered Accountant, he was a keen motorcylist and understood every word in the two wheeler vocabulary.

We were firm friends, for the past antagonisms attached to my appointment to Triumph had rapidly disappeared. I was thankful indeed that I should be fortunate enough to have his guidance and counsel for, to be sure, there were very few days which passed without consultation and this was the strength which made the situation just bearable.

During early convalescence, Sturgeon must have found it difficult to remain comparatively idle for he called a management meeting which was held at an hotel near his home to discuss model changes. Apart from being somewhat bald, he seemed to be particularly fit and he chaired the meeting with such vigour that it was difficult to believe he had undergone major surgery.

We were then contemplating a change to ohc valve operation for the BSA and Triumph engine units, as a means of extending their acceptable life, thus enabling us to concentrate on a new generation plan. I was never too sure that this would be the wisest strategy for really new generation products had been fobbed off too many times with similar suggestions and I felt, instinctively, that we would get by the next year or so with fewer fundamental changes. This would have enabled us to make an earlier start on the real job of work called for by our new look strategy. I felt disgruntled in having to spend a fair slice of time extending the life of engines which had, in the case of Triumph, perpetuated 1936 design philosophy, good though it may have been at the time. Although the BSA twins were always much quieter in operation, the Triumphs were never anything but clatterboxes which could be heard three blocks away. A completely new approach was long overdue and should have taken priority. Our typically British engines were far from oil tight and although this had been accepted in the good old days, and indeed had created a small industry in the USA which was profitably engaged in marketing devices which were designed to minimise this annoyance, the Japanese were showing us the way with their immaculately oil-tight machines. Besides, our new engineering thinking needed to be geared to modern production engineering both for high quantity and repeatability. I felt that it was now or never, for we seemed to have much better prospects than ever before of getting the market logic through to the proliferation of merchant bankers, financiers and accountants in the make up of our Board.

Harry Sturgeon had been very keen to market a 250 cc three cylinder machine and felt that such an engine would have a world beating performance. He persisted until a design which Doug Hele had masterminded a year or so previously was updated. It impressed Harry so much that he gave instructions for prototypes to be made.

The power unit was based on an 83 cc single cylinder module, with a bore of 50 mm and a stroke of 42 mm, the basic essential of which was that the 'scantlings' should have provision for racing performance. From a vast pool of know-how, plus the design ingenuity of Hele, we finalised on a double ohc valve gear with some unusual features, not the least of which were exceptional cooling characteristics.

This was purely a racing engine designed to produce 40 bhp plus which at the time would have been up in the top of its class. An offshoot of this unit, which would be offered as the bread and butter mass production version, was to be very similar in external appearance but have two valves per cylinder, instead of four, and a much simplified ohc drive system along with several other changes to obviate unwarranted expense. The whole unit had a very clean appearance and had provision for electric starting plus a six-speed gearbox that was capable of taking an eight-speed gear cluster as and when the need should arise.

The strategy was to get into the high volume, low capacity market, and Sturgeon felt that important racing successes would be helpful if not necessary, to satisfactorily introduce a new BSA machine into this market sector if we were ever to enjoy a sensible share of world demand.

The BSA Bantam of the mid-1960s.

Chapter Eight

The Bushman version of the BSA Bantam.

Our standard motorcycles were proving very successful in most other types of the sport but I was aware of signs, which left no doubt in my mind, that Harry Sturgeon would take us into Grand Prix Racing. The thought of this horrified me, but I felt satisfied that the development of a pure racing unit, together with its weaker brother, which I hoped would become the first in a new range of machines with thoroughbred muscle, was a reasonably sensible plan. We went to it with gusto.

Sturgeon had been a three cylinder man from the start and our first management meeting after McKinseyisation was one which I clearly remember with a great deal of amusement. Harry had just been appointed and our Chairman called us together for the purpose of introducing him to the Senior Managers. There were about thirty people at the meeting which was chaired by Eric Turner and we had several hours of interesting discussion with a free exchange of views, which seemed to me like a breath of fresh air. One of our Sales Managers, a very capable man, had a habit of stopping many a meeting in its tracks by making momentous and often disturbing statements. These were usually based on snippets of information about up and coming activities of our competitors, and experience had told me that we should always listen most carefully. One of his specialities was to wait until the meeting was on its feet and dispersing and then release his information. We were moving out of the room on this occasion when this fellow said to the Chairman 'Oh by the way, I learned today that Honda will shortly be marketing a 750 cc capacity machine'. This man was a good psychologist and knew precisely at what stage such a statement should be made. As planned, it stopped our Chairman in his tracks and the assembly was sharply brought back to their seats. This seemed to be surprising and disturbing news to our top brass for had they not let it be broadcast, not so long ago, that the Japanese were good little fellows who were obliging us by messing about with the small motorcycles which they were foolish enough to consider worth while. Was it not that they were happily engaged training youngsters on their loss leaders to enable a steady stream of sophisticated riders to buy the big machines in which market we were entrenched?

This thinking had been a little dented by the introduction of the 450 cc Honda but now a monster of 750 cc capacity would be an invasion, so the meeting readjusted itself to a brisk re-appraisal of our management strategy. It is extraordinary that a remark such as this could be the means of producing immediate action at top level, but this is exactly what it did. On reflection, I could not help feeling that our Sales Manager had just given me my first real lesson in the art of instant decision strategy, for it was better than all the marketing and forecasting logic and technical blandishments in the world and I decided that, from now on, I would mend my foolish ways.

I remember that the meeting was silent for just a while. I suppose that some were nonplussed, but eventually Harry Sturgeon looked across and asked me what I had to say. I felt like a criminal, for his attitude seemed to be a little reproachful, as indeed it should have been. He could not have known that in late 1961 I had put forward to the late Managing Director a ready-made plan for a 750 cc triple cylinder motorcycle.

Chris Vincent was remarkably successful racing a BSA twin sidecar machine. Chris and his passenger are here seen in typical style.

Chapter Eight

I told the meeting that a 750 cc twin would be much too much of a shaker (our 650 cc models were already causing great concern) and that by the time that we had developed a suitable balancing device, we would be running very late. I suggested that a three cylinder unit was the quick answer, for such an engine would be comparatively smooth in operation and would be ideally narrow for a motorcycle and could be installed in a similar, if not identical, frame to the Bonneville machine.

Most of those at the meeting seemed to feel that I was sickening for something serious, for at that time a three cylinder motorcycle was a new, if not original, concept. The thought of an odd number of cylinders seemed to make most people back away but not so Mr. Sturgeon, for he quickly grasped the point and asked me

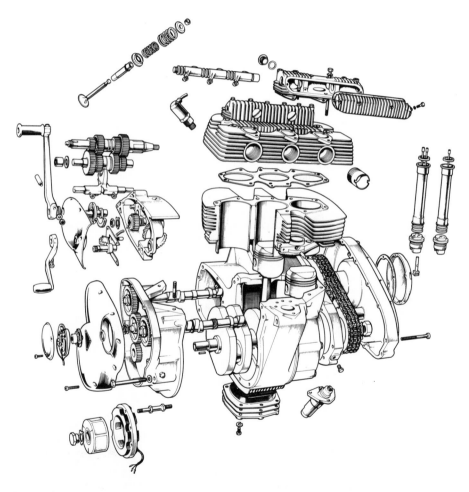

An exploded view of the 750 cc Triumph/BSA three cylinder engine designed originally in early 1963.

how long I thought it would take to design such a unit. He was more than pleased to learn that we had a design almost ready; the drawing was produced there and then and his enthusiasm was such that we were not long in deciding that prototypes should be made forthwith.

I made it clear that such a design, which of course carried all the characteristics of the Speed Twin engine and therefore inherited the 1936 design features which were long overdue for reappraisal, should be considered only as a speedy means of producing a triple engine. There was need to ascertain whether the effect of rotating out of balance forces, inherent in such a design, would enable us to be satisfied that it was a viable proposition when it was installed in a typical motorcycle frame. If this particular power unit proved to be as smooth in operation as we hoped, then there was no reason why it should not go into production. Always, of course, with the proviso that it should be considered only as a short term or stop gap product to serve our immediate purpose and that production expenditure should be geared accordingly.

We had worked on the balance problem mathematically and were very hopeful that in practice it would prove much less severe than those we would encounter with a 750 cc unbalanced parallel twin engine. The forces involved were in the form of a couple related to the engine width, and until such times as we had a new device of this type assembled in a complete motorcycle and under test, it was not possible to be absolutely positive as to the degree of user acceptability.

Harry Sturgeon thought me quite stubborn and unhelpful for he simply could not believe that I would not commit myself to a statement as to the exact percentage of improvement in vibration characteristic that I expected from the new triple in comparison with our present 650 cc twin cylinder machines. I suppose that his aircraft industry background made it difficult for him to understand that the frame of a single track vehicle does not provide the best installation for even the smoothest of engines. We had done our homework, had called in a consultant and compared notes, and we were all agreed that the new engine should give a much smoother ride. Although Sturgeon was all set in his enthusiasm to tell some of our BSA dealers about our new project, I objected very strongly and insisted that until we had a complete motorcycle and had run a few test miles, we should keep our mouths closed and our fingers crossed.

We had a design team busy immediately and Doug Hele came up with a very compact clutch drive and assembly which removed, very largely, the problem of excessive width at the footrest position. Twelve months later we had our first engine under bench test. The power output proved to be 58 bhp at 7,250 rpm and we were more than pleased with the vibration characteristics. Now we had a large capacity machine, much smoother to ride than the smaller twin cylinder models, with a weight increase only 40 lbs above that of our Bonneville model.

To save time, the prototypes had cylinder blocks made in cast iron. Other new **215** components, such as the crankcase, were in sand-cast form and carried a weight penalty because of this. We felt that an aluminium cylinder block was a 'must' if the unit reached the production stage, and we were quite confident that the mass-produced version of the motorcycle would weigh only 420 lbs dry which was not bad at all for a triple engined 750 cc machine developing 58 bhp.

Harry Sturgeon, duly recovered from his indisposition and seemingly with all his old verve, was back with us, pressing himself to the extreme and now anxious to achieve a new and responsible image for the company. I detected a somewhat improving dealer relationship both at home and abroad, particularly in the USA, where he was taking great pains to know the market and the views of our dealer organisation. It seemed to me that, from a first suspicious appraisal, the outside

The original prototype of the Triumph 750 cc triple machine, later to be called the Trident. This machine proved satisfactory from the start and could readily have gone into production, in this form, in 1965.

world was beginning to feel that our new Managing Director meant just what he said. With ample evidence of this dynamic man's personality rubbing out some of the lethargy which had existed, a slightly more optimistic climate began to blossom.

It is a tragedy, however, that not many months had passed before Harry was once more in trouble. It seemed that the major surgery which he had undergone, had not cleared his problem and he was, once more, out of action for a considerable period.

At this stage our Chairman was taking a somewhat more active day to day interest in management matters and, as a consequence, he and I were drawn much closer than hitherto. From our many discussions and a much more intimate

Frontal view of the original prototype 750 cc triple cylinder Triumph machine showing the narrow proportions of the power unit.

knowledge of the man, I became quite certain that if the worst should happen to our Managing Director, it would be quite inconceivable to him that I should succeed as Chief Executive. Our Chairman was a hard working, generous and fair minded man and we got on together reasonably well but our basic thinking and priorities always seemed poles apart. He seemed to effuse an atmosphere almost of contempt for engineers (or shall we say those who had at some time practised the art) who had, somehow, strayed into the world of business. Not that this bothered me for one moment for there was far too much work to be done and even now I did not believe that Harry Sturgeon would die. I think that our Chairman, in turn, may have sensed

Buddy Elmore, on a Triumph 500 cc twin, won the classic 200 mile Daytona race in 1966. Here he is shown during the race.

that I was somewhat fed up with the business approach from which we had suffered for so long and was reflected in the background of accountants, financiers, merchant bankers and consultants which had been the make up of our governing body for as long as I cared to remember.

During the very long periods of Harry Sturgeon's absence. Charles Parker and I shared our Managing Director's working responsibilities in addition to our own day to day management activities. On reflection, very little went amiss during a period

of great change, when production figures had risen by almost 40%.

Buddy Elmore's winning Triumph of 1966 with the racing fairings removed.

A scene from the two wheel sporting front in the USA. The start of the Big Bear Run, which is something in the nature of a mammoth motocross through rough and varying terrain.

I was soon to know the reality that Harry would not return as our Managing Director for he was now desperately ill. Although, towards the end, he did rally, this improvement was short lived and he passed away during 1966. From that moment on, we plunged from slow and painful recovery to an era which was to prove the final countdown for the remnants of an industry which once led the world.

In the all too-short period of Harry Sturgeon's influence, much of our confidence had been restored and we were making positive progress with reorganisation and project thinking, not all of which may have made the grade through to our production lines. But, like others, I felt sure that we had started on the great trek back. He was a great man and was indeed, as he was described, a super-salesman. Had he have survived, I feel certain that we should, somehow, have resolved our only serious divergence of view.

Our Chairman must have made provision for a new Chief Executive long before Harry Sturgeon died, for only a few weeks after I enquired about Harry's progress, **220** and was told that he was getting along well and was likely to be active fairly soon,

A pit scene during the Big Bear Run in California.

I was informed that our new Managing Director, Mr. Jofeh would be joining us. These tactics seemed very strange, but at least I was the first to be given the news which so disgusted me that I resigned on the spot. Although I had no illusions, I did not relish the thought of a further session in a deputy capacity and if, in the view of our Chairman, I did not measure up to the top job, I considered he must find some other person to replace me.

Our Chairman expected me to react in this way and refused to accept my resignation. He gave me the remarkable news that I was certainly the most important executive in the Division and it was essential that our incoming Managing Director be certain of my full support and guidance. I was far from being flattered; rather I was tired and fed up and longed to disassociate myself for I was now anxious to sell my home in the Midlands and enjoy early retirement on the South Coast before my seniors in business finally reduced me to a dithering idiot. However, as there were still several years of my contract to run, my lawyer advised me not to break the agreement.

221

Chapter Eight

I think there was little likelihood of any action being taken if I had walked out, and perhaps I should have done just that but, on reflection, I have to admit that I never aspired or at any time expected to attain the dizzy heights of the Parent Board. My real ambition on re-joining the BSA complex was to succeed to the executive chair at Triumph Engineering, a job which had now been scrubbed from the management chart.

During a further meeting with the Chairman, I remember that I was so disparaging about our business ability that I was surprised he did not react more strenuously. As always, he was gentlemanly and polite and this is the finest antidote for what must have been a degree of rudeness.

I told him that I hoped that his new Chief Executive would prove to be the long awaited answer to the maiden's prayer, for if I were incapable of making a better show in the world of business than one or two important executives whom I had recently propped up, I would be quite prepared to be publicly sacked, as a spectacle, from the platform of a meeting called for that purpose. If terms of reference, such as this, were written into service contracts it would have the effect of shortening the short list and almost certainly guide the Board in making the right choice.

I am afraid that my comments would have had just as much effect if I had been speaking in Swahili. It really was not worth further discussion; Mr. Jofeh was already installed and after all, I had no means of knowing whether he was or was not the business wizard we had all been led to believe.

Chapter Nine
Management dons its learner plates

FROM MY first meeting with our new Managing Director I had some doubts as to our prospects. He made it no secret that he knew all the answers and seemed to be word perfect on our problems and strategy at a very early stage in his adventures in a strange and complicated industry. It struck me as being a bad sign for although, of course, we needed confident leadership, his rather devastating statements regarding the activities of his predecessors, however just, were made somewhat early. I felt it would have been more constructive to make visible progress before being too verbal and I am afraid that I was to draw his attention to this before very long.

On the advice of our late Managing Director, the Chairman had been searching for a building which would be suitable for a new Group Engineering Centre, which hopefully would house the design, development and research facilities for the Division. Quite out of the blue I was asked by Mr. Jofeh to accompany him on a visit to Umberslade Hall, an old country mansion located near Hockley Heath. It was vacant and on offer and was apparently being considered by our Board for this purpose.

The rambling old building was not exactly ideal for the purpose of housing an Engineering Centre but certainly designers could be transferred without too much difficulty, although the multitude of small offices, many with unsuitable natural light, would be far from ideal.

A research and development facility was quite another matter but I understood that a 'fair sum of money could be spent' (in answer to my question 'how much', the answer was 'enough'). My first impression was that although far from ideal, the place was just a possibility with one thing in its favour; it was equidistant from each of our plants at Meriden, Small Heath and Redditch.

Chapter Nine

As always, I talked over the new project with my close colleague, Charles Parker, who felt that he would like to take a look for himself. I telephoned the Estate Agent asking if we could be permitted to do this and I was told that the place was ours. Our Chairman had already made a decision and agreed to take a lease. I suppose that this was fair enough, though rather sudden. Had I been in his position, I would have needed much more time to consider the proposition and some advice, at least, from the engineering executive whose responsibility it would be to set up and run the place, before closing the deal.

We had been searching for some time for a Deputy Engineering Director who would support me and hopefully take over on my retirement, due in 1973, as our directors had, regretfully, taken the view that there was no one within the organisation of this calibre. How they came to this conclusion I cannot say, but it was obvious that someone from another industry would be recruited. I had been anxious that Doug Hele should be given the opportunity, but Sturgeon and others would have none of it. There was no doubt at all in my mind that he had all the ability and needed only the opportunity to absorb more organisation and management knowledge than hitherto.

Hele had the right engineering and academic background and although he seemed always to shy from the prospect of a top administrative position, it would not be until he was promoted as my deputy that he could demonstrate his full ability and latent talents. While working together at Norton Motors I had been convinced that he was endowed with no mean organizing ability but, as all who have met him would

Umberslade Hall, the BSA Group Engineering Centre of the late 1960s and early 1970s.

know, his first love was a complete involvement in the design and development arena and his complete dedication in this direction seemed to convince our various Chief Executives that he would never master the art of delegation. They were quite wrong since he had done a first class job at Triumph in the reorganisation of his department, had been a prime mover in most of our successes and, more important, was steeped in the industry. It was logical that he should have been promoted, rather than have us face the uncertainty of taking on a newcomer from a strange industry. However our new Managing Director would have none of it and in January, 1968, Mike Nedham came to us from the aircraft industry as Deputy Engineering Director. His first assignment was the formation of our new Engineering Centre at Umberslade Hall.

The design staffs were transferred very quickly from our three separate plants for very little needed to be modified to enable them to start working in their new surroundings immediately. The research and development activity, however, needed substantial rebuilding before the new centre could become completely operational and it was not until late 1968 that all the wheels were turning. At this stage there were the beginnings of such violent differences of opinion between the Managing Director and myself that I found it most difficult to continue. Since I was continually by-passed with direct instructions being given to my assistants, I washed my hands of all Umberslade matters and was soon to do the same with the rest of my management activities.

High level jobs with huge salaries and works cars provided were being created at an alarming rate and the management charts were becoming huge clusters, far out-stripping the McKinsey structures. Meanwhile, our new-found aeronautical philosophy developed from strength to strength and it seemed to many of us that the company was powerless in a desperate situation which was moving rapidly beyond the point of no return.

The high rate of job creation generated meetings and discussion groups which grew larger and more numerous until at length the great BSA showroom at the end of Armoury Road, with its vast acreage and its outsize table, was the only place capable of housing these conferences. Each new meeting brought fresh faces and job titles, which were new to our industry but no doubt commonplace in the aircraft world, until each little window on the Managing Director's management chart was filled. From comments between comments amongst our new-found strength I found myself to be almost convinced that 'the motorcycle industry is great fun'.

We were reorganized, co-ordinated, charted and paperised to such a degree that our offices simply were not big enough. They became receptacles for paperwork on such a scale that the reading of it was quite out of the question and the normal filing cabinets were of little or no use. We had a computerised recording system in our Spares Department which ejected miles of paper and was so unreliable as to be useless, such that our dealers gave us up as a bad job and the pirate spare parts **225** business, a lucrative pastime, grew steadily. This happened in spite of being advised by McKinseys not to computerise until such time as our organisation was of the standard demanded to make such a device really meaningful.

Our new-found teams of critical path analysts and product planners were, of course, without any new products or any likelihood of critical paths for us in the near future for, as always, there was no long term strategy. As was confirmed later, we seemed set fast in our bad old ways of yearly cosmetic changes to our products, with the odd frantic crash programme as and when we had news of some new goody about to be marketed by our competitors.

Many of our up-and-coming youngsters were disgusted, for most were passed over when promotion was possible. One can only surmise the feelings of some of our bright ex-apprentices, just out of their indentures. Only a short time previously I had deputised for Mr. Sturgeon at the Annual Apprentices Dinner, where I took the chair. An excerpt from my speech ran as follows: 'The Division is now providing opportunities as never before. Markets and turnover are growing and so is the need for skilled men. When it comes to recruiting men for important jobs we prefer the home-grown brand. It is up to you to make it impossible for us to be unaware of your abilities.'

We had a very fine team of engineering personnel at Small Heath, Meriden and Redditch and I would say with confidence that here was the best collection of talents with which I had ever been associated. It is unforgivable that these men, many of whom had left positive marks in a successful industry, should now find themselves with bosses who knew nothing about motorcycles, but, worse than this and almost without exception, were regarding their new found way of life as some sort of academic mission into the primitive backwoods of two-wheel philosophy.

My opposition to the strategy of our new Managing Director was voiced on every conceivable occasion and at one of the farcical Board Meetings when I ventured to make a point of commercial common sense, I was sharply called to order by our Chairman who told me that he regarded me purely as a 'work provider'. I feel fairly certain that this was not meant to be a compliment, but I may be wrong for I sometimes had language difficulties in this part of the world. Nonetheless I felt somewhat flattered and I suggested that the shop floor and the shareholders would classify everyone round the Board table, including the Chairman, in this manner.

At about this stage I was drawn into an interesting development which indicated that I was by no means the sole critic of our new executive. During a meeting of my management colleagues, at which I took the Chair, any other business resolved itself into a downright sweeping condemnation of our top management. The comments were so bitter and unanimous that I was most surprised. To me this was a new situation for as yet I had made no comment and here we were with every local director feeling very strongly that we were going downhill with the clutch out.

I asked the meeting whether it was felt that we should take the matter further and to my surprise the answer was in the affirmative. I warned them that, in my opinion, each and every one of us should be prepared to resign if the en masse protest brought forth no meaningful results. I was quite willing to write the appropriate letter and to have my signature head the list, but all but one backed down.

If, as a result of such protest, the six top management executives had walked out, I do not think that BSA would have gone broke but I do believe that such goings on would have generated some discussion at Parent Board level as well as through the media. It is conceivable that as a result the final shakedown may have come somewhat sooner and Lord Shawcross would have 'inherited' something much less than the £10m overdraft with which we finally had to cope.

Our accountant intensive Board, egged on by our new Managing Director, seemed to have the impression that our technical half-wits were short of work and to fill in the long day, were amusing themselves by making alterations to components in production. This, they had discovered, was making our machines unnecessarily expensive and uncompetitive. I find it difficult to believe that even they were serious in suggesting that this part of normal activity was in any way connected with the declining image of the British motorcycle industry.

It is true that in every manufacturing activity alterations to parts are sometimes made but, once a product is successfully in production, whether it be a motor car or refrigerator or even a motorcycle, the designer is so thankful that the worrying stage of development to reliability is over, he does not relish further activity in what amounts to going over the same ground.

Of course, components must sometimes be modified to obviate problems which occur in even the best of organisations, although changes after production release are kept to an absolute minimum for obvious reasons. No one knows better than the Engineering Director whether it is necessary or wise to make a change.

Before our management explosion, we were operating a simple modification system, flexible enough to get rapid changes made once a decision had been made that these were essential. The whole production unit was then alerted immediately, to obviate over-stocking of parts being considered for modification. We were never seriously at risk either from delays to the production line or from significantly high obsolescence factors. It was part of our working day, albeit a very small part, and surprise! surprise! the Engineering Director was, at all times fully informed of the financial significance of these activities.

Our invasion by accountancy, however, had created large teams of product planners and evaluators and we had been 'sold' value engineering, a new catchphrase for good design with correct time factors. We were using this like a new toy, with a further team of experts. We had also recruited a goodly team of market researchers, had a substantial marketing team (we had long ago scrubbed the good old word 'selling' from our dictionary) and were once more being advised by management consultants.

227

Chapter Nine

We seemed to be suffering from a bad attack of management indigestion for the engineering modification system broke down completely and ceased to function. It now comprised a committee of twenty people, most of whom were out of touch, so this proved to be one way of stopping the silly games which design engineers get up to in their spare time. However, from this inactivity came chaos, for very urgent work was lost in the system and our products and reputation were beginning to deteriorate at a somewhat more rapid pace.

The product planners and evaluators had, as yet, little to plan for or to evaluate but the 750 cc Triumph triple prototype, which, by now, was being minced about by huge committees, becoming a target for testing their skills. Before long the machine was being subjected to re-design by committee, which is the surest way of creating a piebald hybrid.

Both Doug Hele and I were always certain that the original triple would have sold well, for it was light in weight and a good performer in the Triumph tradition. It would have provided our dealers with a new and smooth superbike and given us good business for five years, by which time we had in mind the new generation plans. But with so many people collecting opinions and making decisions who were completely ignorant of our market, the styling of the motorcycle was so transformed that, to me, it looked a strange mixture. I was beginning to feel that perhaps this recently discovered new market place country was somewhere I ought to visit, although deep down I knew that the market place was just outside my window. If we

The BSA/Triumph three cylinder machine after the original design had been minced about by committees and passed through the hands of consultant stylists. An artist's impression of finalised styling.

The first production version of the BSA triple launched in late 1968.

made a motorcycle which pleased British riders, we were well on the way to pleasing the rest of the world.

The triple machine which found its way to the market in 1968 was a flop and it was not until we reverted to the original prototype style that it started to sell and earn revenue. It could and should have been in production in 1963, thus five years of production were lost, the Japanese became more firmly entrenched and our reputation suffered yet another severe setback.

The first production version of the Triumph Trident launched in late 1968.

Chapter Nine

The truth is that there was nothing wrong with the market assessments which my associates and I had made in the past. All that was needed was a board capable of absorbing the common sense of the proposals and then stepping aside and allowing us to get on with it.

To add to our bewilderment, our costly Market Research Department had forecast a recession in the American motorcycle scene but in a very short time the reverse had happened and demand, particularly for large machines, had doubled almost overnight.

Edward Turner, long since retired, had not been idle and had designed a 350 cc twin cylinder machine with the help of several of our designers who had been loaned to him. As a result, the Board felt that prototypes should be made. I shall never understand the logic of this for we were well advanced with the 250 cc triple which Mr. Sturgeon had authorised and this engine could very easily have been upgraded in capacity, if necessary. All work on this project was stopped forthwith even though we were about to assemble the unit, for one of our top executives had just returned from a visit to the USA and had been told that we now needed a machine of 350 cc capacity. But this was typical of our decision making for we bobbed about like yo-yos. I have no doubt that if the latest suggestion had been a 750 cc single or a 1000 cc six, it would have been equally acceptable.

Edward Turner's design was powered by a double ohc engine and was

It was not until 1971, when the BSA and Triumph triples had been re-designed with more suitable styling, that these machines were accepted by the market. Here is a picture of the 1971 Triumph Trident, almost identical with the original prototype of 1964.

commendably light in weight. Unfortunately many engineering fundamentals had been ignored and, from the start, this motorcycle proved to be most unreliable. But our Managing Director had, for some unaccountable reason, given a preview of this machine, long before it was complete enough for test, to a number of our USA representatives. Not unnaturally they started to press hard, for a lightweight machine of 250 cc or 350 cc capacity would have been more than welcome amongst dealers, who had nothing to offer in this popular size of motorcycle.

I was surprised to be asked by our Managing Director to undertake responsibility for the design work necessary to (as he put it) 'get satisfactory equipment into production at the earliest possible date'. This I refused for, by now, Umberslade was operative and our design and development personnel and resources were scattered in a bureaucracy which was quite unmanageable. Indeed, our skilled designers were lost in a tangle of academic complexity which, I told him, was beyond my power to disentangle.

I did not want the job but there were a few other reasons why I took this attitude and I quote from my letter to Mr. Jofeh written in October 1968.

'You will remember that, when I saw you, I went through, in some detail, the reasons why I refuse to have anything to do with Edward Turner's 350 cc twin cylinder design and I suggested to you that some other person must be made responsible. To refresh your memory, there is so much fundamentally wrong with the design that, if this were corrected, there would be little of the original layout surviving. I told you that no one in his right senses would touch this with a barge pole because, from considerable past experience, I know that he would be accused of causing delays and unnecessarily altering a perfectly sound design.'

However, I was prevailed upon by our Chairman to organise the work and I agreed, with the proviso that in future, Edward Turner should use his own private resources to carry out his design work as by now, he was not part of the company and was negotiating royalty payments for this machine. This was agreed and to confirm, I wrote the Chairman as follows:

I told you that I could not organise the redesign work if we continued to loan to Edward Turner certain of our designers, in this precise manner, and that, in future, his initial designs should be carried out by way of his own resources. They should be dealt with by us in the normal manner, by giving our legitimate engineering staff the opportunity to study such designs at an appropriately early stage and to pass comment and to advise as to whether such designs were meritorious enough to proceed with.'

I disliked the idea of loaning to Turner a staff of design personnel who were located elsewhere and I felt that Mike Nedham, who already had his hands full, could not cope with a separate design group over which he would have no effective control.

Immediately I agreed responsibility for development to the production stage of *231* the new project I became the subject of a disgraceful attack by Edward Turner, who seemed to feel that I had an axe to grind. He wrote to Mr. Jofeh, exactly as I had predicted, suggesting that there could be wilful distortion and that *'Hopwood would delay production for one or two years if I know my man.'*

I was very angry indeed, but more than this, bitterly disappointed that a man of Edward Turner's calibre, whom I had known and worked with for so long, should so reduce himself. I was getting desperately tired of all the ploy and personal politics and purely because Turner's rather damaging letter had been circulated to all and sundry I felt that my point of view should be on file. I wrote the Chairman and Mr. Jofeh, as follows:

'Edward Turner seems to feel that I have an axe to grind but sadly this indicates how little he has learned of me during an association which covers 35 or so years.

For the record it would be true to say that I have been intimately connected from the design stages of most of his successful products but I cannot say this of the unsuccessful ones such as the Tina scooter, the Tigress scooter, the Pixie, the Beagle, the 200 cc ohc Triumph twin and several others which emanated from him and which did not stand the test of time.

As my record is under attack I suggest that we bear in mind that some of the most successful and trouble free BSA machines of the 1950s were master-minded by me and that these made good profits. Also the engine/gear unit of the latest project from our British competitors (the Norton engine) was designed originally by me in 1947.'

A week or so later, when we had a little more time to collect a few more facts, I felt that the whole Board should have a report on exact findings to date for the situation must have seemed somewhat confusing to such people. In late October 1968 I circulated the following letter.

'Our practical experience with the new 350 cc machine bears out the previous report made when I was asked to comment on the design. The engine on bench test has run an equivalent of 1500 road miles, none of these at more than the equivalent of 60 mph and there have been two broken crankshafts and one valve gear drive failure. In other words three very major failures or one every 500 miles.

The complete motorcycle which we have on test now has 5,400 miles registered and in this mileage, 3000 have been completed by a tester who rode most of the time at very low speeds because of severe problems. The machine is using four pints of oil every 100 miles and the tests are worthless because of lack of power. The other 2,400 miles by various riders embraced four complete rebuilds of the engine unit due to the failure of parts such as crankshafts, gudgeon pins and main bearings. The frame of the machine has already been re-designed due to excess flexibility in the main, which constituted a hazard, and the front forks also are considered to be fundamentally unsafe and are at the moment engaging our attention.'

It was necessary to make the matter very clear particularly to the non-engineers of our top management. I had the feeling also that sooner or later the project, once we had got some sense into the operation, would be minced up by committees, which made it doubly important to get some fundamentals straightened out before this happened.

The terms of reference for the engineering part of the operation were that no part of the original design should be modified unless it was essential to do so and this we honestly did our best to achieve, for I was anxious to be rid of it and wash my hands of the whole distasteful affair.

Unfortunately, the heart of the engine, the crankshaft, was hopelessly skimped. Not only was it breaking with monotonous regularity, the flywheel was so small in diameter, and so lacking in effective rotating mass, that it had little or no effect on the cyclic speed variation of the engine. To make matters worse, the inside of the crankcase was so close to the rotating parts that engine oil had no free passage of return to the sump, a serious problem. This meant that crankshaft re-design with a larger flywheel, plus adequate clearance in a larger crankcase, was beginning to spell out changes so drastic as to call for something like a fresh start.

The gear drive to the double ohc operation had proved unreliable and noisy and we had complete agreement on the substitution of a chain drive. This, of course,

The original prototype of the 350 cc twin cylinder machine, designed by Edward Turner in his retirement during the late 1960s. A good looker but extremely badly engineered and very unreliable.

The 350 cc Triumph Bandit due for production in 1971. This motorcycle had an ohc power unit and a five-speed gearbox and electric starter.

necessitated further major changes and consequently the re-designed engine/gear unit seemed to have little in common with the Mark One effort. Items such as valve angles were unmodified, as firmly requested, although I personally would have made these much steeper and thereby have improved the thermal efficiency of the engine.

The frame and front forks had to be re-designed for safety's sake and the machine developed to a high degree of reliability. Although I felt that the styling left much to be desired, it seemed to be regarded as an acceptably competitive motorcycle with an up to date specification and was planned to be launched jointly by BSA and Triumph, in slightly differing versions, as the Fury and Bandit respectively.

It was high time that we concentrated some of our attention towards the smaller engine capacity section of the market and, although the design had been inhibited by the foolish terms of reference, this motorcycle could have been a start in this direction. It was deplorable that the BSA Bantam was allowed to languish and die for, just before Harry Sturgeon passed away, we had given this machine a re-design, more in the nature of a facelift but with the important change of pumped and metered engine lubrication very similar to the Suzuki Autolube system. Engine power had been increased by something like 20% and on the whole the machine, in its new guise, looked more 'with it' and attractive. It would, we felt, have some possibilities in the US market which had hitherto registered no interest, for there the petroil lubrication system had been unacceptable.

We were ready to go ahead, for very little extra tooling had been necessary, but our new management suddenly decided to call it off. I shall never understand why, **234** for the increase in total cost of £3 did not, to me, sound a valid reason for

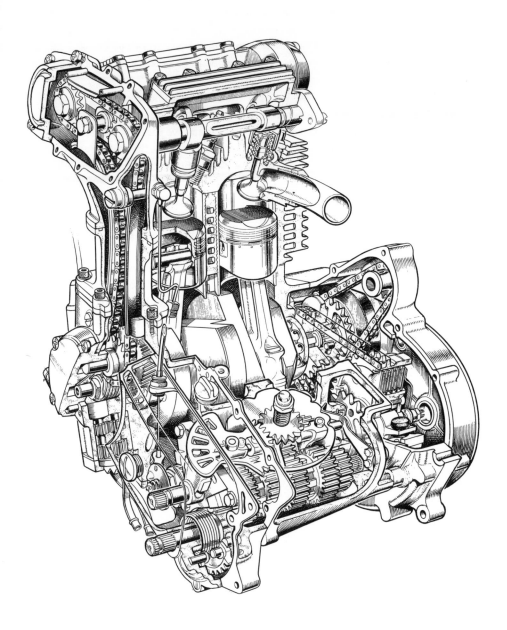

Detail of the 350 cc ohc engine of the Triumph Bandit and BSA Fury models which were planned to be produced during 1971.

abandoning this project. The Bantam was a famous link with the learner rider and it seemed to be a great mistake to cease its manufacture. We should have persevered in the manner that Sturgeon had planned and I am quite sure that the results would have been very rewarding.

In the meantime the Umberslade complex was working on a face lift programme for the rest of our products and seemed to be making very heavy weather of what should have been a straightforward exercise.

I thought then, as I do now, that our time would be better spent in creating a family of new generation products for, by and large, the appearance of our machines was not inhibiting our likely market share. Once again, we seemed to be shirking our responsibilities in ignoring the urgent need to arm our dealers through the world with real power to fight back. There seemed to be little point in making massive changes if these did not do something to improve the image of British machines or reduce the cost or, preferably, a little of both. Where was the business sense in authorising expensive tooling for cosmetic changes, which left the product with the same old clatter, the same old massive oil leaks and the same old range of technically outdated motorcycles?

The changes envisaged for our current range of machines were mainly to the frame and forks and were intended for the 1971 model year. They embraced a degree of rationalisation between the BSA and Triumph models and although this of itself was worthwhile, I felt that it was quite unjustified to develop a completely new frame for this purpose. It would have been far better to have standardised the Triumph

The BSA 650 cc twin cylinder model of the early 1970s. This picture gives an indication of the enormous seat height.

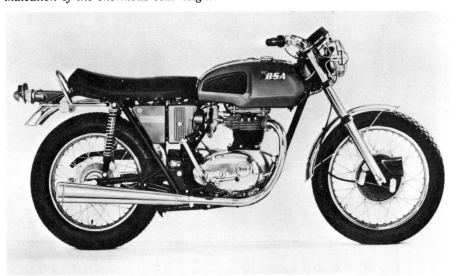

frame on the two makes, so that tooling costs and delays would be minimal, but our new management seemed determined to have a brand new frame with a very large diameter spine in which the engine oil was carried. Although Doug Hele and I exhausted our powers of persuasion, it seemed that the novelty of oil in the frame tube was too good to miss.

I believe that the average motorcyclist doesn't give a hoot where the engine oil is located and I think that it was most foolish to embark on such a massive change for so little return. By the time Umberslade had developed this frame to a state fit for production release, the company found itself hopelessly bogged down with delivery dates almost a year late and as a result suffered huge losses of revenue.

It is remarkable that with the frame change came an increase in saddle height of something like 3 inches, which had the effect of making our new models only suitable for those giants who, from astride the machine, could just reach the ground with their two feet. This, of course, created near havoc with our market acceptability.

The new establishment at Umberslade honestly felt that theirs was the healing breath of fresh air for a sickening industry and no opportunity was lost in making it clear that long experience in our game was a disadvantage for it prevented us seeing the wood for the trees. I suppose the current record of our achievement in the total world market could excuse them for taking this point of view, but their goings on can only be described as the blind leading the blind. By now, our design work in particular was being done at a very low level.

Our American operation, the most important subsidiary of the BSA Group, was by now fully exposed to the wisdom of our home management, who lacked the confidence of the dealer organisation and were totally ignorant of the type of market strategy needed. Yet it had become almost a sixth sense to people like Denis McCormack, who had set up Triumph Baltimore almost two decades ago and was President of the eastern sector of Triumph USA until his retirement. Denis and I are personal friends and there had never been the slightest doubt that his knowledge of product requirements and his almost intuitive feel of the market had been a keystone of Triumph achievements in the USA.

Such men do not grow on trees but there were several other very capable members of the US management team whose experience and expertise had been major factors in our success. They should have been considered for the empty management chair but, once again, our Board ignored completely this wealth of latent talent. Instead, they appointed a powerful sounding stranger to the newly created job of President, BSA Inc. USA, an all embracing new company with its headquarters in Verona, New Jersey.

Lavish expenditure and plush headquarters did nothing to stem a serious deterioration of morale which now permeated our US organisation. Our new President's first manifesto to his dealers made mention of 'a complete and sweeping realignment of our operation and executive responsibilities and the building of greater **237**

The ill-fated Ariel 3 launched in July 1970.

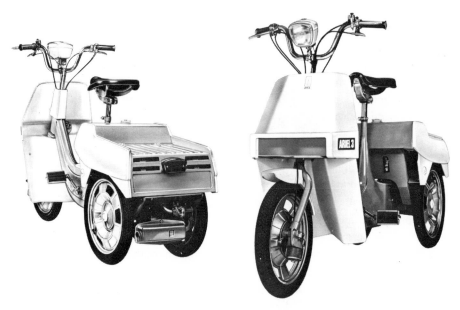

and greater consumer demand, meaning more profit and a series of dramatic changes designed to capture for us all a greater share of the growing motorcycle market to meet the challenge of the 1970s.'

It seemed to me that this sort of talk was a bit childish and simply was not on with dealers who were struggling desperately and loyally with brands which were outdated and had growing quality problems. I know that they would have been more encouraged if some mention had been made of realistic moves to counter these problems rather than babbling about great new worlds which are waiting just round the corner for us to conquer. Of course, a man with knowledge of our market would have known that the dish of goodies which we were about to release as our 1971 range of products would not allow us to survive, let alone 'make more profit from a greater share of the market challenge of the 1970s.'

Early in 1969 our Board was offered the option on manufacturing rights for a small tricycle powered by a 50 cc engine with pedal assisting gear, having a pivoted frame which enabled the front wheel to tilt in the appropriate sideways direction when cornering. This unusual moped was designed to have so small a lateral span for its rear wheels that it came within the legal requirements to be licensed as a single track motorcycle. It was a project that might have enjoyed a better market reception if our stylists had left well alone and developed the simple design which had been offered to us.

The peculiar styling of the production version seemed to provoke feelings of distrust rather than safety and there is no doubt that an adult tended to look a little strange when riding one of these machines. This unusual moped did not have the riding stability that was expected of it, due to a fundamental fault in basic geometry, which was pointed out by Donald Bastow, our retained consultant. His advice was ignored yet although we could have made the handling characteristics infinitely better, I am sure that this would not have affected the final outcome.

When launched in July 1970 as the Ariel three-wheeler, the new moped was fitted with a two-stroke engine of Dutch origin, but the price was high in comparison with most conventional machines. Contrary to the forecasting of a powerful market research programme which had predicted a brilliant future, sales were a mere trickle and eventually petered out. It seemed that none but the brave were ready or willing to create a new fashion on wheels.

By late 1969 our Chief Executive himself must have started to worry about the efficiency of our new engineering set up, for as time went on we were becoming more bogged down with paperwork and conferences. Although we now boasted a design engineering staff of over 300, the product planning and product reliability situation worsened daily.

My office was at the Meriden Works and by arrangement, the Umberslade organisation had been the responsibility of our Deputy Engineering Director working in close harmony with the Managing Director himself. So I was a little surprised to *239* have our Managing Director call me to his office and ask me to help 'straighten out the situation' and for this purpose to 'install' myself at Umberslade and come back to him with my recommendations. I must admit that I did not relish the prospect for, as my retirement date drew nearer, I was beginning of late, to feel thankful that soon I would be clear of the once great company which was now reduced to a management mess. But I could not bring myself to refuse this request and I duly installed myself at Umberslade for a week or two. In November 1969 I was able to give our Managing Director the following report:

'I am most concerned by very real problems at Umberslade and I feel that a drastic re-assessment of personnel together with a considerably modified organisation plan is necessary forthwith if we are to achieve our engineering plans for the future.

With more than 300 people working on engineering design and development we should be able to cope, but this is not so and the reason is a fundamental one of poor organisation and poor choice of manpower. Unless we are able to implement important changes, which I shall outline later in this report, our 1971 model year will be a disaster. Agreement between us on my suggestions is necessary as quickly as possible.

We must obviate the fragmentation and inefficiency of our operation and we must generate a correctly master-minded activity and above all we must obviate creative design being carried out at the low levels of experience and expertise now being permitted. We should re-organise our design groups into teams, each one of which should nurse the product through to the production stage.

The development side should concentrate on first things first (we were currently doing the reverse) and must be properly master-minded with each team of men autonomous, to enable the technical thinking to be correctly balanced and to shorten time factors in the release of final drawings.

We are fortunate enough to have a number of very experienced design engineers who are steeped in the motorcycle industry and these specialised men must be put in charge of teams for the purpose of bringing our design resources back to the standard required and also to give our newcomers adequate training.

Most of our recent senior appointments have weakened us, mainly because of unsuitability, and this reflects in feelings of frustration and disillusionment and the over working of our experienced personnel.

The intake of new staff at lower levels is badly organised and this reflects itself in a situation which is bringing about a 'floating population' with the result that we can look forward to be dealing with the 'dross' of the industry from which we are likely to draw our replacements.

I had hoped that the Umberslade project would provide us with a means of bringing intensive forward engineering to our product lines and no longer would the company find itself mass producing inadequately engineered products, but we find ourselves now entering the 1971 product year with the likelihood of more inadequate design and development than ever before. Never have I personally experienced such a mass production release of parts for new models, many of which have not been given even an assembly check, let alone any sort of test.

The situation cannot be corrected while the present type of organisation persists. An immediate re-assessment of middle management is needed, as a first essential, to put into use the skills and long experience of our top engineers each of whom should head a small team and be allowed to manage as managers and be responsible to the appropriate director.'

My report then went into great detail but the text of this would make boring reading. In short I pressed for a much more streamlined design operation and stressed the need to bring our top designers back into orbit. Most of them were now taking instructions from amateurs and the rest seemed to have developed into progress chasers, whereas the need was to have them back at the drawing board.

We had created a Department of Technical Services which, to me, appeared to be a free ranging discussion group which seemed to be enjoying itself immensely but was producing no results. Worse than that, they were wasting much effort by occupying the time of many other busy people.

In the same way, on the development side, I stressed the need to re-orientate forthwith and to have our top technicians heading teams and specializing on projects right through the development process to production release. The reverse of this was now happening and the amateurish management of each development effort and the mixed pottage of so-called planning seemed to be getting us nowhere very fast.

The average reader will, perhaps, think it strange that I should spend my time stressing management matters which were so elementary, but one needed close association with our Umberslade operation to realise that we were not just in the clouds but on the moon. My recipe for good health was back to the simple life, or else!

We had a three cornered meeting consisting of the Managing Director, myself and our Deputy Engineering Director for the purpose of discussing my report and I was quite surprised that Mr. Jofeh seemed, in the main, to agree with my recommendations. However, the minutes of this meeting proved ambiguous with much of the content not agreed by me. Worse than this, it seemed to be just another sheet of paper with no directive for any action other than a journey to the filing cabinet. This was enough for me and I felt that it was time that our Managing Director and I parted company. I wrote to him on 30th January 1970, as follows.

'Your notes dated 21st January indicate to me that my recommendations are not understood and have been something of a waste of time. A group of   **241**

Chapter Nine

As out products deteriorated, our advertising took on a new sophistication.

headings of this type will in no way help the problem which, as I have pointed out, is mainly that of applied management.

This matter culminates a series of similar situations and makes me certain that there is little point in further prolonging our business association. I am now seeking a meeting with the Chairman so that he may put this into effect.'

I felt relieved, beyond measure, to be disassociating myself from a management sham which was now in top gear but our Chairman seemed anxious to bridge the rift and asked me to sleep on it and come back for a discussion in a week or so.

I was no longer concerned about the huge bureaucratic management structure which now operated throughout the company for I had, long ago, adopted an attitude which made it just possible for me to be a small part of it and still preserve my sanity. But the sheer incompetence of decision making, in my sphere, was something that I did not intend to support for a moment longer. I was quite certain that our 1971 financial year would be a disaster as I had already indicated to the Board, and I now told the Chairman that I did not intend to help our Managing Director bring this about.

Hindsight, of course, now makes this all so clear but our Chairman and our Managing Director should have known, in spite of their lack of motorcycle knowledge, that it simply was not on to keep 'tarting' up the same old noisy, dirty and expensive motorcycles. The public were waiting, vainly it seemed, for us to live up to some of our recent bold statements and to demonstrate to a motorcycle hungry market that BSA and British was worth the wait.

Even now I have great difficulty in believing that after nearly three years of operation, our Engineering Department at Umberslade with its staff of 300 were unable to generate more than such a pitiful programme. My feelings are that it was this particular section of the Jofeh administration that finally broke the company; poor management can often just scrape through with good products but with nondescript marketing material, the finest of organisations will go bust.

In a last ditch attempt at further compromise, the Chairman seemed to favour, at first, my suggestion that we form a separate company for the sole purpose of long term product design and development, with myself as its Managing Director. The idea was that such a company would undertake the design and development of forward models and would be responsible through to the prototype stage, at which point, Umberslade would take over. Eric Turner was, however, persuaded that everything in the garden was lovely and the idea was dropped.

I relinquished my executive position, such as it now was, but remained on the Divisional Board in a non-executive capacity and agreed to be available on a part time basis for consultancy if need be, with the proviso that I should 'assist the racing activity'.

It was important that we put up a good show on the race tracks of the USA if we were to hold our tiny percentage of the market and the Daytona 200 mile **243** classic, in early spring each year, was the most publicised of a string of national events over there. For the 1970 race our management did not authorise the necessary work until November 1969, which left just 3 months to design, manufacture, develop and ship the racing motorcycles to the USA. It is not surprising that we did not pull off the Daytona event although Mike Hailwood on a BSA led the race for a time and Gene Romero on a Triumph finished in second place. By the end of the 1970 season we not only won the American Racing Championship but riders of our machines took the first 5 places in this series.

The brilliance of Doug Hele, who was firmly in charge of the racing activity, was already being reflected in the successes of Triumph machines in production type racing at home and abroad and now our Board had, at the last minute, decided that we must make our mark in the US classics. In the three short months available, a new version of the triple had been designed and developed and was soon to make its mark by winning almost every race in which it competed and breaking many world records.

The racing triple had a new frame for reasons of ideal geometry, weight saving and rigidity and mainly because of the acute time factor, we enlisted outside help from Rob North, a man who made a small living by building special racing frames. He came up with a structure that proved to be satisfactory right from scratch. The engine was not very different from standard but had changes to the crankshaft, pistons, carburettors and had a capacitor ignition system. It had a power output of 84 bhp at 8,250 rpm.

These new Daytona type machines were handsome motorcycles, handled very well indeed and were much lighter than the production type Triumph and BSA

The Triumph three cylinder racing machine which was used during the 1971 season. In this picture the race fairing has been removed.

triples. Since the main change was the frame, which was much cheaper to produce than its production counterpart, it seemed to us that this type of motorcycle would be much more acceptable to the market than our current product with its rather outdated styling.

I knew that we were on the verge of a breakthrough with the racing machine and I wrote to the Chairman in March 1970, as follows, urging him to give instructions to productionise the Daytona triples.

The Triumph racing three cylinder machine for the 1971 season shown here in full race trim. It had a three-into-one exhaust system.

'It would be a comparatively simple job to productionise the Daytona triple to enable Triumph and BSA machines to use a common engine (the BSA engine had slight exterior differences) much more acceptable in appearance than our catalogue models and with a great family resemblance to the racers, which are very handsome motorcycles.

We should then have a 3-cylinder motor cycle in mass production which would, at once, be suitable for production racing throughout the world and, **245** *more important would achieve substantial savings in weight and cost of our present mass produced product.*

One would think that such a machine would be in great demand and would enable us to increase our present production figures in a lucrative section of the market.'

I did not receive a reply and maybe neither he nor Mr. Jofeh grasped the significance of such a suggestion. Had we have done just this, there is no doubt that we would have sold every machine that we could have made. During the 1970 season, riders of these racing motorcycles had carried off the coveted American Racing Championship, but in 1971 we swept the board in this type of racing throughout the world.

All of the technical and engineering work to create six racing machines, which were to prove so successful, was carried out by a handful of engineers under the leadership of Doug Hele, in three months. This gives at least some indication of the insignificance of time and cost factors, had we taken this grand opportunity and phased out the current triples at the 1970 Motor Cycle Show.

I regard the indifference of our management, on this occasion, as a major disaster for BSA as tooling expenditure would have been peanuts and all development costs had already been met via the international race circuits. High volume sales of a trouble-free machine would have resulted, these in the most lucrative section of the market, for it was during this period (1970 – 1971) that our fortunes were in dire need of a straightforward boost such as this. We felt that it was fortunate (although in the event it proved to be unimportant) that the engineering side of our race department was left severely alone and unbedevilled by the top crust of our hierarchy although they were, at all times, kept full informed. It was they who rubber stamped the strategy en route to the outside world and one of my last memos to our new Engineering Director read as follows:

'I would strongly urge you to give consideration to the following suggestions and, if you agree and decide to re-organise in this manner, that you make this strategy fully understood both here and in the USA.

A. The 8 American riders shall be the sole responsibility of Pete Colman (our US Technical Director) and that they shall be instructed to use machines of proven reliability, ie. the 1970 type with such minor improvements which are known to exist and which certainly will not jeopardise chances of success through lack of development.

B. A small development team under your jurisdiction and headed by Mr. Hele, with 2 riders (probably Percy Tait and Paul Smart), 2 mechanics and 1 aero-dynamicist, be allowed to participate at Daytona 1971. The 2 machines to be used on this exercise would be, what is known as our 1971 type, which are fully experimental.

By clearly separating the 2 operations the strategy becomes very sound for these reasons:-

(1) Colman would be clear of any responsibility for engineering development work because the machines in his charge would be known and reliable.

(2) A continous development programme under your jurisdiction and headed by Mr. Hele, would be running parallel. It is impossible to develop the new features without race participation at all times and this would enable you to have a sensible forward strategy and also the ability, on occasions if need be, to have experimental machines in the first line of defence.

(3) This plan would generate much more harmony and would be a commercially sensible arrangement with Colman managing known riders and machines and Mr. Hele devoting his time to the forward element which is most difficult to achieve with our present mixture of activity.

(4) The new system would ensure that loss of championship points by riders due to experimentation would be obviated.'

Our advice was accepted and the brilliance of Doug Hele, as engineer and organizer together with some of the world's finest riders, enabled the company, sometimes labelled BSA and sometimes Triumph, to scoop almost every race in which these machines were entered.

I had been particularly anxious that we should be seen to be following a well defined path in our racing activity, mainly because of the silly problems and bitterness generated by the partisan attitude in the company which Harry Sturgeon had seemed determined to do something about. Although I was never optimistic that we could completely avoid this sort of thing in a group such as ours, he did, without doubt, bring about some noticeable improvement. However, our present administration had, from the start, seemed determined to make Triumph the underdog rather than employing management skills to improve the efficiency of both companies. It was in this climate that the feuding politics of the BSA and Triumph activities returned to the surface.

A classic example of the attitude of our Managing Director on this particular issue is, perhaps, the punch line of his speech made to the senior staff of Triumph on the occasion of the annual Christmas lunch in 1970. He referred to the forthcoming racing season and made it very clear that if any person was found to be promoting or favouring, in any way, the Triumph brand of racing machinery, that person would immediately 'get his cards'.

This was, perhaps, a peculiar way of saying that the BSA and Triumph racing machinery must be equally well prepared, but on this convivial occasion, the spirit **247** of those sitting round the table was very much watered down. This was a poor way of spreading goodwill, much less a demonstration of inspired leadership.

In point of fact so identical in power output and everything else were these Triumph and BSA machines that the racing rider, with his special skills was, of course, the final arbiter of our success or failure. There were many simple ways of getting BSA riders over the finishing line in front of their Triumph counterparts and our management should have been masters of this simple situation without giving everyone indigestion for Christmas.

By mid-1970 it had been obvious that target production dates for the 1971 range of motorcycles could not be met and, at times, there was near panic on the engineering side. There was much table thumping by our Managing Director but this did not help such a situation.

Our Chairman had asked for the Board of Directors to be given a preview of the range of prototypes and these gentlemen sat in the showroom at Small Heath while Mike Nedham (very ably, I thought) talked through the technical points as each machine was wheeled forward. The Deputy Engineering Director was very much a Wankel enthusiast and, much to Nedham's dismay (I am surprised that they did not come to terms before such a meeting) took control for a few wild moments and explained to the Board why the Wankel device was so simple, so cheap to produce, so reliable, so quiet in operation and indeed why piston type engines were now completely outdated.

I shall never forget the reaction of Lord Shawcross, a comparatively new member of our Board, who appeared to be puzzled that our Umberslade team had laboured so hard and so long to dish up, once more, power units which they were now telling him were already outdated because they were piston operated. Not unnaturally his Lordship asked the 64 million dollar question and from the welter of replies which he received I was left with the suspicion that he was more puzzled than satisfied.

I had been invited to the meeting as an act of courtesy and when it was all over, I was asked by Jack Sangster, who was still a Board Member, what I thought of the projected 1971 model range. He added the comment 'I cannot think that these machines are going to be very successful'. I felt very cross with him, for rather than make such a comment to me, he should have expressed himself at the appropriate Board Meetings long ago while there was still time to do something about it. I could not help feeling that the sickness of our industry was not solely due to the antics of our new army of management.

We went into the 1971 selling year with our updated model range arriving on the showroom floors much too late to have the desired impact and the later part of the selling season found us with extremely high dealer and warehouse stocks. Added to this, our brand new 350 cc Bandit and Fury machines were still some distance from a realistic production release date. The end of summer, a year later, was now

The appallingly tall machines, produced by BSA and Triumphs during 1971, could have been reduced in seat height by at least two inches without any loss of stock, and the change could have been accomplished in two weeks without delaying production. The prototype, above, shows the changes made and compares with the production version below.

predicted and this lowered our credibility factor to near zero in the States. Publicity had been enormous and dealers were keyed up and waiting but their showrooms were empty at peak selling time and then full of our stuff when it was much too late.

To them it looked remarkably like the same old medicine. Our products proved much more difficult to sell because the seat was so lofty that none but long-legged giants could cope. To add to their misery, our quality control seemed to have taken a turn for the worst, resulting in huge rectification problems, aggravated by a severe lack of spare parts due to our system going haywire.

By May, 1971, a loss of £1m was being tipped in some financial circles and in June that year, Peter Thornton, the President of our US operation, resigned, having served less than two years in office.

During July, Mr. Jofeh, our Managing Director, agreed to resign his position. On July 30th the directors of BSA revealed that the company made losses of about £3m during the financial year and warned that the financial position could hardly be more serious.

Institutional shareholders were now very restive and our Board commissioned a well-known name of management consultants, to study and report on the situation. Their recommendation was that a new management structure was needed and, in particular, a new Managing Director of high calibre should be recruited to fill the vacancy in the Motorcycle Division. I have yet to hear the equal of these two platitudes:

The Motorcycle Division had planned a turnover of around £40m and had achieved only £26.7m. Our stocks had piled up to £15.6m from £9m a year previous so our liquidity was negative and something had to be done very quickly. It was now disclosed that Eric Turner, our Chairman, felt that it would help the creation of a new image if he resigned as soon as another could take his place and the Board invited Lord Shawcross to take the Chair, with the Bank expressing a strong wish that he should accept. Accordingly he agreed to take it on, but as he was already a very busy man and by no means young, he proposed to remain Chairman only until we were 'over the hump', as he put it, or a better man became available on a more permanent basis.

At an extraordinary shareholders meeting held on November 2nd, a financial reorganisation plan to keep BSA afloat received approval. The outgoing Chairman, Eric Turner, faced an hour of tough questioning from the 100 or so angry shareholders present.

In agreeing the financial reorganisation, shareholders and stockholders gave Barclays Bank a charge on the company's assets in return for a £10m loan. The incoming Chairman, Lord Shawcross, admitted that there had been mistakes in management but added that 'with the full support of all concerned, and especially the full understanding of employees and trade unions, prosperity could be restored.'

Chapter Ten

The legacy of the past decade and an exciting new effort

A NEW Chief Executive, Brian Eustace, joined the Group in November and on the first day of his new appointment he spoke to the employees at Small Heath works. They had already been warned of redundancies, and he told them that his most important task would be to save the jobs of those being retained.

Brian was 49 years old and an ex-GKN executive, with a vast experience of general management in large companies. Recently he had spent three years in India where, as Chief Executive of an engineering company with 13,000 employees, he had a tough but successful time weathering a number of strikes, during which he was subject to a good deal of abuse. Nonetheless he left the company in much better shape than that in which he had found it.

Brian had a long chat with me some time in November. My first impressions of the man were very encouraging for he was, above all, cautious, and he seemed to have a great deal of drive, knew his subject and also knew that the job he had undertaken needed all the help he could muster from all levels, which he admitted freely. A few days later he asked me whether I would be prepared to work, once more, on a full time basis and I was agreeable to do so, but only until the company was safely on the way to a new generation of products. I was anxious, by now, to retire before long and was hoping that two or three years at the most would suffice.

He seemed happy about this and I recommended full activity with no job title. This did not matter for there was so much to be done and Mike Nedham, the Engineering Director, needed help in a big way. I simply waded in and was thankful that I knew my way thoroughly in all the plants so that I could offer advice in many areas, without causing any upsets whatsoever.

I was very surprised indeed when, early in December, I was invited to join the Parent Board of Birmingham Small Arms, with executive responsibilities for design **251** engineering in the Motorcycle Division. I accepted, knowing that from now on, every Board Member must be in possession of clearly understood and factual pictures of product proposals if the right decisions were to be made and it was now entirely up to me.

The AGM was held in London on December 15th 1971 and this was the first occasion I had of meeting my Board colleagues, for I had not, so far, been part of any discussions or decision making at this level. Lord Shawcross gave a masterly resume of the situation in which he indicated that we were disposing of some of the group's peripheral activities (we were just then negotiating the sale of our Metal Components Division) and this would leave the motorcycle business constituting about 80% of the group's whole activity. He also indicated that, in the last few months, 3000 redundancies had been made at Small Heath and BSA motorcycle assembly was to be transferred to the Meriden works, which would enable us to sell about 75% of the Small Heath site, the remainder continuing to house the gun and general engineering production facilities.

The trading loss for the year had amounted to a little over $£2\frac{3}{4}$m but in addition, very heavy and exceptional provisions were being made during the 1972 financial year, of $£1\frac{1}{4}$m in respect of write-offs due to a decision to discontinue the manufacture of certain models. A further sum of $£4\frac{1}{4}$m was needed to cover the estimated cost of product and factory rationalisation.

In simple language, from a Group turnover of £40m (which was £2m higher than that of the previous year) we had finished with a debit balance of $£8\frac{1}{2}$m and our overdraft was a staggering £10m. We would need to make the best part of £1m profit in order to pay the interest charge on this overdraft alone.

By this time Denis McCormack, the ex-president of Triumph USA had been brought out of retirement to take charge of the total USA operation. This restored a little dealer confidence, although there was much to do before our motorcycles could be regarded as being readily saleable, and it was now realised that substantial discounts had to be offered in order to clear stocks, which in the USA alone totalled just under 11,000 machines.

Unfortunately both Triumph and BSA triple cylinder engines were being manufactured at the Small Heath works, which was now being drastically reorganised and this was affecting availability of these units. The introduction of the new 'Vetter' model (an American-styled sports version of the BSA triple) was deferred until the 1972/3 model year because of this and the need to restrict immediate cash spending.

It had been planned also to switch production from 650 cc to 750 cc capacity twin cylinder machines at Triumph but, thankfully, I arrived just in time to prevent this until such time as the proposed change had been thoroughly tested and approved by us. My action made me thoroughly unpopular in certain quarters, particularly with, of all people, certain members of our Management Consultants. Goodness knows how they felt able to put the OK stamp on a design which, as yet, had no test background.

As was usual, certain of our sporting dealers in the USA had bored out a number of standard 650 cc engines to 750 cc capacity and these were being raced in short track events. On investigation I found that in many cases important components like crankshafts were renewed for each race, to avoid the risk of breakage. I had stumbled on to this by querying a very large batch of crankshafts which were being diverted from our Spares Department for shipment to the USA.

These American 750 cc machines were certainly carrying off many short track events, and on the face of it, were ready to go into mass production. But it was a short life and a happy one; prize money was high and it did not matter a hoot to fairly successful riders how many times a crankshaft was renewed to ensure that the engine remained in one piece until the finishing line.

Had we a 750 cc machine available, our task would have been more simple, for the market was screaming for this capacity, but the production build up of 750 cc triples was painfully slow. We were turning out more 650 cc twins each week and adding to a stockpile, particularly in the USA, of motorcycles which were difficult to move because they were of the wrong capacity, poor quality and too tall to attract the hardcore of Triumph enthusiasts.

The Vetter X75 three cylinder Triumph Hurricane. Styled by Craig Vetter in the USA this model was produced in limited quantities during 1972, for sale in the US market.

Chapter Ten

I felt like a criminal in vetoing the mass production schedule but I knew that we could not survive if new products were not fully developed here at the centre of manufacture. I simply could not bring myself to take the risk, much as it would have pleased our Management Consultants apparently, of releasing this important variant of which there was, as yet, no real prototype.

In a matter of weeks we had things on the move and we were soon to learn how wise we had been, for many important changes were necessary to obviate crankshaft breakages, seemingly incurable head gasket and oil leakages and the extremely bad vibration characteristics of the new engine. All of the necessary changes were simple enough but took a little time to sort out. I am glad that we took this course for it would, otherwise, have been another disaster; in the event the new 750 cc Triumph twin went on to become a very reliable machine and indeed it is still being manufactured at Meriden.

Brian Eustace had recently returned from the USA and had, of course, been up against it with some of our dealers there. He had asked me to make a trip with him to hear and diagnose their complaints at first hand, but since I had already started the 'instant surgery' necessary for our problem I felt that this part of my work should be completed before I wandered too far.

We agreed that we should not have any particular time programme for the re-designs but should update our models, week by week if necessary, as each particular problem had been overcome, and that we should give no indication to our dealers that improvements were being made, otherwise our warehouse stocks would look pretty sick. This is a rather naughty way of management but, in a life or death situation we felt justified in operating in this manner. I am glad that we did for, by April 1972, we had eliminated most of the important problems and were safely in production with somewhat more saleable products.

This may seem a staggering accomplishment and indeed it was, but only the unstinted energy and keenness of the employees involved and their anxiety to create something they were more proud of, made it possible.

It was fortunate that we had all the drawings ready for the most important changes to correct the seat height long before I took over, for Doug Hele and I had engineered a prototype to correct this fault a few weeks after Mr. Jofeh had departed. This had been offered to our late Chairman by Denis McCormack, as an 'immediate must'. But, as was then usual, a huge meeting was convened to consider the matter (even the Personnel Director was there) and it was turned down flat by the assembly, most of whom were trying to learn the ABC of the world of motorcycles.

I had a few harsh words with Denis as he really should have been master of the situation. His job, it now was, to market these unsatisfactory machines and had he been forceful, this particular change could have been in production by September 1971, seven months earlier.

Details of the 750 cc Triumph twin cylinder engine which went into mass-production early in 1973.

Chapter Ten

The new administration now had many of the unsatisfactory machines on their hands, seven months of unnecessary production in fact, but the return of Dennis did a great deal to restore order in the gargantuan task we had set ourselves in liquidating 1972 model stocks before such changes as we had in mind for 1973 were due for release.

At the Board Meeting of February 1972, Lord Shawcross was anxious to have a clearly defined engineering action plan in being as soon as possible and between times in our frantic product surgery, I was able to begin to formulate some possibilities and time factors for an ongoing programme of action. It was tragic that we were now so poor that the fluctuations of our borrowings, as they were called, were a major concern to every member of the Board. Barclays, if not exactly big brother, were undoubtedly in close touch with the situation at all times for our maximum borrowing limit was not to be exceeded.

This is all very well in a reasonably healthy company but it seemed to me that our maximum borrowing power was never very different from our actual borrowing and I must confess that the prospect seemed very dismal against the time when we should need finance for tooling new products. Obviously the great BSA organisation must learn to walk again before it ran and any action plan must be seen in this light. Also I realized that, sooner or later, we should need fairly massive help, with interest-free finance for a time, if we were to survive. Every member of the Board, of course, knew this but at first we were so busy concentrating on our immediate plan, each in his own sphere, to generate a more viable management structure and to achieve a somewhat brighter balance sheet, that this point was not fully discussed until a later date.

By March 1972, I had sufficient work done in detail to form the basis for a Board discussion on engineering policy and our immediate action plan and so, on the 13th of the month, a meeting of all the Directors was held at Meriden. I outlined to them the present engineering situation, as I saw it, and our suggestions for coping with the immediate future.

Our real need was for a new generation of machines with a greater spread of engine capacity, but this was not yet discussed, although some design work had started. We knew that it would take roughly three years from the conceptual design stage to get the first of a series of motorcycles safely into production. I must confess that, at that time, I personally was not too concerned as to the whereabouts of the finance necessary to mount the long term product strategy which would be needed to save us, so that this did not inhibit our initial thinking in this area.

From the start we had planned a three stage engineering programme, the first phase of which I dubbed 'instant surgery' and applied to our current range. Thankfully, this work was now complete and we were turning out more acceptable machines with little or no material being written off, whilst production flow was not affected by the many re-designs which had extended through a three months period.

I had not been relishing this part of the job but, once over and done with, I realised from reports we were receiving, that it had been well worth the united effort which had been made, particularly at Meriden works.

Phase two of our programme involved the design and development engineering necessary to support our next two model years (1972 to 1974) and much of this work was already in hand.

Phase three was, of course, the product revolution. Nothing short of this would, I felt, put us in a position of strength from 1975 onwards and I told the Board that by December 1972, design preparation must be well in hand. This part of our plan would need some heavy financing which obviously was beyond our means in the foreseeable future. Right now we had merely outlined some possibilities in this area but we agreed that, unless by 1975/76 we were seen to be positively breaking into the Japanese domination of the world market, we may survive for only a year or two but it would be no more than a lingering end.

We were too busy fighting to survive to have our sights set too firmly on 1975 and thereafter, but we certainly had Board discussions and there is no doubt that it was realized that we should have to seek some sort of Government assistance when it came to financing and launching the first, at least, of our new family of products.

Lord Shawcross, our Chairman, was a delightfully lucid individual and without exception, The Board was thankful that a man of such calibre should have agreed to take us through a period which, at best, would be somewhat thankless and certainly very difficult. I understand he felt that, as a member of the old Board (albeit a latecomer), it was something of a duty to see the company 'over the hump' as he put it, and but for the lack of insight of certain members of the then Conservative government, he would, I think, have succeeded.

In March our overdraft was critically near the Barclays Bank limit of £10m, plus £2m bridging accommodation which had been agreed, pending the sale of our Metal Components Division, a profitable section of the Group. However, the best offer so far had been £1½m, which we felt was totally inadequate and rather than accept a give-away price, the Bank agreed to extend the extra facility until the end of the financial year.

For the trading year ending July 31st 1972, we had planned a profit of £900,000 gross, with overdraft interest bringing the figure down to £173,000 but, by April, it was clear that this result would not be achieved. Sporadic industrial disputes within the Motorcycle Division, plus an increase in bank interest charges, were significantly affecting our performance. This was very disappointing for me personally and was not very encouraging for a Board which was unified in a hard slog with a plan needing the support of every employee in the Motorcycle Division if we were to be saved from the brink. With the aid of some discounting, our stocks of the old 1971 models in the USA were on the move. We could sell every triple cylinder machine we could now produce, and all round sales were on the up and up. **257**

Chapter Ten

Unfortunately serious shortfalls in production, due to strike action, created a scarcity situation during the peak selling months, which simply improved Honda sales.

It would be a long awaited performance of real leadership if the 'economists' of the trade union hierarchy spread some real wisdom, in a brotherly way, to the shop floor. In March, due to petty industrial action, we enjoyed only 14 days production instead of 20 and our loss in the Motorcycle Division for the month amounted to £181,000 instead of a planned profit of £12,000.

Our plans for the 1973 season, which commenced in August 1972. were now being finalised and I admit that I was surprised by the level of interest which was shown at our Board Meetings for we had only two Directors who had an engineering background and I fully expected decision making to be somewhat laborious. In fact, it was quite the reverse and I understand that it had been a very long time indeed since such detailed product discussions had taken place within the confines of that stately room in London's St. James Street. I recall feeling that the state of our industry could have been much happier if the executives responsible in the 1950s and 1960s had taken the trouble to generate a similar atmosphere.

By April 1972, the Motorcycle Division showed a profit of £105,000 and although industrial action continued, mainly at the Meriden works, the month of May returned a profit figure of £393,000. Although these figures were somewhat short of those planned I was beginning to feel a little more encouraged for, to me, there seemed little doubt that we could be on the way if our workforce would get behind us. With this in mind, I spoke to Brian Eustace, suggesting that it might be worth a try if I could be allowed to see the Meriden shop stewards and, if necessary, all the workers there and explain it to them, in their language, what we were up against and what we were doing about it. We were all wasting our time if we could not get production stability forthwith and I did not doubt that the works management team were doing their best in difficult circumstances. However, the leadership was new and seemed to rely on the showing of huge charts and many giant pictures indicating our planned and actual performance, which were projected in such a way that many who attended the mass meetings felt that much of the shop floor neither understood nor trusted this approach.

I knew the men and all of the shop stewards at Triumph very well and my face dated back, so far as many were concerned, to the late 1930s. I was prepared to talk to them in their own terms, as I had done when I was General Manager not so very long ago. Anything is worth a try when one is bleeding to death and I simply did not understand Brian's attitude in fobbing this suggestion off with a somewhat facetious remark that he understood I was 'busy with engineering'.

He was quite right, I was indeed, and we had, of course, a works management set up whose job it was to cope with the situation. But I am sure that something could have been worked out to enable me to have a try, without seriously upsetting local management, before the situation deteriorated further.

The legacy of the past decade and an exciting new effort

In April we appointed a Chief Executive for BSA Inc. USA and although a very able man indeed, I seemed to be alone in voicing doubts as to the wisdom of such an appointment, which came to most of the Board as a fait accompli and seemed to have been more or less forced through by our management advisers. No doubt they felt that our US operation was in immediate need of high power expertise from without. I had written to Brian, just prior to the appointment being made public, and pleaded with him to give up the idea, for the moment, and upgrade one of the many capable executives we had over there, in a caretaker capacity. I pointed out that our operation was short of sophisticated products, not personnel, and was just recovering from being turned upside down by other management wizards; such an appointment would emphasise this in the eyes of our dealer organisation and our excellent staff who simply were waiting for us to 'give them the tools'. I pointed out that it seemed like 'taking a 50 ton press to crack a nut' for our dealer organisation was good and we were staffed by personnel who knew the business backwards. Right now, we would run the risk of being seen as irresponsible and spendthrifts when we should really have been concerned with cutting costs.

Such a man would, I felt, reorganise at a time when we needed stability in that area and I could not imagine how we could justify such a highly paid appointment until we could be seen, in the eyes of our dealers in particular, to be coming through positively. Once more I received the raised eyebrow and the hint that engineering should be keeping me busy. In May 1972, Felix Kalinsky was appointed and also given a seat on the London Board.

He was a first class executive with a very clear mind, capable of taking charge of this very important part of our operation. Although I admired him very much and he worked prodigiously, I felt a little sad that a man of such high qualification, who was every bit a professional, should have at this stage such poor material with which to revitalize our weary dealers.

During May, the Board gave much consideration to problems which were bedevilling our spare parts supply situation, for this very lucrative sector of our business had been falling short of profit estimates for a number of years. For some reason, which still escapes me, our resident Managing Consultants were asked to make a survey of the situation and their report, in my opinion, over-elaborated a simple situation which if accepted, would lead us into a costly maze of over-management.

If I was earning a reputation for consultant bashing it was not intentional but I did feel, quite strongly, that this type of habitual consultancy was a dangerous habit, tending to deprive us of our basic management function which right now was largely a matter of our own particular abilities plus a generous helping of common sense.

To part with good money and to be told as a result that a replacement part supply operation can be profitable was just too much for me to take. From long **259** experience I knew that this side of our business was not only the simplest but also the most profitable and needed none of the complicated management changes which were suggested, which would only increase our already excessive overheads. We had a huge backlog of unfulfilled orders for spare parts which had created a pirate supply business in the USA and naturally our dealers were no longer bothering with us. During our visits to the USA we established that the information we had been receiving, relating to customer needs, was often unreliable and that in addition, our prices were somewhat high.

We tended to starve our Spares Department of parts when the motorcycle production tracks were busy, but this was a simple point to deal with and did not need costly new staff, for we had all the facilities. It was essential that we manufacture and despatch items on time, and plan a production shedule based on a realistic yearly call up which did not run hot and cold. With such an operation, our costs could be adjusted accordingly. A unanimous decision by the Board enabled us to commence operating on these lines within a matter of six weeks.

By this time our total turnover in the USA was slightly ahead of plan but in the rest of the world our stocks of machines, of which there was still a sprinkle of 1971 types, were proving very difficult to move. It was important that we dispose of these, particularly the ageing baddies before our new programme launch in August. We had little option but to indulge in heavy discounting at a further cost of £100,000.

By June we had appointed a new Marketing Director, whose responsibilities would embrace markets other than the USA, a newcomer to the trade who had, I understand, been found for us, once more, by our resident Consultants. I was hot under the collar again and had a down to earth discussion with our Chief Executive which at least established, between us, that I was no longer willing to accept further appointments of this sort which had not been fully discussed and agreed by the Board. Although we did not always see eye to eye I had much respect for Brian as he was impressive in most aspects of management. He was a man of vast energy who was holding us together well and despite this wretched big brother watchdog condition which prevailed, he was coping well in difficult circumstances.

The new appointment, like that of Felix Kalinsky, was premature, for at that time we had no material which would serve as the starting point for any new marketing expertise. I had to repeat that it was important that we should not rock the boat and further disenchant, not only the outside world, but also our very capable staff, some of whom were beginning to query whether the new Board of BSA were any more 'with it' than their predecessors.

There was no doubt in my mind that our resident watchdog consultants, or call them what you will, had some inhibiting effect on certain members of our Board, for at no time were we free from text book type reports, many of which highlighted management deficiencies of which the executive section were fully aware and were working on systematically. I knew that the time-absorbing probings and questioning,

The legacy of the past decade and an exciting new effort

The BSA Wankel-engined motorcycle prototype photographed during 1973.

often by individuals comparatively fresh from college with no practical background, and the somewhat amazing 'discoveries' and long winded pronouncements, were tending to reduce the credibility of the Board in the eyes of our workforce. Time factors did not allow me to concern myself overmuch with this for now we had formed a substantial forward design section of first rate men and were fairly deep into plans for our new generation of products.

It was much too early to have discussions at Board level as it was felt that nothing meaningful could be achieved until a folder was produced which would be comprehensive enough to be clearly understood by every member of the Board. Decision making had got to be right or we should go bust and it was hardly

The BSA Wankel engine under development in 1973.

reasonable to expect Board members, whose background was mainly financial, to cope adequately unless the engineer did his job properly and projected the technical picture simply and clearly together with life-like illustrations of our new range.

We were expecting to be in a position to present such a plan to the Board in the spring of 1973, by which time it would be necessary for us to be giving consideration to a range of machines from small to large. Hopefully, by then, we would be in the position to authorise the manufacture of prototypes of the first model of our new series.

My terms of reference, agreed after much discussion, were to embrace a range of piston-engined motorcycles from small to large (later agreed to be from 198 cc to 1000 cc engine capacity) to cater for most classes of rider, but excluding the moped type of machine. It was fully agreed that the Wankel engine principle should be further explored and my folder should include 'positive recommendations in this area'.

It is necessary to explain that, for the previous five or six years our Group Research Department had been developing a Wankel type engine and a prototype motorcycle was now under test. As we did not have a Wankel licence it had been necessary to link up with someone who did and we had a working arrangement with Fichtel and Sachs, a well-known firm of engine manufacturers in West Germany, who had produced the components which needed the technique so peculiar to this type of engine and which were controlled by expensive licensing arrangements dictated by Audi-NSU in Neckarsölm, West Germany.

Our engine was a single rotor air-cooled type which had a carburettor intake system drawing its air supply through an attenuated tract which embraced vital engine cooling surfaces. The cooling air supply was dictated by the air consumption of the engine and simply was not adequate. Also, the carburettor was called upon to deal with air supplies of greatly varying temperatures (the carburettor inlet air had already passed over and cooled the engine), a fundamental fault. It could, of course, have been corrected with the addition to the air system of an intercooler, although this would have been an expensive way of dealing with this problem.

We had to make up our minds, very quickly, where we had arrived in our six or seven years of development and I am afraid that it was soon realised that we were not very far from square one. Severe cooling and wear problems prevented any road work and the frequent breakdowns disassembled for my inspection were to become known as the 'burnt offerings'. We had to start again and do the job properly, as good engineers, or forget about the Wankel system altogether.

We were not too happy, at this particular time, to discard work on this system entirely, for the Japanese motorcycle and car industry, we knew, were well on the way with engines of this type. Indeed, the Mazda rotary-engined car was proving to be very reliable and highly successful.

One of the many considerations in our future policy was the need for a clean and reliable final drive system, particularly for the larger capacity machines, to supersede the short lived and filthy exposed rear chain drives, normal on most motorcycles. Although we had in mind a novel means of complete chain enclosure, which we felt should put the problem behind us, I felt that we should be investigating the shaft drive principle as an additional choice for certain machines, depending on comparative cost and market acceptability. The possibility of a Wankel powered motorcycle with shaft final drive had led to the design of a two rotor power unit with contra-rotating rotors coupled in parallel, an unusual design of which more will be revealed later.

Chapter Ten

In June 1972 the BSA Board were faced with a difficult decision as NSU Wankel had a manufacturing licence which was on offer. It was about this time, a very large and well known British group of manufacturers approached us with the suggestion that we should join forces on Wankel development. Their offer was to foot the total bill for the manufacture and development of six prototype machines and to provide adequate design and development personnel who would work together with a small team of BSA engineers; all costs would be met by them through to the pre-production stage. The new Wankel machine had been designed to have as optional equipment either a six-speed manually-operated gearbox or a fully-automatic transmission, with torque converter, similar to that already being offered on certain Mini cars. The Company responsible for the manufacture of this transmission equipment had agreed to 'hold our hand' through the rather tricky design and development stage with regard to the control gear for the automatic drive. It is necessary for the reader to have this knowledge of our total 'Wankel' package to understand, a little more clearly, why a company such as BSA with dire financial problems, finally decided to invest in a Wankel licence.

By the end of June 1972, the Board had discussed at great length and on several occasions the Wankel system, in an effort to arrive at a decision on whether or not we should take up the manufacturing licence offer from Audi-NSU. It was during these meetings that I was impressed by the thoroughness and probing interest of everyone at the Board table. I was anxious that my colleagues should not get the impression that I was promoting the Wankel principle in any way and I had indicated, from the start, that such a licence could, for the time being, be regarded only as an insurance policy. Nonetheless, we had to make an immediate decision for the offer was linked with a time limit.

Lord Shawcross queried whether we could afford to continue the technical work necessary, but the offer made by the well-known manufacturing group to link up with us and meet most of our engineering costs came shortly after these discussions. It cleared any doubts about our involvement in high engineering costs.

The real issue at this stage was whether it made good business sense to take up a licence, at a cost of something like £100,000. As the majority of the Board felt that we should continue some investigation work on this type of engine, it seemed obvious that, if we continued our link with Fichtel and Sachs, they would wish to recoup some of their licence fees to NSU, by supplying us with complete engines, should we decide to produce. This would not have been attractive and, in addition, it was understood that Fichtel and Sachs did not have licensing rights to manufacture engines in the horsepower bracket which interested us.

For some reason which escapes me, the Wankel licence was on offer as a horsepower package rather than an arrangement based on engine capacity, and the costs, in terms of value, made little or no sense to us. For instance, a licence to manufacture engines between 0.5 to 20 hp would cost £54,000, one to manufacture between 20 to 35 hp would cost £117,000 and one to manufacture 35 to 50 hp would cost £78,000.

I felt that this type of engine, with its inherent smoothness, would have more to offer in a large capacity machine, where vibration problems with normal single cylinder or twin cylinder piston engines were unacceptable and with the current trend towards three or more cylinders. The Wankel engine would be difficult to manufacture for a number of years and it seemed obvious that a large machine, with this type of power unit, would be more viable than a small one.

Finally, the Board was unanimous in deciding that we take up the licence offer and for reasons of cost, we restricted this to horsepower capacity between 35 and 60 at 5000 rpm. Consequently the arrangement was finalised at a cost of £129,000.

By August 1972 our 1973 model changes were due for production and the work involved, which had occupied our Engineering Department for the past nine months or so, would, I hoped, be the last major effort on basically ageing designs for, by now, a great deal had been done towards the final phase of our forward plan. I was beginning to see daylight and was hopeful that, by the year's end, a master plan with several options would be ready for consideration.

There were three so-called new 1973 models and, in addition, the whole range carried detail improvements, with disc brakes and five-speed gearboxes fitted as standard equipment on all machines of 650 cc capacity and upwards.

The first of our 'new' models, the Triumph T50T, had a 500 cc twin cylinder engine and was an 'off road' machine for sale in the USA where this addition to our range would tap a new and growing market which catered for the sporting cross country rider. Secondly, we planned a limited production of a BSA 'Vetter' Rocket, a variation of the triple cylinder machine but with a vastly different appearance. It had been styled by Craig Vetter, a young American, to appeal to what I can only describe as the 'trendy' type of rider whose numbers were increasing fast in the States.

The third new model was the 750 cc Triumph twin, basically a bored out version of the 650 cc Bonneville which it would replace and which would sell at a substantially higher price. Because of the many problems which had needed solving in the development of what must seem to be a very simple change, this model was not due for production until December 1972 but the 650 cc market was declining rapidly and we were working desperately to improve our target.

We would have liked to ditch the frame in use on our best selling models, which had been 'inherited' from Umberslade, but consideration of tooling expense, time and obsolescence factors prevented us doing so at this particular juncture. It is sad to record that this frame, which had caused so much embarassment in the 1971 model year, and which we were now producing in large quantities, was heavier, more costly and had more accessibility problems than its predecessor, in spite of the opening fanfare to the contrary. The huge engineering development and tooling costs involved **265**

The new Thunderbird III prototype. Due to be launched early in 1973, events were to overtake us and this machine did not quite reach the production stage. The three cylinder engine, uprated to 850 cc capacity, developed 67 bhp at 8300 rpm and the noise level was 4dB lower than the Triumph machines then in production.

were a sheer waste of money.

By September 1972, we were well on the way with a rejuvenation of our triple cylinder motorcycle featuring much of our world beating racing model, which was due for production early in 1973. The 750 cc engine unit had been upgraded in capacity to 830 cc, with a power output of 67 bhp at 8,300 rpm and with electric starting as standard equipment. Doug Hele had achieved something of a break-through with an exhaust system which greatly improved middle torque and reduced exhaust noise by 4 db.

It was planned that this model would replace both the BSA Rocket and the Triumph Trident, with no major structural differences to either name. I am sorry indeed that our planning engineers were not able to see eye to eye with me on possible production dates, for I was sure that with this machine we had a winner from modest tooling expenditure. If we could have recaptured some of the old Triumph 'get up and go' and made a determined effort as a team to force through a more realistic production date, we would have sold at a premium every machine we could have made.

The lack of a Managing Director for the Motorcycle Division created a fundamental problem, for co-ordination between the Meriden and Small Heath plants was vital because the latter was now manufacturing much of the material for final assembly at Meriden. If we did not very soon create a leadership which had more determination to break a few production planning records and improve some of the silly target dates which the Board was being given, we were likely to miss the next selling season in the USA and find ourselves, once more, manufacturing for stock.

It simply was not on for our Chief Executive to take on the responsibility of running this Division for he had the overall responsibility of the whole BSA complex and it seemed strange that the operation which represented some 80% of the total capital employed by the Group should be jogging on in this way. It is difficult to understand why our resident Management Consultants did not appear to find it necessary to underline this novel arrangement and press hard for action to be taken, for I certainly made a point of expressing myself on several occasions. Brian seemed to think that our capability was sufficient and he did not agree with me that our applied management technique, particularly in the manufacturing corner, left much to be desired.

We needed now a managing director who had real knowledge of our specialised business, who knew when his leg was being pulled and who was capable of putting the Division on emergency and knock to pieces all of the silly production target dates and effort rating which appeared to be some relic of our past administration and which I flatly did not accept. Also we needed production and more production, with no stoppages, and we needed to have Meriden overheads cut down to size by a redundancy of something in excess of 300, in order to trim our wage bill by £1m and make a sensible profit.

A 650 cc Bonneville power unit is coaxed into the frame and cycle parts of the 350 Triumph Bandit. A compact motorcycle with a very attractive power/weight ratio, it is a pity that this project was abandoned.

The legacy of the past decade and an exciting new effort

My views, which were shared by David Probert, our Financial Director, were backed up by experience in running the Meriden company during a very profitable period. It is unfortunate that serious events were to overtake us for I am sure that David and I had the answers to the major problems at Triumph and I had it on very sound authority that the shop floor would have welcomed some of the old medicine

An experimental Triumph Bonneville machine with a balancing device on the crankshaft. The results were quite encouraging.

even though it may, at first, have tasted a little bitter.

Writing in this vein is, of course, very easy but I was being approached, almost daily, by many of our Meriden workforce who seemed to know that drastic surgery was needed and indeed expected. I felt certain that right now we had a fighting chance to straighten out Triumph and get back well into the black.

However the completion of our set of forward project packages, together with in-depth feasibility studies, were fully occupying me and although we could now see a great deal of daylight, I estimated that it would be Spring 1973 before the Board could have all the engineering and marketing information we should need in order to arrive at conclusions.

In the meantime Felix Kalinsky had toured his dealers in the USA and, not surprisingly, had been told that our outdated lines were becoming more unacceptable and that our 650 cc twin cylinder machines must be upgraded in engine capacity forthwith. The nett effect of this was to inject a little ginger into the production lead times and the new 750 cc Bonneville machine, with its 52 bhp engine started to roll off the production lines in September 1972.

With our 1973 model range safely launched, much of our effort was now fully focused on our new generation engineering, a very different kettle of fish from the yearly updating of the current line. The first moves were planned to seek the financial assistance which would be required for us to go ahead with the first of our models.

Our huge overdraft facility was not everlasting as Barclays Bank had made clear, but to continue the motorcycle operation within the present cash scene meant, at best, that we may manage minor design improvements. Now the message was loud and clear that nothing short of a product revolution was needed and to soldier on with yearly cosmetic changes would mean reaching the point where voluntary liquidation would be the only alternative.

Our forward plans were blossoming and we were encouraged by the designs which had emerged, giving us confidence that we would be competitive through the late 1970s and into the 1980s, with a full range of modern machines to enable us to go for a turnover more in keeping with our total facilities,

It is true that our plan was ambitious (it was designed for a reviving activity and not a dying one) and embraced a range of machines from 198 cc to 1250 cc capacity, together with a Wankel-engined motorcycle. In addition, we had plans to embrace automatic transmission and shaft driven machines as well as a new means of enclosed rear chain transmission. The logic throughout was comprehensive readiness, something of which the industry had never been guilty. We resolved to obviate the spasmodic design rushes, which were, as often as not, too little and too late, and which in the past had not been coupled to intelligent forward market research. We knew, of course, that it would not be possible to plunge in with a new range but it could be possible for the first of our new models to be in production by 1975. To achieve this, we agreed that an interest-free cash injection of at least £5m would be necessary.

In June 1972 we had approached the Department of Trade and Industry, a Government Department, requesting that financial assistance be given to the BSA's Motorcycle Division on the understanding that the initial intention of such assistance would be 'to enable BSA Motor Cycles Ltd. to remain in business and market more

Ray Pickrell sweeps his Triumph Trident through Waterworks during the 1972 Superbike Production TT race. He went on to win the race, setting up a new lap record of 101.61 mph, with a race average of exactly 100 mph.

competitive products. To obviate direct interest charges it was first suggested that BSA would form its Motorcycle Division into a separate limited company and the financial assistance provided by the DTI used to purchase part of the equity of the Company.

Preliminary discussions with senior representatives of the DTI left me neither impressed nor encouraged, for the people we saw did not comprehend the real difficulties of our operation which I, as an engineer, felt was primarily the early introduction of a re-vitalized range of products which were fully competitive. Other members of our Board thought, perhaps rightly, that I over-simplified the situation but the management improvements, financial control and marketing expertise we had achieved during the past few months simply would not impress any motorcyclist. If **271**

After winning the Superbike Production TT race earlier in the week, Ray Pickrell, here seen taking his 750 cc Triumph through Signpost Corner, carried off a TT double by winning the 1972 Formula 750 TT race. He pushed the lap record to a staggering 105.68 mph and averaged 104.23 mph for the race.

I had been in charge of this investigation on behalf of Her Majesty's Conservative Government, I would have concentrated on the strategy, which BSA was planning, to match or better Japanese competition. I would have expected a master plan, which we now had, and I would have needed to have explored such a plan, in great detail, and with much advice before I should have felt capable of going back to the Minister. I would have been more satisfied, of course, if I had found that the current management structure was good, but even if it had been found to be bad, the logic and viability of the forward product strategy would have been my top priority in forming conclusions, for management can be corrected, if necessary, much more quickly and easily than products can be created.

The legacy of the past decade and an exciting new effort

Apart from one short meeting during which I explained, in answer to their request, how we intended to 'soldier on' with our current outdated models, there never was a query as to what we had in mind for the future. Although, at the time, I was shocked and annoyed, I now realize that these gentlemen were not a bit interested in helping BSA, for events would indicate that they had already reached a conclusion.

Our 1972 balance sheet was somewhat depressing, with a trading loss of £465,000. With a bank interest charge of £674,000 having been absorbed it gives some idea of the fragile state of our finances. The interest charge seems surprisingly low however, in view of our indebtedness, and was a result of the excellent financial control strategy of David Probert who, however, was powerless in obviating a loss of income of £300,000 resulting from the devaluation of the dollar during the trading period. The Board had planned for a break-even figure and indeed a profit was made during the second half, but this was not sufficient to wipe out the loss of £1,151,000 in the first half year.

It is tragic that Eric Turner did not allow the design changes suggested by me to go into production immediately Mr. Jofeh resigned, for these would have enabled us to have started the 1973 year with machines which would have been somewhat more acceptable. Certainly it would have obviated something like £½m expenditure in forced sales and it is tragic that the trade union activists, mainly at Meriden, did not have the gumption to give the new Board a crack of the whip.

But for these two problems, and in spite of the dollar devaluation loss, there would have been a small profit and our background may have been just a little more impressive at Government Minister level. Although the new Board had been in action for only seven months of the trading year, and the Balance Sheet, of course, drew comparison with the previous year's loss of nearly £3m, I found little consolation in comparing losses of any sort.

By late November 1972, our Chairman had met the DTI who now were prepared to provide up to £20m towards establishing a British motorcycle industry, but the condition was that the two largest manufacturers, BSA and Norton should merge. It seems that Dennis Poore, the Chairman of Norton was agreeable and the DTI requested a working party between the two companies 'to consider and recommend how their merged companies would meet the opportunities of the market'.

We had the option of approaching a merger enthusiastically or to continue independently without government help. Our Chairman's view was that Barclays would be unlikely to support the latter course without definite indication of profit making. After long hours of discussion, we favoured the merger alternative but we felt that Norton must be made aware of the BSA position because it appeared that they had intimated that BSA, unlike themselves, were 'doing badly' and they (Norton) would be the continuing profitable partner which would be exploited **273** accordingly. The Norton balance sheet, which was not yet due, would prove this to be quite untrue for they were a sick enterprise with little achievement and less to offer for the future. The plain facts were that both companies were in need of Government help.

A meeting of principals of both companies was held on November 30th 1972, and had, in attendance, representatives from our resident Management Consultants and our Merchant Bankers. It was, of course, essential that during the negotiating period complete secrecy should be observed. Accordingly all discussions, letters or papers of any sort were confined to the Board Room and Norton were referred to as 'Zebra' and BSA as 'Longlegs'.

I was never in attendance at any of these early meetings and cannot pass comment as to how the DTI managed to conclude that Mr. Poore was the man capable of saving the British motorcycle industry, but it was quite obvious that no doubt ever existed. From the start, the negotiations were so weighted that I felt we were fortunate indeed to be joining forces with a company which, obviously, must be masterminded by a brilliant individual.

The Conservative Ministers concerned seemed spellbound and I was genuinely delighted with the prospect of more strength to our elbow because although we at BSA were nearing maturity with our new generation plan and were, by now, rig testing some of the more unusual engineering which formed part of our new approach, I welcomed the possibility that the Norton concern must be nursing some winners, with which to rock the Japanese boat. I cared little from which source the master plan emanated so long as it did indeed come, and soon. At that precise time, I thought that the combining of effort was a means of strengthening us as an industry.

However, perhaps it may be thought that my engineering background was affecting my management vision and that I over emphasised the product part of our sickness but as the negotiations went on, I had nagging doubts that the DTI did not realise that money and management would not, as they put it 'restore the fortune of the industry'.

I am aware, of course, that product strategy is part of management but the word management was far too loose a term to satisfy me and it needed qualifying in some detail. We at BSA in the last decade or so had been inundated with industrialists and management specialists, with very good pedigrees and fine business records, who had failed miserably because they had no product background and were unable to comprehend the situation that existed in the business to which they had graduated. They were equally unable to recognise the solution to our problem, for to them a motorcycle was no more than two wheels with an engine roughly midway.

By the beginning of 1973 our new generation plan was in an advanced stage, **274** with the options having been considered thoroughly. However, the negotiations

Triumph mounted race marshals for the TT races of 1973.

which were going on and the lack of final agreement on any plan which would enable us to break through with the finance which now was urgent, prevented us from moving ahead with the first prototype.

The new family of products had the following requirements firmly established as guidelines:

(1) A range of motorcycles from small to large to cater for most classes of rider and to provide comprehensive coverage of the world motorcycle market.

(2) A range of products designed to take advantage of modern manufacturing techniques and lending itself to automated production processes.

(3) A range of products sufficiently advanced, technically, to justify six years of quantity production without fundamental change.

(4) A range of products with a minimum of assembly problems and designed to eliminate the need for frequent maintenance.

From frequent excursions into various approaches we had established to the complete satisfaction of our technical and marketing staff that a range of motorcycles on a modular principle would be of great benefit. But in taking this approach, the fundamental had been established that no technical sacrifices must be made with any of the units in order to satisfy this principle.

The single cylinder engine unit or module embraced everything we could give it from our combined experience and most up to date thinking on ohc valve gear **275**

The new generation 200 cc motorcycle due for launch during the 1975 model year. The engine unit was designed to be uprated to 250 cc at a later stage and formed the basic module on which other engines, in a new generation range of products, were based.

operation and our most ideal engine geometry aimed at optimum volumetric efficiency. This approach was extended by multiplication through a range of five piston engines of varying capacities, in multiples of the module, to achieve a minimum variety of components without impairing design efficiency in any way. Each engine unit was designed with an ideal capacity in mind, but past experience indicated that after the first flush of production runs the pattern of demand may dictate somewhat larger capacities and in view of this, each unit had been designed to enable a 25% upgrading in capacity for a negligible capital expenditure. This approach was attractive because it enabled new models to be introduced after a while with a minimum of engineering and production lead times and with minimal tooling costs.

The range of piston engines by capacity and type together with the option on capacity increases were as follows:

200 cc Single cylinder unit could be upgraded to 250 cc
400 cc Twin cylinder unit could be upgraded to 500 cc
600 cc Three cylinder unit could be upgraded to 750 cc
800 cc Four cylinder unit could be upgraded to 1000 cc
1000 cc Five cylinder unit could be upgraded to 1250 cc

The single and twin cylinder units were fully balanced by a simple mechanism which had no chain or gear drives and should therefore have been reliable and silent. Power units with more than two cylinders had no balancing mechanism as this was

considered unnecessary.

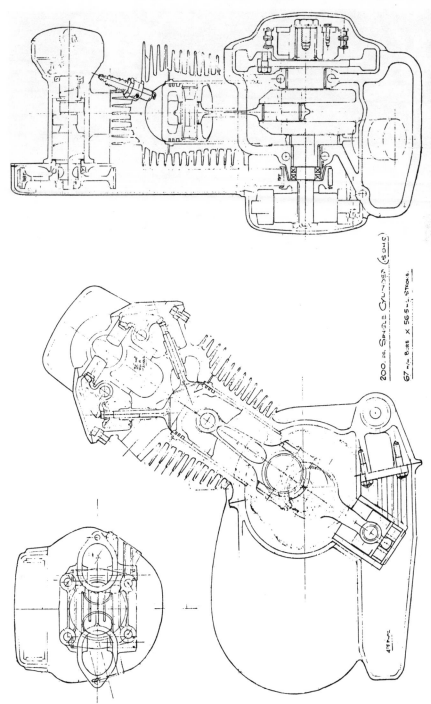

200. cc. Single Cylinder (sohc)

67 m/m Bore x 56.5 m/m Stroke.

The new generation 200/250 cc single cylinder engine module. A new type of crankcase construction embraced the fully integral oil-sump and a crankshaft driven balance device served also as a simple, valveless double acting oil pump.

277

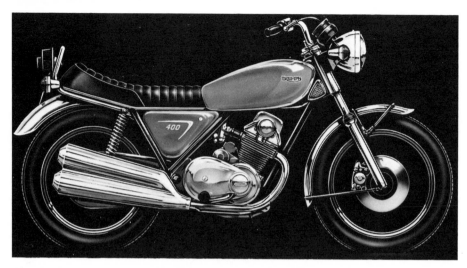

The new generation twin cylinder machine of 400/500 cc capacity.

Much attention had been paid to oil leak problems, hitherto a serious defect on most British machines. As a consequence, the total surface area of joint faces, which must be oil tight, was reduced to an absolute minimum. Each power unit could be produced with or without an electric start facility and this had been achieved without the need for additional chain drives or the like. Every engine had a simple ohc valve gear, a unique design, which featured very simple tappet adjustment and a camshaft operating in an oil filled chamber. This enabled camshafts to be manufactured from cheap materials like cast iron without creating wear problems and because the valve

Details of the new generation 400/500 cc twin cylinder machine.

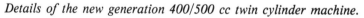

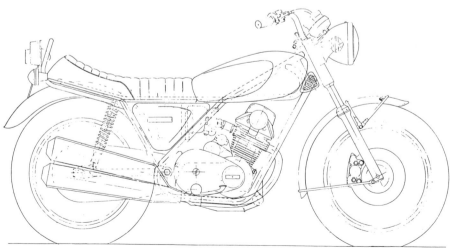

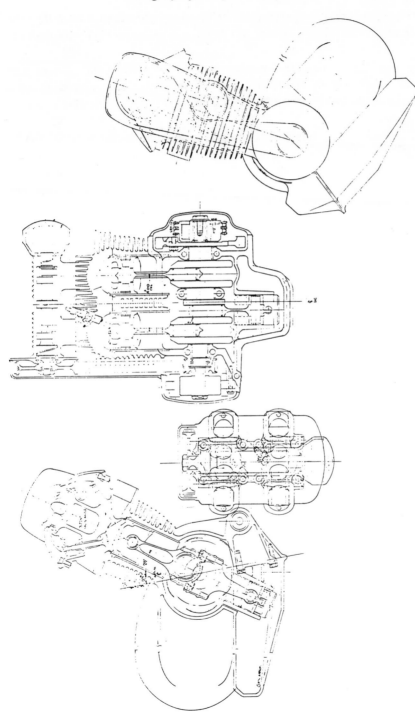

Engine details of the 400/500 cc new generation twin cylinder unit, designed to develop 36 bhp at 9000 rpm in 400 cc capacity or 44 bhp at 9600 rpm if fitted with an eight valve cylinder head.

spring chambers were quite separate, we achieved semi-dry conditions at the valve guide surfaces, to obviate oil leakage at this point, a major problem with most ohc engines.

The balancing mechanism on the single cylinder and twin cylinder units functioned also as a double-acting valveless oil pump and seemed to be a breakthrough in the design of a much more simple and reliable lubricating system for a motorcycle.

All the power units were designed to accept pressure die-casting techniques for aluminium components because this process, as our Japanese friends were demonstrating, enabled cheaper and better finished castings to be made and reduced much machining time. A novel crankcase design achieved a one-piece construction of a normal assembly of several components, thus simplifying the machining operation, reducing cost and obviating a multiplicity of joint faces which normally would be potential oil leakage points. Each engine through the range was designed with an option of either two or four valves per cylinder, the latter, of course, developing higher power, and this had been achieved with exactly similar camshaft drive gear for both types. Thus one had the option of standardising one type or marketing standard and sporting versions simply by changing the cylinder head assembly.

The rear wheel drive of our outgoing range of motorcycles was by means of a chain which was almost completely exposed and on high powered machines, in particular, the chain wore very rapidly. The former difficulties of chain enclosure and lubrication had been overcome with a massive, single member, suspension arm reminiscent of well proven principles in motor car engineering. This enabled a simple enclosed rear drive construction with the wheel mounted on one side and the chain drive located on the other side of the central member. Each gear transmission unit was operated through a five-speed gearbox and reliability, cost saving, mechanical efficiency and silence were the main considerations in our approach. The whole range of machines was catered for with two basic gear clusters and transmission units, one being a miniature of the other.

Die-cast wheels in magnesium alloy had been designed which looked most attractive and we were progressing with tests which I hoped would enable cheaper wheels than the spoked type to be produced. Hopefully our company would pioneer the use of tubeless tyres on mass-produced motorcycles with better safety factors, earning us a pat on the back from the now very active safety legislation makers.

Each machine had been styled in two forms, one basically to satisfy the US market and the other for the European continent. Although the illustrations cannot make this clear the new motorcycles were much smaller than their equivalents in current production, the whole effect adding up to a much more attractive range with better handling and a lower seat height.

Because it enabled our discussions to be more practical and helpful in decision

making, particularly with the non-engineering type executives in mind, art work was

The legacy of the past decade and an exciting new effort

The new generation 600/750 cc three cylinder Mini Superbike. Styled to suit the US market with cast alloy wheels and new rear transmission system intended as standard equipment.

The new generation 600/750 cc three cylinder Mini Superbike, styled for European tastes.

Chapter Ten

Details of the 600/750 cc Mini Superbike triple.

superimposed on engineers' drawings of the machines, to present life like impressions. These were not artists' impressions, full of fancy licence, but working drawings of the real thing.

It was inevitable that there would be unusual features in a range of motorcycles which would, I hoped, take us through six years or so, but we had completed much of our homework and as a result, our engineering staff was full of confidence. The rather unusual ohc valve gear, featured on all the units, had been under test for some time on a Triumph Trident, which had been updated in this manner. The balancing mechanisms, which would enable us to go to the market with smooth running singles and twins, and which doubled up as the oil pump, were being rig tested and had already exceeded the performance of the current Triumph lubrication system.

The unusual five cylinder engine had been the subject of much theoretical study and we had done a great deal to enable us to feel that problems of balance would present us with nothing more serious than those encountered on a normal triple-cylinder engine. However, in all probability, it may have meant a choice between the four or the five cylinder engine units rather than the manufacture of both, and we had this point very much in mind. Although the five cylinder engine package of 1250 cc capacity was very much smaller overall than the current 750 cc triple, and did not look at all 'busy' in appearance, it was necessary to be very sure of market acceptability of this unusual machine before plunging in with too much expenditure.

The new rear transmission system, something of a breakaway for motorcycles, was somewhat time-absorbing to make up in prototype form, particularly with little finance available, but we were busy converting a Triumph Bonneville machine in this way and this prototype was due for test in July 1973.

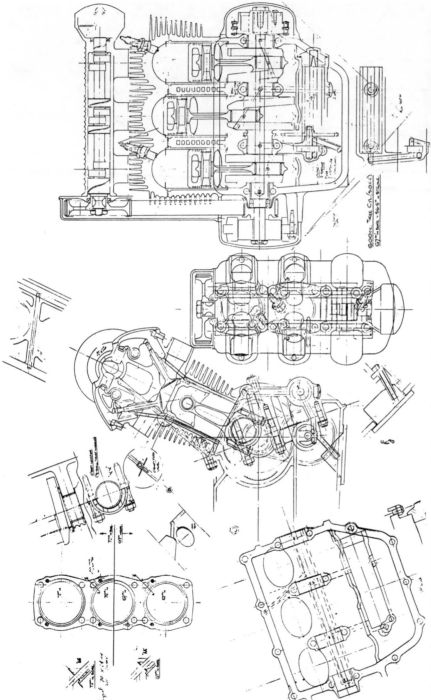

Engine details of the 600/750 cc three cylinder engine unit designed to develop 54 bhp at 9000 rpm in 600 cc form or with a twelve valve cylinder head change, 66 bhp at 9600 rpm.

283

The new generation 1000/1250 cc five cylinder Grand Superbike in livery suitable for the US market.
The new generation 1000/1250 cc five cylinder Grand Superbike with European styling.

The legacy of the past decade and an exciting new effort

Details of the 1000/1250 cc five cylinder Grand Superbike.

Much groundwork had been completed relative to the 200 cc module and with bore and stroke of 67 mm x 56.6 mm respectively, our output figures were projected at 18 bhp at 9000 rpm with two valves and 22 bhp at 9600 rpm with four valves, both sets of figures from engines in standard trim, with no 'racing tune' whatsoever.

So much for our new piston-engined family of machines. Our planning strategy also needed to include a machine of a very different type, powered by an engine operating on the Wankel principle. We had in our engineering work catered for a revolutionary new motorcycle with an engine unit having two rotors, each of 600 cc capacity. In making the choice of 1200 cc, it will be recalled that the BSA Board, at the time the Wankel licence was under consideration, had decided on a 60 bhp limit of 5000 rpm and our experience indicated that this choice of capacity came nearest to satisfying the rather strange engine power and speed limitations imposed by the wording of the licence. At the same time it would provide a power output in keeping with the large piston-engined machines with which we must compete, although this approach would, I think, have commanded a much higher price.

The main requirement was the achievement of air cooling, if possible, but to include provision for liquid cooling if this was found to be necessary during development. With five years development experience behind us on charge-cooled rotors (where cooling air passes through the rotor on its way to the carburettor) it was now obvious that the rotors must be oil cooled and this was featured in our new design. The rotor housings were air-cooled but could quite easily be liquid cooled if experience showed this to be necessary.

The engine was novel, having two contra-rotating rotors which provided a cancelling effect on the total rotating inertia of the unit, a great advantage for our motorcycle, which had shaft driven rear transmission.

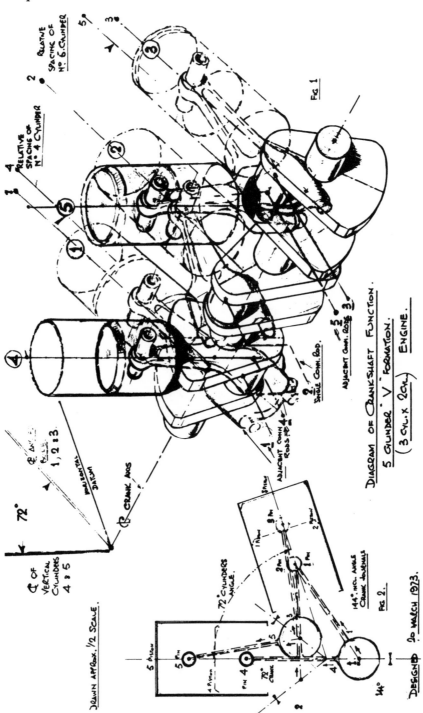

Details of the five cylinder engine crankshaft.

The legacy of the past decade and an exciting new effort

It was important that we should seriously investigate the possibilities of shaft driven rear transmission as a possibility for all of our larger machines as, although we had designed what seemed to be a very sound chain drive which should have solved our problem, we had not, as yet, tested this device. Despite the confidence of our engineers I felt that we needed an option and I strongly recommended that we gained experience both ways and made our final decision from 'devils we knew'.

Additionally, I was determined that we should investigate the possibilities of automatic transmission for motorcycles using the Wankel machine as the test bed. Our design would cater for the option of a 5-speed manually-operated gearbox, or automatic transmission via a torque converter. Top level discussions had taken place with the manufacturers of a Mini car automatic drive and it had been arranged that our engine would accept an offshoot of this unit.

The Wankel machine looked a handsome design and attracted a gread deal of interest when the news leaked, as it inevitably does, of this enterprise. In particular, the free publicity which we unintentionally enjoyed worldwide, even though many accounts were wildly inaccurate, penetrated our USA dealer network and seemed to give a little encouragement in their long and patient wait for the 'Limeys', as they put it to 'get off their butts'.

I felt, as never before, that we were doing just that and by early Spring 1973 we had fully explored all avenues of our new generation plan and engineering-wise were in a position to get moving with our first new model. However, events were to overtake us and our progress was delayed, although we continued to finalise our design work.

Meanwhile, for reasons which completely escaped every member of the BSA Board, the DTI had concluded that their help would be forthcoming only if Mr. Poore became the Chairman of the merged companies. Lord Shawcross was glad, we knew, that a new Chairman seemed to be emerging, for he had indicated from the start that he desired just this. Most of the Board were somewhat puzzled, for there seemed to be no reason whatever to suppose that Norton, with its insignificant achievements as a company, had the brand of management to lead the combined motorcycle industry to the promised land. The sign had certainly not been evidenced by me, but nonetheless we, as a Board, having been given this 'take it or leave it' ultimatum, were anxious that the shareholders, creditors and employees should have the benefit of the best scheme we could get out of the negotiations.

On March 14th 1973, our Merchant Bankers printed the first draft of a circular to our shareholders, recommending a scheme which involved the acquisition by BSA of Norton Villiers, and the sale by BSA to Manganese Bronze of their non-motorcycle activities. The equity in the reconstituted company was to be equally divided between the shareholders and Manganese Bronze, who owned Norton Villiers. The Government support would be via a special issue of preference shares. Mr. Poore would become Chairman of the reconstituted company and Lord *287*

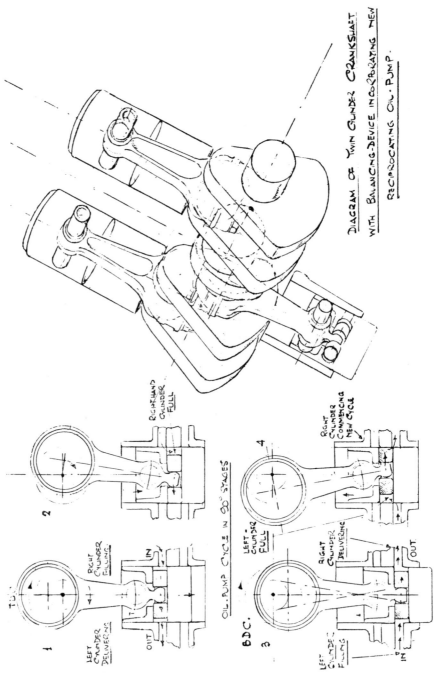

DIAGRAM OF TWIN CYLINDER CRANKSHAFT WITH BALANCING-DEVICE INCORPORATING NEW RECIPROCATING OIL-PUMP.

Details of the balance mechanism-cum oil pump designed for the single and two cylinder engines.

The legacy of the past decade and an exciting new effort

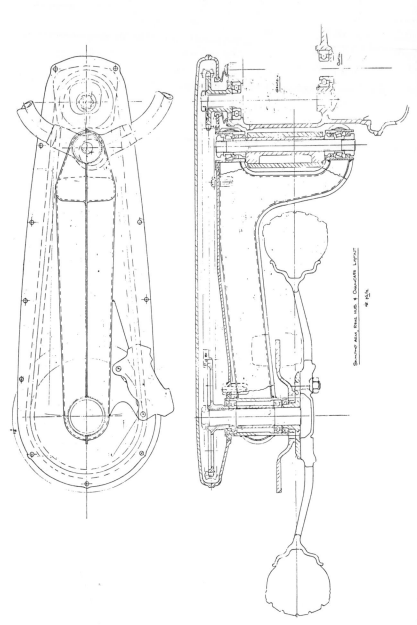

Details of new swinging arm transmission system for certain of the new generation piston engine range of machines. The design caters for a simple, unobstructed oil bath chain drive on one side of the swinging arm and a quickly detachable rear wheel on the other side.

Shawcross was invited to become Deputy Chairman, although he had not so committed himself. The scheme required for its viability, in addition to government assistance, substantial support from Barclays Bank, who had indicated a willingness to provide it.

On that very day of March 14th, a leakage into which the Stock Exchange later held an enquiry caused BSA shares to slump to virtually no value. Dealings had to be suspended, although it was fully realized by us that this would gravely prejudice the prospects of government aid, not yet formally agreed.

Mr. Poore subsequently put forward amended proposals on March 17th, the terms of which were a DTI subscription of £4,872,000, the sale by BSA to Manganese Bronze Holdings (MBH) of its non-motorcycle interests for a total cash sum of £3,500,000 and a further sum of £2m from MBH in exchange for shares in a new company which would be named Norton Villiers Triumph. The full capital structure of this new company would be on the following lines:-

A. Redeemable preference shares of £1 each £3,500,000
B. Convertible redeemable preference shares of £1 each £1,372,000
C. Convertible redeemable preference shares of £1 each £1,372,000

Ordinary shares of 10p each £4,012,472

The A and B shares were to be held by the DTI and the C shares by MBH. The ordinary share capital would be owned half by MBH and half by the present shareholders of BSA.

Immediate consideration was given to the new proposal but most members on the BSA Board felt that the offer of £3,500,000 for our non-motorcycle interests, most of which were profitable, was inadequate. While we were desperately trying to achieve a somewhat better deal, it was suggested that Mr. Poore and I should meet for the purpose of an exchange of ideas relative to the future development of the industry. I am afraid that my nagging fears were now to be confirmed, for Mr. Poore admitted that his company had no positive plan and few major product changes in mind apart from a large capacity two cylinder racing engine, on which a firm of engineering consultants was working, with possibly a large four cylinder engine from the same source.

I was beginning to feel greatly concerned that, very soon, together with my colleagues on the Board, I should be asked to support a recommendation to the BSA shareholders and I was now extremely doubtful that 'Zebra' had a management that could build a viable industry. History would, I hoped, clear up the mystery as to how the DTI had been able to make their early conclusions.

Back at Meriden we had, at last, fully agreed on the gross overmanning situation and had set this right with a voluntary redundancy of 300 employees. This had been a reasonably smooth operation and it seemed that our remaining workforce were facing up to difficulties with a degree of responsibility long overdue. Our new-

The new generation 1200 Wankel-engined motorcycle. Designed with shaft drive and planned with the option of manual or automatic transmission.

Details of the new generation 1200 Wankel-engined motorcycle.

found urge was such that the trading result of the Motorcycle Division for the month of April 1973 produced a surplus of £390,000. This was some indicaton of what was possible for, with a labour force now in near balance and a brisk demand for our big machines, we simply needed the industrial peace we had enjoyed during this month to produce a startling reversal and maybe an opportunity to have second thoughts about Mr. Poore and his merry men.

At a BSA Board Meeting on 2nd April 1973, reference was made to recent unwarranted press reports discrediting BSA management and in particular, unfair and intolerable personal attacks on the Chairman. The Board recorded its resentment and went further, with a pledge of support by a unanimous vote of confidence in our Chairman, Lord Shawcross.

It was particularly deplorable that Edward Turner, now retired for some five years, chose to make an attack in the Press in which he placed the blame for the company's current plight entirely on poor management. He went on to say *'Lord Shawcross may be a distinguished lawyer, but this does not mean he is an expert on motorcycles. Machines sell on the whims of fashionable young men. These fads are constantly changing. BSA Triumph are still trying to sell the stuff I designed 30 years and more ago. I can visualise machines which would make even the Japanese superbikes look old fashioned'.*

This is typically Turner but I am quite sure that Lord Shawcross would have been the first to admit that he was not 'an expert on motorcycles' nor did he ever pose as such, if indeed this remarkable fact needed a press announcement. I think that we all agreed, and said so at the time, that bad management was the main cause of our problems. Our Chairman had inherited a disaster born of a canker which had taken hold in the late 1950s, when motorcycle men were occupying the very top positions in the BSA organization with Turner himself Chief Executive of the Motor Cycle Division, with a seat on the parent Board. The smother of successive administrations with which we were plagued through the 1960s did not trigger off our disease; they merely accelerated its growth. The logic of this latest outburst from Edward Turner savoured of self-condemnation but at least he now was taking on the Japanese and making them look silly, if only through the media.

During the long and memorable Board Meeting on 2nd April, Brian Eustace reminded us that it had been obvious since October 1971 that the company's vital need was a major injection of capital. Continuous effort in numerous directions, including a direct approach to the Government, had failed right up to the time a merger with Norton Villiers had been mooted. He expressed management disappointment that now, with labour difficulties apparently resolved, motorcycle production expanded to an acceptable level and demand for machines currently reaching record figures, both in the USA and the rest of the world, the only hope of survival was to be taken over by our Government-assisted smaller rival.

292   My comments were that the three phase product plan which had been set for the Motor Cycle Division had now been achieved and the new generation of piston engined and Wankel type machines (the final phase) was about to be embarked upon. I felt confident that the company had a very viable forward product policy, provided capital could be found to provide the machinery to produce the new range. Without such a plan, and this Norton Villiers, on their own admission did not possess, I felt that it was quite impossible to set up a British motorcycle industry capable of competing with Japan. These views were endorsed by the other Executive Directors. Lord Shawcross agreed that the stuation was a tragedy but said it could be that Norton has presented a more detailed plan to the DTI, although this seemed extremely doubtful.

It was admittedly very disappointing that the greatly improved performance of the Motor Cycle Division could not influence present negotiations and BSA could not continue on its own as the Board would wish, for HM Government had firmly refused separate financial aid. Similar lines were taken by the FCI and the Export Credits Guarantee Department, so our job now was to consider whether the final offer, when it came, would be better than the alternative, a receivership.

The need now was to bridge the period between our consideration of the offer and the acceptance thereof by the BSA shareholders, for the market collapse of our shares had badly damaged the confidence which, up till then, our suppliers had felt. The production hiatus, due to the shortage of critical components from these suppliers, was overcome by them accepting our proposal that a short moratorium be placed on existing debts. The directors believed that if they would cooperate in this way, it would be possible to pay for all new supplies and services.

While the bid was being considered we were able to get their support on this basis and a committee was formed to represent our major creditors during this time, so that they could be kept in touch with events.

Unfortunately we were soon to run into new labour disputes at Meriden and the arrival of machines in the USA was severely limited. Although our recent production performance had been on target, earlier disputes had created a situation whereby our cumulative sales, by April, were only 65% of the plan. We seemed to have regained a great deal of confidence in the market square and we had a very satisfactory order book. With complaints and FOC replacements now at reasonable levels, we needed steady production as never before. However the trade union movement at Meriden definitely thought otherwise and I, like many of my Board colleagues, was forced to the conclusion that once more we heard the declaration, this time from the shop floor, 'to hell with the British motorcycle industry'.

We were mindful that the market collapse of BSA shares and the uncertainties surrounding the merger negotiations were having a devastating effect on our workforce. However, I regard this as no excuse as most of our staff were pulling out all the stops and certainly none of us deserved the frustration of this final sell out. It is true that certain aspects of our middle management approaches tended to annoy **293** and antagonise many of the Meriden shop stewards and this was, to some extent, a result of partisan attitudes towards BSA personnel who were involved at this level. It was nothing that could not have been resolved if some good old gumption had been forthcoming from the trade union side.

The Board, particularly the executive members, needed every support to cope with executive duties as well as Board Meetings which, at this crucial period, were very frequent and sometimes of marathon duration. It was clear that the message 'work or die' had not penetrated and with Meriden works settling down to a blissful strike-bound future, we seemed to be busy fools indeed. We went on sadly to prepare a satisfactory draft of Mr. Poore's final offer, to place before the BSA shareholders.

There was no possibility of BSA being able to continue in its present form, for our inability to supply a market now screaming for our products indicated a loss for the 1973 financial year of at least £2m. The only alternative to acceptance of the terms offered by Norton Villiers, harsh as they might appear to us, seemed to be the appointment of a Receiver.

The document, which needed to be agreed between the BSA Board and that of Norton Villiers, was re-drafted no less than ten times before being fully acceptable (it would be most boring for me to go into details) and by mid-May 1973, we were fully agreed but, as there were further delays, mainly due to difficulties regarding arrangements with Barclays Bank and the Export Credits Guarantee Department, the details of the offer, together with voting papers, did not go out to BSA shareholders until early in June.

The sale to Manganese Bronze Holdings of BSA's non-motorcycle interests was the part of the deal which left me with a feeling almost bordering on guilt and I knew that every Board member had similar naggings; here was a group of subsidiary companies, all currently profitable and with bright prospects, about to change hands at 'book value' as part of the deal.

Having witnessed accountants with high reputations wrangling from various angles about book values, I must confess that I felt out of my depth, although my main problem seemed to be language difficulties. Nonetheless, after listening carefully, I felt that as a non-accountant I probably had a better appreciation of the real future of these particular businesses in terms of product acceptability, future planning and applied management formula. It seemed to me that these successful subsidiaries were worth much more than the £3.5m offered and in my mind I had something like double that figure. My reasoning must have seemed half-baked, as indeed it may have been, but time was fast running out. The national press were becoming highly critical of the BSA Board for allegedly dragging its feet and this was, I am afraid, the best offer we had or were likely to have within our critical time factor.

I can only say that Manganese Bronze Ltd., aided by Her Majesty's Labour

Government, picked up a very good parcel indeed, for the BSA subsidiaries were:

Carbodies — manufacturers of motor vehicle bodies and, in particular, makers of the London taxi-cab.

BSA Metal Components Division — a group of companies manufacturing sand cast and shell moulded castings and also castings by the lost wax process, components made by powder metallurgy technique, and manufacturers of pre-alloyed metal powders for sintering and metal spraying.

BSA Guns — manufacturers of shot-guns, air rifles etc.

Birtley Ltd. — manufacturers of building products and general engineering products.

BSA Heating — manufacturers of central heating boilers and equipment in which company Birmingham Small Arms had a substantial holding.

These subsidiaries of Birmingham Small Arms Ltd. had, between them, achieved a profit of £576,000 for the seven months ended 22nd February 1973, and were confidently expected slightly to exceed the forecast profit of £1,053,000 for the twelve month period.

On June 7th under the new company heading of Norton, Villiers, Triumph (NVT) Ltd. documents were posted to all BSA stockholders giving full details of offers on behalf of NVT to acquire the whole of the issued share capital of BSA. They read as follows:

'The offers are one ordinary share in NVT for every ordinary stock unit of BSA and ten ordinary shares in NVT for every £3 nominal of A or B cumulative preference stock of BSA.

NVT is the new company set up to combine the two major British motorcycle manufacturers to which the government has conditionally agreed to provide financial assistance of nearly £5m by way of an investment in preference shares to help in building a healthy motor cycle industry in Britain, capable of competing successfully for world markets. BSA stockholders will initially own approximately half of the equity of NVT. MBH, which has already agreed to sell its subsidiary, Norton Villiers Ltd., the other motorcycle manufacturer, to NVT, will also own approximately half of the equity of NVT.

The Board of BSA is recommending acceptance of the offers'.

Mr. Poore then went on to say.

'The first task of the Directors will be to build upon the product lines of Triumph and Norton motorcycles and create a healthy British industry. This particular objective will require an accelerated expenditure on the design and development of a new generation of motorcycles and in due course the **295**

concessioning of up to date plant to manufacture them economically. The availability of nearly £5m from the DTI with no requirement to pay dividends on it for three years should provide time to lay the foundations for the profitable continuation of an important British exporting industry and is an opportunity of which NVT intends to take the maximum advantage'.

Chapter Eleven

Countdown

BY AUGUST the vast majority of BSA shareholders had accepted the offer, which was then unconditional, and with the prospering non-motorcycle subsidiaries of BSA absorbed by MBH, the new company, NVT, began to operate. The ailing Norton company was now linked to its sick brothers at Small Heath and Meriden, with a back-up of public money to form a single and presumably more effective motorcycle enterprise.

Not surprisingly, the new Chairman seemed to have little time for any of the former BSA Board and although Lord Shawcross had been invited to join the new Board, he had already indicated that he would not accept the offer.

I had been spending a great deal of time with Mr. Poore, at his request, hopefully, for my part, to survey a future plan of action for the new company. Alas, it was now becoming increasingly clear that my worst fears were well founded and that our new philosophy was to be the same old medicine which had soured world appetite for British motorcycles.

The approach was decidedly sterile and, in addition, the new leader of the reconstituted British motorcycle industry seemed to have decided that perfectly sound manufacturing units should be closed rather than firmly returned to the profitable trading status, which had been almost a habit until comparatively recently. I well remember Mr. Poore, at a working lunch, testing my reactions to the possibility of closing Meriden Works, long before he tried to do so, and I remember equally well my warning which predicted the fight and seige that eventually happened.

By now I was somewhat surprised that there appeared to be no plan whatsoever to cope with even the near future, apart from a racing two cylinder engine being developed by a firm of consultants. It would be raced and if successful could have been followed by a four cylinder unit from the same source. I was quite shocked by **297** the importance which Mr. Poore seemed to attach to racing for this surely was a luxury, although a most fascinating one which two recently merged and poverty stricken motorcycle companies could well put off until happier days. Much as I loved motorcycle racing, I had long since been convinced that before we cavorted on the race track and indulged the cream of our technical staff and engineers in this fascinating and enjoyable activity, we had a duty to our shareholders to get our house in order and make a profit.

A new Managing Director had been appointed, another stranger to our industry, and after a few days our new Chairman called a meeting at which most of the top management were present. Mr. Hele and I were invited, for the purpose of initial discussions on our forward product strategy and this meeting, I am afraid, fully convinced me that it would be most foolish of me to waste any more of my life with such a set up.

I remember the classic opening statement from the chair in which we were told *'Our new company had great responsibilities and we were now very much in the public eye'* and he, the Chairman, was *'now entrusted with the task of creating a viable British industry'* and although I suppose that I more than most should have been unmoved, I must confess that I was shocked to hear him say *'I do not know how this is going to be done'*. This may have been purely a figure of speech but I could not resist the comment *'We had better find out pretty damn quick'*.

The detailed strategy which we had worked on so enthusiastically for the past twelve months, was thrown out forthwith as being far too ambitious and in any case *'we do not intend to interest ourselves in the smaller machines which carry no profit margin.'* The same old business outlook was emerging and the same old thing was being said all over again which fully justified our reputation of an industry run by 'fuddy duddies'. Because I could see no possibility of a management being formed that would, at best, allow these pitiful fragments of the British motorcycle world to survive, let alone create a healthy British industry, I handed in my resignation.

I was taken aback when the Chairman expressed his surprise and I was asked to delay a final decision until I had been given an opportunity of visiting the Norton Villiers Wolverhampton works, to meet and chat with most of the management, and take a look around the production plant. I agreed, but this, if anything, made me more depressed and I immediately confirmed my resignation by letter to Mr. Poore on August 21st, which ran as follows:-

Thank you for giving up so much of your time to me last Friday and particularly for the conducted tour round the production unit at Wolverhampton, which I agreed to make, hopefully expecting to find some mitigating circumstance which would set me off anew.

However, the visit only confirmed my original thinking and I regret that I must ask you to accept my resignation as from this date.

It would be quite wrong for me to continue, in any capacity, with an enterprise which I feel sure is doomed to failure with the present management orientation and, for the record, I repeat my assessment of the situation, which was given to you verbally on August 16th.

(1)   *The segregation of the motorcycle operation into two or three management companies is about the worst formula, particularly at this moment in time. Ours is not that sort of business and the remoteness of groups of management of this pattern will merely prolong the agony.*

(2)   *Yet another Managing Director and what is more, a newcomer to the industry, is a surprising appointment. I hasten to add that I do not mean to cast any aspersions but this position is all important right now, particularly because the man has almost negative time factors to cope with and I do not rate the propects of success as being very high.*

(3)   *You appear to be all set in committing the company to the Norton forward product plan (a racing twin cylinder engine of 750 cc capacity) which is generated by an outside consultant. The BSA plan is, in my opinion, more logical for the reasons given in the folder which I prepared for the BSA Board. Although I realize that you are committed to some extent by contract, it is necessary, I feel, to have full control of product design 'in house'. You have made statements that you are likely to have advantages on pollution and power problems but my comments on these two points are as follows.*

   You did not realize the extent of the work already carried out by BSA and the results so far achieved relative to pollution.

   The BSA new generation piston engine is versatile and up to date, particularly for motorcycle work and there is no reason why our design will not be as pollution free as any. Incidentally your power figures recently quoted for your new racing engine were bettered at Small Heath as early as 1952, nearly 20 years ago.

   It is dangerous to assume that by 1975 the superbike must be liquid-cooled and your design certainly leaves no avenue of escape to air-cooling. The BSA design is the reverse as it originates in air-cooled form but can quite readily be liquid-cooled.

   You appear to be completely disregarding the tremendous ability and potential contained within BSA/Triumph personnel, who have carried the company through a succession of disastrous top management structures. The new order seems to be a Norton benefit and this, to me, is inexcusable because we need strength in depth through personnel steeped in the industry.

This is not a matter of opinion, it is fact, and has been proven so many times during the last 20 years of the company's history. One would have thought that you needed this strength as management, particularly as your own Norton enterprise presents itself as being far from strong in this respect and indeed will finish up with a sorry balance sheet for the final year.

I can only hope that, particularly for the sake of the many loyal and hard working employees you now have, some of whom having spent a lifetime in the motorcycle industry, I am wrong in my assumptions and indeed if this proves to be the case, I will be the first to express pleasure and satisfaction.'

This letter, as intended, left no doubt that there was an unworkable rift of opinion and my resignation was, of course, accepted. It was time for me to pull away from an industry that had attracted me for the best part of a lifetime and move my home, as I had always wished, to the South West in Devonshire.

A curious vacuum seemed to envelope me for two or three months and during this time, I was made to realize just how much work had been packed into the previous short 18 months and how very much our achievements, such as they were, had meant to me.

With the reputation which I have of being a traditional pessimist, it seems that, in the final stages of the exercise, my optimism was infectious enough to spread far beyond the brilliant engineering team who had given everything in this effort. Until the sorry collapse of BSA shares on the stock market, a new feeling of hope was spreading within the company.

It seemed to me that, for the first time, the top brass of the motorcycle industry had considered and unanimously agreed a comprehensive forward product strategy which they fully understood and had stopped talking silly nonsense about the Japanese being unbeatable in certain capacity classes but more vulnerable in others. Much of the spadework of development on the more unusual engineering features had been completed and, in addition, an agreement had been reached on Wankel development which would have given BSA its prototypes without any engineering costs other than the salaries of a handful of technicians. There is still no doubt at all, in my mind, that if the British Government had helped BSA to launch the first of its new models instead of insisting on the merger nonsense, the year 1976 would have indicated that the British motorcycle industry was back in business. Rather than put up the shutters, which NVT have seemed so anxious to do, we should have needed all the space we had to satisfy a healthy market which had been growing in the USA alone at 15% each year.

Brave words, I know, but during its short but eventful existence, the BSA Board was slowly coming to terms with the disaster they had taken on and, so far as I could **300** see, the loss of production through silly strikes at Meriden was the biggest single problem left for us to solve. This, I am quite sure, would have been accomplished, for I was determined that our Chief Executive should be forced to take a new approach with communication between workers and management by people whom the former knew and trusted.

I have strong reason to believe that this would have worked and had we taken this line our improving financial performance would have strengthened enormously and would have made nonsense of any suggestion that the ailing Norton company should join us to take our hand and lead us to the promised land. We should, of course, have needed the interest-free finance for which we had asked the then Conservative Government and this would have been a cheap package by comparison with the expensive events which were to overtake the Poore administration.

Manganese Bronze Holdings Ltd, with the help of the DTI, had ditched its lame duck and absorbed the profitable division of the BSA Group and it is right that these healthy manufacturing units should have been freed from the impossible financial situation which the motorcycle group had generated. What next, now that the two sick motorcycle companies had been lumped together? After all, we had been told that the sole purpose of this Government-sponsored manoeuvre was to revitalise the motorcycle industry.

It is now all too clear that the merger, and I hesitate in using this term, had not a cat in hell's chance of succeeding. The whole strategy of the new operation was negative and I tend to feel that this approach was the means that enabled bureaucracy to help sign *finis* to the remnants of an industry which, in the last stages of its struggle to survive, was probably becoming something of a pain in the neck.

The trade union sham which generated the situation whereby production was halted at Meriden just when our finances were improving and our products were in great demand, finally slammed the door on the BSA Board.

It would be amusing, were it not so serious, to recall the picture of those self-same individuals at Meriden, who had so recently refused to work, exhorting the right to work some months later, with typical trade union jargon and, during their long and cold picket duties, being described by certain press journalists as martyrs to some sort of cause.

The Meriden works has now freed itself from NVT after the workers' blockade and the eventual formation of a workers' co-operative. With some Government backing it is producing the same big Triumph machines which were due to be phased out during 1976.

The NVT operation seems to have thinned out somewhat and there seems to be no sign, from this direction, that the company is *'building a healthy motorcycle industry in Britain capable of competing successfully for world markets.'*

The years drift by and much has been written about what went wrong with the British motorcycle industry. One impressive piece of journalism cited *'lack of infusion of new management blood that might have opened up new marketing* **301** *prospects in an industry noted for its introspective management,'* This sounds good and I specially like the bit about opening up new marketing prospects but as always it is very vague as to what exactly would be used to do the 'opening up'.

It cannot be as simple as this for the real drift within BSA made itself felt during the 1960s, when the influx of new management blood was so prolific that new executives, most with brilliant backgrounds, were part of a way of life. Edward Turner, after he had left the company, blamed bad management in one public outburst but, although his remarks were aimed in another direction, he unwittingly condemned his own policy making during the long period when he was the top executive.

In his book *Meriden : Odyssey of a Lame Duck,* Jock Bruce Gardyne seems to imply that, but for the workers' blockade of the Triumph factory at Meriden in September 1973, NVT might have become a force in the world's motorcycle industry. However, in another part of this work one is led to believe that the British motorcycle industry was as good as dead even before the Government rescue and the formation of NVT. This seems to be highly contradictory but my own feeling is that the workers' blockade merely accelerated the run-down of Mr. Poore's new operation. It would be wrong to blame this for the failure of NVT for it was doomed from the start as a likely force in the world's motorcycle industry even though it may have trickled on for a year or two.

Various other reasons for our demise have been given by people who ought to know. For instance, Mr. Poore seems to put the blame for his failure squarely on the politicians involved and this may not be far from the truth in his particular case. The Chairman of BSA appeared to feel that the weather had something to do with the loss of revenue in 1969 when we were on our way to the brink. During the same year, when taking part in a television programme, the BSA Chairman blamed the minicar for falling motorcycle sales, and also accused the Japanese of copying our big bike designs.

Motorcycles are sold, in the main, to the young generation who know exactly what they like and they are rarely weaned from fixations by the salesman, hence the saying that motorcycles are bought, not sold. Far from getting to grips with the realities of life and absorbing a little of our customer attitudes several of the top brass, in the last two decades of the BSA saga, disliked if not hated motorcycles. One of these gentlemen made some very disparaging comments about the two-wheeled world a short time before he graduated to the hot seat.

The story of our failure is indeed one of gross mismanagement for at no time in the last twenty years or so of our operation did we master the arts of assembling the right expertise and planning management strategy based on the collected knowledge and advice of those people who are always to be found within a company with any background. The big names in the industry with whom I have been

302 associated never seemed able to realize this and bring themselves to respect the wealth of management talent which was readily available to them at all times.

This part of applied management philosophy is the most important and must be absolutely on target. A company that boasts a first class product line, which is in great demand, will survive, at least for a while, a mediocre business leadership.

It is in this field of management where the various chief executives of the BSA/Triumph operation had failed miserably but the Board, as a whole, must take responsibility for the serious erosion of the industry from a period as early as the mid-1950s. Neither those in power who had the advantage of a deep knowledge of the motorcycle 'game', nor those who did not, seemed to grasp the importance of this part of their function.

Those in the former category, who had a background of the motorcycle world and fully understood all the language, seemed to be too lazy or too arrogant to take note. Rather than stand aside and allow strategy to be generated by the more able management which supported them, they were instrumental in opening the floodgates to newcomers who were as much at home in our industry as would be a horse doctor in the sphere of human brain surgery. Those in the latter category, who had no such background, but came to us from the consultants' short lists with fine management records, simply did not realize that they had entered an industry with a high specialization factor and it would be wise to listen. But this they did not do and with a further influx of experts from other fields we were finally overrun by an upper/middle management who, it is true, were now in consumer durables. Never for one moment did they seem to grasp that these particular things were motorcycles and that we were supposed to be earning a living making them.

Index

Index

Index